BEING ENGLISH

BEING ENGLISH

NARRATIVES, IDIOMS, AND PERFORMANCES OF NATIONAL IDENTITY FROM COLERIDGE TO TROLLOPE

JULIAN WOLFREYS

STATE UNIVERSITY OF NEW YORK PRESS

Published by
State University of New York Press, Albany

© 1994 State University of New York

For information, address State University of New York Press,
State University Plaza, Albany, N.Y. 12246

Production by M. R. Mulholland
Marketing by Dana E. Yanulavich

Library of Congress Cataloging-in-Publication Data

Wolfreys, Julian, 1958-
    Being English : narratives, idioms & performances of national
identity from Coleridge to Trollope / Julian Wolfreys.
        p.   cm.
    Includes bibliographical references and index.
    ISBN 0-7914-2101-5 (alk. paper). — ISBN 0-7914-2102-3 (pbk. :
alk. paper)
    1. English literature—19th century—History and criticism.
2. National characteristics, English, in literature. 3. England—In
literature. 4. Narration (Rhetoric) I. Title.
PR468.N297W65 1994
820.9′008—dc20   93-43551
                                                              CIP

10 9 8 7 6 5 4 3 2 1

CONTENTS

ACKNOWLEDGMENTS

Anthony Trollope once remarked that there are some works that just will not bear a preface. I have the feeling this is one of them, so I shall keep this brief.

My grateful thanks go to the following, all of whom are, in some fashion, at different moments in time, responsible for this study, or its good points at least: John Haddon and Jenny Skipper; At the University of Southern California, Peggy Kamuf, for her patient and benevolent discussions of Jacques Derrida; James Kincaid for everything else and more than can or should be put into words; also at USC, Peter Manning, Margaret Russett and Richard Tithecott; William Baker at Northern Illinois University; at Clark University, Marcia Butzel and Virginia Mason Vaughan; Peter Stallybrass; at the City University of New York, Edward Guiliano, Alicia Carroll, and the anonymous reader for *Dickens Studies Annual*, whose comments on an earlier version of the Trollope chapter were both kind and perceptive; Bernd Lenz; at the University of Sussex, Michael Jamieson, David Mellor, and Geoff Hemstedt; and especially Jenny Bourne Taylor, whose friendship, commentary, discussion and suggestions have been invaluable, and largely the reason for the completion of this study. At SUNY Press, Carola Sautter has been of immense help, and always patient when confronted with numerous questions and 'phone calls; thanks also are due to the readers for SUNY, whose gracious criticisms allowed me full view of my own blind spots. Also, Megeen Mulholland at SUNY. Finally, Ruth Robbins at the University of Luton, for her scrupulous and diligent proof-reading.

Slightly altered versions of the chapters on George Eliot and Anthony Trollope have appeared in *George Eliot–George Henry Lewes Studies* and *Dickens Studies Annual* and are reprinted here with permission of the editors.

Introduction: The "Seemingly Indecipherable Metaphysics of Being" English or, Where to Begin?

> ... the text unravels multiple and simultaneous codes, whose systematics we do not see at first, or better still: which we cannot immediately *name*. Everything concurs, in effect, to render the structures one is seeking innocent, even absent.
>
> —Roland Barthes

> If the Tories have their way, English Literature will become the linguistic equivalent of the Tower of London.
>
> —Terry Eagleton

Where to Begin?[1]

An important insight of Derridean philosophy is that we read in several epochs simultaneously. The "epochs" or, at least, the historical sites in and against which the readings in this work take place in more or less oblique ways, belong both to the last fifteen years, and the nineteenth century signalled in the use of proper names in the subtitle of this study. A central concern behind this work will be, through a series of close readings, to question on an implicit level the notion of "Victorian values" which has been used to shore up a sense of national identity in the last decade. This study will show, through readings in nineteenth-century literature, how "Victorian values" (as an homogenised package) do not exist *as such*. Rather, the values of the nineteenth century, with regard to the question of national identity, when read in all their complexity provide us with a fragmented and often paradoxical vision of Englishness. It is to these fragments and contradictions that this study (re)turns as a means of understanding national identity, because, as Benedict Anderson has argued with regard to nationalism, national identity is most thoroughly understood, not by comprehending "self-consciously held political ideologies but . . . [the] cultural systems . . . out of

which—as well as against which . . . [identity] came into being."[2]
Anderson's definition points both to what Homi K. Bhabha identifies as
"cultural signification" and its importance to identity,[3] and to the tensions ("out of which," "against which") that exist as the necessary structure of any cultural system. The cultural system with which this study
therefore engages is "literature" in the nineteenth century, its mediations
and performances of national identity, and the "idioms" of those performances.

But to invert historical order for a moment: as a brief prehistory to
the situation of these readings, it is necessary in this preface to offer a
sketched context for this study. During the Thatcher years, Englishness
came to be defined in part by Thatcher's polemical recourse to the concept of "Victorian values," as is now well known. These values centred on
the twin figures of the nuclear family and the aggressively competitive
(heterosexual) individual. Society, according to Margaret Thatcher, did
not exist; there were only individuals, families and the nation. The
rhetoric of the New Right structured a seemingly unified and normative
model of national identity out of these elements, naming them
"Victorian" in the process, against which you measured yourself. If you
were not "English," if you could not identify in yourself those ideological
markers that were held to be paramount in Thatcherite discourse, then,
equally clearly, you did not exist. Not only did you have no right to a
voice, in reality *you had no voice.* A coercive, homogeneous national identity, and identification with that transcendental Identity, were the pretexts of one's own Being within the context of "Englishness." Thatcher's
rhetoric of unity was not abstract, however. Although it relied for its
emotional appeal and cogency on the idea of national identity as a metaphysical category beyond critique, it did not belong to the grand gesture
of metaphysical speculation, but was carefully, locally orientated—in typically English fashion—in the discourses of nineteenth-century liberalism. Hence Thatcher's Victorian referent as a means of grounding otherwise otiose and grandiloquent rhetorical flourishes.

Thus provisionally defined, it should be stressed that Thatcherism,
in the words of Anna Marie Smith, is but "one variant of authoritarian
discourse, [and] must be understood as a floating signifier, and not as a
project which naturally belongs to a fixed constituency and which is
naturally opposed by another fixed constituency."[4] Thatcherism is
merely a proper name which in effect defines a subject but prohibits further critical thinking about that subject. Equally, both liberalism and a
more traditional Tory ideology can be read, like Thatcherism, as having
a unifying project, although their authoritarianism has been more hidden because of the absence of a self-asserting, hyperbolic figure such as

Margaret Thatcher. Traditional socialism is also culpable of authoritarian thinking, having chosen in the past to ignore issues of gender and race in favour of a left-wing authoritarian concept of the "proletariat." All of these constituencies have, at times, mobilised their own particular versions/visions of Englishness for their own political purposes. Thatcherism was merely one discourse which had recourse to what Etienne Balibar calls the myth of national continuity, an "ideological form, in which the imaginary singularity of national formations is constructed daily, by moving back from the present into the past."[5]

However, if Margaret Thatcher has—or should have—taught the left anything, it is that unified and totalitarian concepts with fixed, eternal meanings are to be distrusted; distrusted for what they ignore, what they forget and for what they self-actively seek to marginalise and oppress. Thatcher's invocation of the Victorian epoch as an unproblematic, concerted moment in the historicity of identity is a paradigmatic narrative of the absolutist project, and thus serves this preface as a single—although by no means unique—moment from which this study stems, and against which it is positioned. Narratives of identity need not, *should not*, be unified, absolute and written with the immanence of transcendence. Rather, narratives of identity have to be read for contradiction and with a respect for difference. Hence, this study's re-reading of Victorian narratives for performances of identity as models of non-unified, often problematised mediations of Englishness in the nineteenth century.

The issue being raised is obviously that of the narration (and possible other narrations) of national identity. As the New Right demonstrated in the 1980s, the "proper" narrative form and the propriety of that narrative's contents depend on choosing the right idiom with which to perform identity. Part of that idiom for the New Right was the rewriting of the past through nostalgia. Margaret Thatcher's vision and narrative of Englishness have provided but one access in recent history to the politics of national identity. Such a narrative, with its "organicist and essentialist overtones whereby the part incarnates the whole,"[6] relies heavily on the organic and essential as routes through to the "singular universal"[7] which thus constructed is not open to critique whilst hiding its present political agenda focused on the issue of national identity. This political narrative is not only Thatcherite. As Jacques Derrida, Robert Young and others have shown, such narratives have long been part of a more general, and humanist western project of rethinking and appropriating the West's Others, both outside and within itself.[8] My concern is precisely to counter such political narratives in the domestic scene with an alternative, fragmentary politics of national identity, as it comes to be represented and performed in fictional narratives of the nineteenth century, which narratives are precursors to our sense of modern identity; and which narratives also tell numerous tales of a sense of a profound crisis of national identity, which is still with us today.

Paradoxically, and despite all attempts at the suggestion of unity, Thatcherite discourse makes us aware that Victorian narrative in all its fragmentary and labyrinthine complexity is still very much with us. Crises of (the unity of) identity, of the type which provide the contexts of Eliot's and Trollope's fictions (discussed in chapters 6 and 7) are still present as constituent elements in current thinking on Englishness. Trollope was perhaps gifted with an uncanny prescience, albeit momentarily, when he showed us his Prime Minister, Plantagenet Palliser, the supposed head of a coalition government, unable to bring into being his dream for the decimalisation of English currency. John Major was having as little luck with his own wayward backbenchers in 1992 over an issue of equal importance to certain versions of Englishness, the ratification of an amendment to the Maastricht Bill. The Conservative party is now in a state of internal disarray and crisis, precisely over the issue of national identity, as the debates on Maastricht have shown. The division within the Tory party between Cabinet and backbenchers (a narrative worthy of Trollope's satire) is being fought precisely because of differently defined structures of Englishness and a perceived threat to those structures. And it is perhaps a sign of the extent of the crisis of Englishness, that the Labour party are unable to offer any alternative sense of national identity, and take any coherent oppositional position against the Tories, despite the opportunities afforded by events such as Maastricht, the threatened and actual closure of mines, and the radical cuts to the National Health Service, all of which speak urgently about the question of identity. And while all this was happening, in 1992 the £10 note was re-designed in order to show on its obverse side a picture of Charles Dickens and a sickly cute cartoon of the Dingley Dell-All Muggleton cricket match. In this one image, with its village green, its Norman church spire in the background, the evocation of a time of good humour and fair play, all the discourses of a forced pseudo-Victorianism were brought into play, as if to remind us that we are much more Victorian than we think, and that a certain version of the nineteenth century is only ever as far away as your wallet.

This brief excursion into the current condition of "England" should help to show how Englishness cannot be thought of as a fixed object. Correspondingly, this study does not have a central thesis by which it attempts to master its subject, because it seeks to oppose such totalising narratives of identity. Instead, it seeks to elucidate a more strategically incoherent and differentiated notion of national identity, which respects difference-in-identity as part of a broader politics, grounded in the comprehension of the rights of otherness. Part of the reading strategy employed throughout is one of close reading which does not seek to construct a historical context for the texts in question in the manner of, say, New Historicism. Such a process is an attempt to validate a particular reading by constructing a supportive framework of narratives of a (highly selective view of the) past from extra-literary materials. This does not in itself retrieve the past as such. Close reading does not pretend to produce the past, nor does it imply that there is a past which can be recuperated unproblematically. Of course, close reading can be comprehended as part of a conservative hermeneutics of reading ignoring all political and cultural contexts, which charge has been levelled at both Leavisian textual analysis and deconstruction. However, What I am seeking to effect, through implied readings of certain theoretical models, is that close reading can be used against its own conservative hermeneutic. Leavisian readings and their kind became in the forties and fifties the paradigm for literary analysis, and thus were used, whether consciously or not, to reinforce a particular identity of readership. I have attempted to reappropriate close reading against its production of that unified identity by reading, in some cases, much closer than close reading would allow; paying attention to one line or a proper name for several pages at a time. This may well prove uncomfortable for some readers because the closeness is somehow improper. At the same time I have made various assumptions about the reader: the "Victorian" reader, the reader of nineteenth-century literature today, the reader of this study. What I have not sought is to imply that all readers are identifiable as a single readership. There may be a community of readers, but that community is not forged into a single, monolithic reader. The assumptions around readership are intended as a means of including many different readers, rather than excluding anyone.

Thus, this study does not assume that the subject of Englishness is in any way fixed, unified, or fully identifiable *as such*. And if, as part of that ethics and politics, this study avoids a central thesis, so, also, Englishness is properly to be considered as merely one more effect of practices and discourses which are themselves not fixed, to paraphrase Peter Mason.[9] Englishness, or national identity is "the product of an economic mode of structuring discourse which produces in the act of discourse that very object which it purports to describe."[10] Thus, the literature which is questioned in this study is read for the ways in which it can be re-read; we can reconstitute the narratives of Englishness from the poems, essays and novels not for the stories they seem to be telling "naturally," but for the subject positions that they perform, consciously and unconsciously.

This study therefore concerns itself with various responses by writers of poetry and prose in the nineteenth century to issues of national and cultural identity. Such a study throws up numerous questions. How do poets and novelists perceive, mediate and produce a sense of "Englishness"? What are the politics and poetics of cultural identity and identification? By the means of which narratives do writers such as Coleridge, Gaskell or Trollope either legitimise or criticise the ideology of the English middle class? What traces can we read as being enunciations of a sense of cultural self? And how do the writers in question work against, coalesce with, or become co-opted by what they—and we—perceive to be the stultifying, enervating, or galvanising aspects of their culture? While not all of these questions can be answered fully—each constituting a field of enquiry demanding rigorous investigation—they can at least open up for us the complex nature of the problematic of identity.

This study attempts to be sensitive to the particular, local economy of a single text. Often, and as part of its own political programme, its efforts are directed towards producing estranged versions of the writers and the works concerned; estranged, that is, from traditional and canonical readings. The purpose in doing so is to make available other cultural identities, to produce an other Englishness, other Englishnesses.

Working with the texts of Coleridge and Wordsworth, Matthew Arnold, Gaskell and Collins, Eliot and Trollope, certain gaps open up in the questioning of English identity. The authors that have been chosen have not been selected because they best serve the purpose of proving any single point about Englishness. As I hope these essays demonstrate, certain authors share largely coincidental similarities while, in the main, most are notable for the differences between their ideological and philosophical perspectives. There is not a single "Victorian" vision of national identity which persists throughout literary production during the 1800s. Where similarities do exist, I have tried to emphasise the subtle differences between the similarities, opening up small gaps to forestall absolute resemblance. The selection of authors and works is not wholly canonical; nor is it wholly marginal. In many cases, this study has sought to foreground less well known texts of well-known authors, in order to introduce contradictions into the received wisdom about those authors. As Terry Eagleton has argued, replacing Shakespeare with Alice Walker does not liberate the study of literature from its co-option into right or liberal ideological positions. Broadening the canon does not mean breaking the canon. More importantly, an implicit recognition behind the generation of these readings is the political necessity to "get to the point where classical literature [has] been emancipated from the oppressive ideologies it has historically served."[11]

The list of interchangeable names which could have been selected for this study is as broad as the nineteenth century itself. Charlotte Brontë, Charles Dickens, Ruskin and Tennyson are justifiably as crucial to any study of national identity. So also are Mary Braddon, Walter Pater, Bram Stoker and H. Rider Haggard. To paraphrase Peter Mason once more, while juxtaposing various texts and the positions they can be read as enacting, it is not assumed that the texts in question constitute a corpus or a single vision.[12] The texts and the gaps between them are often fragmentary, incomprehensible; the texts resist being gathered up as much as they are readable for similar ideological and philosophical traces and effects. The "Victorians" themselves—or, at least, writers in the nineteenth century—can be read often in the act of resisting ideological or typographical compartmentalisation in their various mediations of English cultural identity.

Throughout, this study has pragmatic and polemical recourse to the thought of Jacques Derrida in its approaches, as much as it is committed to a politics of the left. Particularly, I have had constant recourse to Derrida's more recent thinking on the subject of nationalism, national identity and the politics of the subject within such discourses in order to assist the comprehension of national identity as a "system" mobilised by differences and paradoxes.[13] Although this is not the place to go into an over-hasty analysis or too-brief regurgitation of Derrida's thought, it is important to recognise Derrida's opening of the question of idiom, of national idiom as a structure with which to engage in the texts that are defined as "literature" (by this, Derrida means both fictional and non-fictional, poetic and philosophic; indeed, his questioning of the national idiom has taken the form of undoing the boundaries of particular genres, which boundaries hide the very question of the idiom as idiomatic, pertaining to national identity itself). In beginning to comprehend this aspect of Derrida's work, certain questions, not traditionally part of literary-critical analysis, can be formulated, thereby providing worthwhile tools in the work of reading. Analytical tools, such as the political dimension of deconstructive thought that Derrida's thinking on national identity and spirit makes available, can be employed in reading(s) of Victorian texts, not to declare a level of indeterminacy of meaning (as is the habit of a more conventional version of deconstruction), but to make visible the various, often contradictory structures and discourses that serve as the means of producing the English subject and the ideologies of Englishness. In so doing, we can begin to counter unifying, universalising and authoritarian positions as those typified in the language of the New Right through such critical situations. In reviewing the ideological paradoxes of the "natural" and "common sensical," we can offer the possibility of taking part in the construction of a space for cultural reformation.

In order to understand how national identity has come to be situated today, the discourses of Englishness in nineteenth-century literature are important in discerning how and in what ways our identity is performed, and how we act as (sometimes unwitting) accomplices in the performance. This is obviously a large claim belonging to a project larger than the one at hand, and needs to be qualified. What is important to this particular study is the production of dissident readings of national identity in its various mediations and narrative structures as these are understood from a narrow range of texts. In comprehending specific sites and places inhabited by Englishness, this study pays attention to the pretexts and contexts, the affirmations and contradictions of identity; without policing texts for their "true meaning," this study attempts to move towards the possibilities of "differenced" articulations of identity by means of situational re-readings and re-writings of national identity, foregrounding not its coherences but its ambiguities, paradoxes and the fissures in its edifices.

The fissures are readable, but need careful opening. That part of the subtitle to this introduction which is in quotation marks—the "seemingly indecipherably metaphysics of being" English—is taken from an essay by Iain Chambers.[14] Chambers's convoluted play of terms provides us with a glimpse at the extent to which the ideological imperatives have been hidden, mystified and naturalised in the maintenance of particular dominant normative models of national identity. As Chambers's phrase insinuates, if the "metaphysics" in question—"metaphysics" composed merely of the economy of exploited concepts and terms—are not *actually* indecipherable but only seemingly so, then we are already on the way to finding a crack in the surface of identity's unified image, into which we can situate a critical analysis. We can read the invocation of an illusory metaphysics of Englishness, with English identity *as* the metaphysical appealing to the notion of a unified identity somewhere "out there," not available for questioning, and to which we should all aspire. We should read in this proposition a sleight of hand as part of an effort to construct a coercive simulacrum, that elides cultural difference and enforces the fiction of a single English identity.

In opening the topic of Victorian literature to questions of identity and relating that to the recent past and the present, right-liberal and traditional Tory versions of national identity should be comprehensible as on-going products of their own discourses, all with the potential for critique and dismantling. The English identity that has at its core "Victorian values" is not immutable. It is paradoxical within itself, and this can best be understood by a return to Victorian culture, and the re-reading of that culture. This study is therefore also involved with analysing the generation of cultural meanings for political purposes, and to show how those meanings are themselves composed of other discursive traces. It seeks to mediate against a politics of identity as only a politics of unity by analysing that which is discontinuous in identity. In order to effect such analyses, it is necessary to read the fragmentary, fragmented epochality shared by both ourselves and the Victorians; hence, certain of these readings will produce versions of the writers concerned as implicitly modern or even postmodern, and not "Victorian" at all. Such readings hopefully bring into question the historical trajectory of the middle classes as the dominant class of the last 170 years. Regardless of political parties and of traditional vertical and static models of national hierarchy, the social power of national identity and its cultural power have been and still are vested in and across the large, often contradictory, body of the middle class, who are themselves produced by the negotiations of specific economic structures. The Tory and Liberal middle classes who claim both explicitly and implicitly to be the representatives of national identity are what Matthew Arnold called the heart of England (see Chapter 3, below). However, this heart does not have a central location; hence the problems in seeking to define its organisation and means of operation.

Therefore, in order to consider the function of the "heart of Englishness," it is necessary to stress the idea of the heart as only a provisional focal point of numerous arteries and veins; of practices, discourses, institutions, philosophies, structures, all of which are mobilised for a particular unifying political purpose. It is necessary to give up the notion of a focal or central point; for this image is itself of the order of absolute definition, which unifying narratives produce. In reading behind the mystification which such definition effects, the discourses of totalitarian unification can read against the grain of their naturalising tendencies that seek a consolidated identity in the face of a disparate, feared other, which feared other is the departure point for this study.

In the first chapter, I look at the uses of the female image and its relation to national identity in two short poems by Coleridge and Wordsworth. The structure of the essay is a double horizontal column, the study of Coleridge occupying the upper part of the page, the analysis of Wordsworth the lower. The purpose of the structure is to introduce the subject of the book—Englishness—by a double opening, in order to avoid the implication that there is a single, originary site from which is generated the modern sense of English identity. This chapter indicates obliquely both Romantic and modern points of entry. The upper and lower texts are related in their concerns, but not necessarily by any comparison of the two authors and their works. The two analyses introduce the subject of national identity from different perspectives, thereby intimating some of concepts and formulations which inhabit and haunt the idea of Englishness in the nineteenth century and which will be examined in the chapters that follow.

Structurally, this double beginning also serves as an oblique commentary on the break between romanticism and modernism, a gap which cannot be closed and which is caught up in any literary conception of Englishness. This obviously Derridean structure is also introduced in order to put Wordsworth briefly in a subordinate position to Coleridge, to invert the conventional thinking on the hierarchical relationship between the two signatures in the canon of English literature.

Despite the different concerns of each poet with regard to Englishness which are elucidated in this chapter, both men are seen to rely on the female image as a means by which they can return home to their native identity in its psychic and ideological contexts. However, while Coleridge's use of the female is analogous to an addictive fix, Wordsworth's control is more assured, bearing the mark of sacrifice. Both poets can be read for the ways in which the reader is implicated in the construction of national identity, and so serve as exemplary figures from which to begin any consideration of Englishness in the age of Victoria. For, although they predate the Victorian period strictly speaking, their joint involvement with the cultural identity of the nation foreshadows issues and questions of identity throughout both the nineteenth century and the latter part of the twentieth.

In Chapter 2, the question of Arnold's Wordsworth is touched upon, as I look at the pertinence of the question of national identity and spirit in Matthew Arnold's writing. In this chapter, I look at the issue of national identity, nationalism and Arnold's often Wordsworthian sense of spirit—of spirit as knowledge, the knowledge of a people aware of their own identity, and the immanent hollowing out of that identity, as their heritage—as expressed in poems from the 1840s to the 1870s. Also given attention here is Arnold's attempt to engage with the problematic nature of Englishness, mentioned at the close of the previous chapter. Like Coleridge, Arnold experiences identity through a sense of fear and shock at the possible, imminent collapse of that identity. Unlike Coleridge, however, Arnold attempts to respond to this collapse by recalling the literary-historical culture of England as the structure on which to reform national identity. Yet Arnold's problem is that he is unable to reconcile poetic pursuits with an ethical commitment to social engagement on the part of the artist. As Arnold gradually eschews a purely poetic identity in favour of a more quotidian discourse, his writing maps the transition from poetry to prose.

The transition from poetry to prose lies in Matthew Arnold's essay "My Countrymen," which is explored in Chapter 3. Arnold seeks out new philosophical paradigms for the performance of a sustained social and cultural critique which itself draws on pre-existing cultural paradigms of Englishness, rather than trying to stand outside of the culture. This marks a transition for Arnold, who had sought unsuccessfully in his poetic experiments for a vehicle of criticism at once both polemically engaged and yet attentive to certain aesthetic traditions.

Arnold finds a partial answer in prose forms themselves. This answer is itself part of a wider transition from poetry to fiction as the art form closest to the realities of the age. In being essentially bourgeois media for a bourgeois readership, the essay, the novel, and fiction in general, were the vehicles through which models of national identity could be formed, mediated, questioned, criticised and reformed. Yet as this reading of Arnold shows, one also has to be aware of the cultural and historical blind spots. It is because of such lapses into cultural unconsciousness, lapses which are themselves the necessary condition of identity, that the writers often mark their own Englishness. Arnold's recourse to a continental philosophical model, one that is recognisably Hegelian, offers an escape route from the snares of identity and into the very heart of Englishness. Thus Arnold's prose can be read as positing a structure of alterity within national identity.

The idea of allowing alterity to speak in its various voices from within the dominant identity is at the heart of Elizabeth Gaskell's fiction. Such an attempt to write the other is fraught with problems for any concerted exegesis of Gaskell's texts. This interpretative difficulty is due to Gaskell's anticipation, and inclusion, of several differing, often contradictory, ideological voices in the space of a single text. Gaskell gathers into her writing many positions and situations that are broadly political, often mutually contradictory. She resists positive criticism and from the sounding of an authoritative voice, so as to leave the possibility of silence in which there can be heard various political discourses and thus affirmation of other identities. Gaskell's texts do not attempt to avoid the snares of traditional modes of thought; such evasion, she realises, is impossible. However, in the face of formal structures of thinking, Gaskell opens gaps through which dissidence is enunciated.

The problematic of the single reading is therefore further compounded by Gaskell's refusal to allow a particular voice either hierarchical or hegemonic primacy. Depending on which character is speaking in any particular novel, the text appears Tory, Whig or radical in its polemical undercurrent. No simple or full identity is more than partly established, without that structure being, in some fashion, critically solicited at an other textual instance. The narratorial voice is never absolutely identifiable with one ideology. Such obscurity is not, again, equivalent to the assumption of superiority, but is, instead, part of Gaskell's recognition of political identity's paradoxical nature within a national context. Furthermore, such recognition incorporates a true democratisation of narratorial enunciation. Gaskell's writing foregrounds the inscription of the "truths" of cultural identity and reality in all their fragmented complexity.

The fifth chapter moves to Wilkie Collins who, like Elizabeth Gaskell, is critical of the shaping of national identity and so focuses, again like Gaskell, on seemingly insignificant details of everyday, middle-class life in mid-Victorian England. Such details form the network of the English way of life for Collins. Out of such details, Collins mediates his own critical visions of England's dominant class. Through attention to the details of English life, Collins unfolds the troubles, contradictions, hypocrisy and corruptions that comprise the architecture of the heart of English middle-class culture.

The next chapter offers a reading of *Daniel Deronda*. Eliot's last novel attempts a dual function; a critical narrative of the English upper-middle-class, which shows them to be the exhausted performers of a self-reflexive and hollowed-out culture, and the search for an alternative national identity, rooted in the ideal of the spirit. Eliot achieves her double narrative through the figure of Daniel Deronda, who is most typically of the English upper-middle-class, having an English education and being thoroughly English, whilst also being Jewish. His analytical mind allows us a critical window on the sterile world of the Mallingers and their social circle. The life of the novel, the life that is not part of a series of arch descriptions on Eliot's part that have more to do with theatricality than essential identity, is the Jewish life, portrayed through Mira's family and the composer Klesmer, as well as through Daniel, albeit unknowingly.

Daniel's search for an alternative to the dead end of purely, narrowly English existence leads him to embrace Judaism. Yet the critical problem for Eliot in envisioning this alternative culture and the possibility of a vital identity is that Judaism is idealised and sealed off from the social flow. Daniel's quest becomes an idealistic inquisition after a utopian culture. Thus Eliot's narrative, in having Daniel leave England, finally marginalises Daniel's alternative identity. So threatening is the possibility of alterity for Eliot that she marginalises both Daniel and Jewish culture while recuperating her narrative into the English tradition that she has sought to criticise.

The final chapter, Chapter 7, turns its attention to Anthony Trollope, as a means of offering an alternative to the dead end of idealism, up against which George Eliot had run in her final novel. As Trollope shows us, the answer is not to look outside Englishness, but to look within it from (and for) an alternative perspective. The question of Englishness is mapped comprehensively by Trollope in the Palliser novels, and problematised by that mapping. These novels are readable as being heavily traced by crises of identity that Trollope reveals as located specifically in the local and the political. Trollope unfolds for us the hegemonic situation of the English bourgeoisie in the 1870s. In foregrounding the social milieu of the upper middle class, Trollope comprehends conservative projects, such as a call for a return to supposedly "Victorian" values, as being part of a particular ideological narrativization, and questions the illusion of unity that serves as the base of such projects.

Trollope questions the ideal of unity as political strategy as he displaces supposedly eternal values and the narratives that perpetuate them. He does so through the ironic questioning of cultural categories such as "the gentleman" that are employed as crucial props in the maintenance of national identity by the middle class. Trollope also employs the strategic placement of dissident, questioning figures such as Phineas Finn, who are placed within particular cultural, social and political situations in order to read those situations against the grain. This chapter moves from a reading of Finn as an "outsider within" whose trajectory dismantles social structures to a reading of what is at stake in Trollope's soliciting of the discourses of "the gentleman," "liberalism" and "the coalition." In doing so, it reads the redundancy of traditional categories which need to be shaken with ironic laughter. Trollope shows us, whether directly or indirectly, that we should not fear the other-within, because the other is vital to our own sense of national identity.

In order not to fear the other, we need to know ourselves, we need to recognise exactly what part we play in the politics of identity, how that politics has been constructed, and what questions we need to ask from inside that identity in order to re-shape it, in order that we might attain a fairer, more open politics of identity; an identity that is not homogeneous; an identity which respects difference as difference without attempting to police it or enclose it. We need a politics of identity which, to paraphrase Rosalind Brunt, is adequately informed by the genealogy of that identity, informed by readings in the historicity of identity's culture.[15] Literature is one of the most immediate accesses we have to our past identities; from a knowledge of past representations of identity we can begin to reformulate our own identity, In being so informed, we can begin to comprehend how it is the very idea of a monolithic identity—a "Victorian" concept of Englishness, if you will— which prevents us from moving along the road to "active political agency."[15] Only from such comprehension can we posit the idea of what Brunt calls "unity-in-difference."[16] Brunt cites as an example of the potential for unity-in-difference the widespread support for the miners' strikes of 1984-1985. In 1992, we have been witness to and, hopefully, participants in a similar voicing of support for the miners, threatened with illegal pit closures. It is only through thinking and working with such events that we can take hold of the question of identity, in order to have a say in its shaping. Despite the closure of some pits in 1993 the mining communities have demonstrated the necessity of action, the necessity of asserting an other identity, even in the face of seemingly immovable opposition. To those mining communities, this study is dedicated.

1

OF DETOURS, RETURNS, ADDICTIONS AND WOMEN: COLERIDGE, WORDSWORTH AND NATIONAL IDENTITY[1]

Mon desir ne va qu'à la distance invisible/
My desire goes only so far as the invisible
distance

—Jacques Derrida

He had a world about him—'twas his own
He made it—for it only lived to him

—Wordsworth,
The Ruined Cottage
(87-88, MS B)

A savage place! as holy and enchanted
As e'er beneath a waning moon was haunted
By woman wailing for her demon-lover

—*Kubla Khan* (14-16)

She was a Phantom of delight
When first she gleamed upon my sight . . .
I saw her upon nearer view,
A Spirit, yet a Woman too!

—Wordsworth,
She was a Phantom of delight
(1-2, 11-12)

A Damsel with a dulcimer
In a vision once I saw:
An Abyssinian maid,
And on her Dulcimer she played,
Singing of Mount Abora.
Could I revive within me
Her symphony and song,
To such a deep delight 'twould win me . . .

—*Kubla Khan* (37-44)

A Negro Woman like a Lady gay,
Yet silent as a woman fearing blame;

—Wordsworth,
September 1st, 1802 (3-4)

I

What is the purpose of the two female images that Coleridge inscribes into his opium-induced, self-confessedly fragmentary poem, *Kubla Khan?*[1]

Why are they there, what is their relation to the subject of cultural identity, and how should we read them?

Coleridge's application of the female belongs to a broad cultural discourse of feminine representation and national identity. Through the figure of the female, Coleridge is partly able to construct a return home to the site of domestic desires, more familiar in their strangeness than the foreign, Oriental other of Xanadu. Furthermore, Coleridge's recourse to the female figure is analogous with the addictive fix. The user desires, yet simultaneously fears, the "substance" in question and the loss of control that both the drug and the female supposedly induce. Both female images in the poem comprise visual and aural elements designed to distract the reader, to entrance, enthral and transport, in much the same manner as an imbibed toxic substance.[3] In the case of the second image, that of the Abyssinian maid (39), the poem implicates the reader into itself, speaking directly to us of an addiction shared by all readers.

Moreover, *Kubla Khan* also involves questions of domestic identity and foreignness. Specifically, the Western discourse on Orientalism is at stake. Coleridge's invocation of the Oriental has, again, to do with a fear of losing control. It is a question, as John Barrell puts it with regard to Thomas De Quincey, of ingesting the East as well as throwing it away.[4] Coleridge attempts to resolve the paradox of the rush of desire and its concomitant lack of control by "injecting" the female into the Oriental vision. Coleridge, when apparently straight as in his introduction to the poem, knows that he cannot direct his responses to the opium when high. He cannot even bring the opium under his discipline once it is in him and of him, although the drug is under his control inasmuch as he decides whether to take it; nor can Coleridge "subdue" the Orient. In this, he typifies and represents the attitude of the English towards the idea of the Orient. This is part of a greater white fear of which the opium is merely a privileged signifier. However, Coleridge seeks to effect domination over his others, as do many Englishmen. He does so through an attempted colonisation in the form of a return to, a detour known as, the female, which is simultaneously both domestic

---

Wordsworth is always returning. He returns to Nature repeatedly. He returns to Tintern Abbey and its surroundings ("and again I hear . . .") after five years; he returns to the "writers of reformation England," as Geoffrey Hartman reminds us;[5] to his youth, and to his various performed identities in The Prelude, *amongst other poems; to* The Prelude *itself, through seemingly endless revisions; and to England from France (to comprehend Englishness, we must understand Europe, before the Orient, as England's Other). In fact, all of Wordsworth's life and work is dedicated to, governed and guaranteed by the idea and the promise of the return. To reiterate: the*

and foreign. Coleridge's contamination of the Orient with the female permits a partial domestication of the foreign, thus making the Other safe because the presence of the female image as desired object universalises the Other. These are, however, only brief considerations. A more thoughtful and less addicted, less jumpy, response to my initial questions requires two brief detours.

Consider, for instance, the detour that "Coleridge" has always already taken. As he rehearses and performs the growth of his own writerly and poetic identities in the 1790s, Coleridge takes the detour or deviation named William Wordsworth from an originary or essential sense of self. Today, we are unable to read Coleridge except as Wordsworth's Coleridge. There is no Coleridge as poet or writer other than that which is a form of self-translation or sublimation, on Coleridge's part, through what he perceives to be the mastery of Wordsworth, and under which mastery he willingly places himself in subjection. Coleridge cannot avoid the Wordsworthian side-track. It is this detour that, in his Eastern fantasy of 1798, allows us the possibility of reading in the figure of the Khan's stately pleasure dome(2) other architectural structures, written as poetic or allegorical sites of the Romantic imagination.

We can read, for example, the ruins of Tintern Abbey (which had been impinging on Wordsworth's memory for five years) and the ruined cottage and cottages through various manuscripts and versions) of *The Ruined Cottage*,[6] begun by Wordsworth in the previous year, 1797, the year which Coleridge had mistakenly dated *Kubla Khan*.[7] We can also read behind the exotic scene the homely cottage wherein Coleridge takes his fix. No matter where the imagination roams, the architecture comforts, even in its desolation, by referring to home, specifically, a safe English home.

Architecture and, especially, ruined architecture is an important figure both in and for the Romantic imagination. Wordsworth com-

---

return is guaranteed with (and by) Wordsworth; it is, in sum, the very worth of his words. So, the implication of this teleology is that, if the return is guaranteed, the investment is safe. Wordsworth is a sure bet as an, no, the English tour guide.

This question of the guaranteed return leads, however, to an anterior question or two at least; notice immediately how the economic logic of Wordsworth forces itself upon us; we also, always return: What is it that is being invested in by Wordsworth? What does his ineluctable return guarantee?

ments on his own poetry as being architectural. In his "Preface" to *The Excursion, The Prelude* is described as being "the ante-chapel . . . to the body of a gothic church," while minor poems are described as "little cells, oratories, and sepulchral recesses, ordinarily included in those edifices."[8] As Wordsworth's metaphors of church architecture attest, ruins and architectural decay provide the signature of what is lost and desired, what cannot be named but what is obliquely indicated. What is desired, therefore, may well be an Englishness of identity that is forever lost both to Wordsworth and Coleridge. The architecture of decay insists in Romantic poetics as the haunting, obsessive trace, as another residual effect of the Romantic addiction, of Romanticism *as* addiction. Of particular relevance in this context is Thomas De Quincey's recollections of Coleridge's description of Piranesi's *Imaginary Prisons*, being etchings of the artist's delirious visions.[9] Mistakenly, but tellingly, De Quincey describes the classical architecture of the etchings (which he had not seen) as gothic. He also recalls from Coleridge's description the labyrinthine and infinite qualities of the imaginary architecture, recalling Piranesi "standing on the very brink of the abyss."[10] De Quincey goes on to remark that the splendours of his opium dreams were chiefly architectural. The Romantic unconscious, an unconscious always hungry for another fix, is filled with exotic architecture, mapped by labyrinthine and abyssal landscapes, inhabited by the ruins of other worlds, which are, we suspect, really our own. In both Coleridge and Wordsworth, in their evening walks, country rambles, and even in "The Rime of the Ancient Mariner," we can read the desire to return home, to a lost, desired England. We can thus map out motifs of circularity which "can lead one to think that the law of economy is the—circular—return to the point of departure, to the origin, also to the home."[11]

The other detour, already alluded to, is not particular to Coleridge and is broader than a single signature, however big a name that may be. Orientalism is the deviation in question, considered especially as the

One possible answer to this is national identity, or Englishness which is itself the guarantor of Liberty in the Wordsworthian economy. For the poet Englishness does more than guarantee Liberty, freedom, and other associated concepts and fetishes related to any sense of national Being. In Wordsworth's vocabulary, English identity guarantees freedom because the terms are ideally interchangeable; Englishness is Liberty, and, to be free truly, absolutely, is to be English, regardless of one's actual birthplace or nationality (I shall return to this point). And Wordsworth is so sure of that which constitutes Englishness that he can, unequivocally, confidently corre-

confluence of imperial and commercial discourses. No doubt there is a poetic "value" in the fact that Coleridge's almost cataleptic state—he writes of himself in the third person as being "[t]he Author . . . in a profound sleep, at least of the external senses"[12]—that produced his vision of a labyrinthine, inscrutable other, was induced by his indulgence in opium, *the* drug of the "Orient." It is as if opium transports Coleridge, chemically, against his will, yet because of his desire, to the place where the "anodyne"[14] is grown, harvested and manufactured.[15] It is as though, reading a little obliquely, we can say that the drug carries, traced in its chemical properties, the mythological texts of its imagined, conflated geographical sites; and that the enigmas constructed in the West about its composite Oriental Other are inscribed, sedimented, in the very soil that nurtures the poppy. Taking the opiate transports one back to the supposed origin of the other; except that, this "origin" is, of course, the displaced figure for the desire of the Occidental subject.

There are, then, two possible locations at least as the sources or goals of our detours (deviations that are both ours and Coleridge's). First, the seemingly symbolic architectural structures that figure the following: a gothic excess or decadence (the pleasure dome itself), the broken writing of feudal Catholicism (Tintern Abbey), and the more humble, yet, for Wordsworth, more universal, decaying, familiar habitation of spent, dispersed humanity (the ruined cottage; the cottage is more poignant and, therefore, endowed with greater resonance for Wordsworth because it is non-sectarian). An economy of mordant, yet idealised, spirit remarks each architectural space.

Secondly, yet having to do equally with an issue of spirit, we have an imaginary discursive and (implied) geographical space—at least in Coleridge's fragment which is my main concern—of cultural otherness. If detour, in leading away, always already premises a re-turn, bringing the reader to the architectural and geographical as sites (or even citations) in the poetic imagination of loss, memory, the foreign, alterity, desire, and

---

spond on that which is proper to an English Garden.

In a letter to Lady Beaumont, written from Coleorton in January 1807, the poet, donning his gardener's hat, gives details of his winter garden.[13] *Ignoring the anomaly that, in some cases such as the Laurustinus, he has to refer to plants by their Latin names, Wordsworth writes of the "English winter shrubs and flowers, intermingled with some foreign shrubs as are so common in* english *(sic.) cottage Gardens as to be almost naturalized" (my emphases). Wordsworth's eye is still able to discern the foreignness of imported plants, despite their being almost naturalized. Yet it is because of their domes-*

fear, what is the overdetermining figure for all such configurations and displacements? In sum, what, poetically and economically, historically and philosophically, in Western culture has the greatest exchange value, the greatest exploitative potential as the figuring of all figuration?

The female, or femininity, which, as ultimate object of desire, and as ultimate fix, apparently engendering that desire, haunts poetic structures as both keystone and seismic disturbance.

II

Coleridge, by his own account, published *Kubla Khan* at the request of Lord Byron.[16] (Byron documented his own desire for the female repeatedly, at length, *obsessively*, in his letters from Venice, an archetypal geographical non-space, composed of fluidity and at the commercial conjunction of East and West.[17]) Coleridge rejects the poem as poem, reading it instead as a "psychological curiosity" only.[18] Coleridge's two comments, dismissive and yet desirous of a certain kind of reading, inscribe a lack of will on the poet's part. Coleridge directs his efforts towards disowning the text. He seeks to displace it as being unworthy of his signature and authority, while attempting also to deflect aesthetic and formal analysis, and any readerly imposition of coherency inthe second. The poet tells us how to read and what we should not read.

In the subtitle itself, "Or, a Vision in a Dream. A Fragment," Coleridge has already begun to direct the reading of his text in particular ways. While we are not to read this as a poem, we are, nonetheless, being policed as readers. Paradoxically, Coleridge desires that, in reading, we read otherwise. The insistence on the interiority of the poem's genesis, that it is not merely a dream but a vision in a dream, is a violent displacement of responsibility for the vision—and the

---

tication, that he will allow them to appear, their proximity to English flora and fauna no doubt legitimising and taming them. However despite this touch of infiltration, Wordsworth desires that he should be able to see an "English spire," the presence of home-grown architecture reassuring him that he is still at home. And it is the inspiration of this sight that leads him to remark: "I would have in all its ornaments entirely English." The foreign shrubs stay close to the ground where they belong, surrounded and towered over by all things proper to an English cottage garden. To paraphrase John Barrell's commentary on the title of Thomas De Quincey's autobiographical

dream—on Coleridge's part. He protests too much, so excessive is his desire. The displacements proliferate, spreading out even as they register a condensation of the dispersed pieces. The vision *in* the dream becomes a ruin or dismembered body, whether architectural or human, in being re-marked as a fragment. Or is it not the vision within which is the fragment but the dream itself? Or both? Or neither?

The problem is that reading, any reading, involves the accretion of components. Yet nothing in this subtitle indicates the possibility for any such accretion, in order that we might be able to read or translate this. In the structure of the subtitle, the phrase, "a fragment," is itself a fragment of the subtitle, being a piece—both connected and disconnected—of the title *Kubla Khan*. "A fragment" is not part of, nor does it belong to any complete sentence. It is an absolutely faithful mimetic figure of and for itself; it names itself, its own function. We get the sense of architectural disarray, of imminent collapse, and the idea that structure is always predicated on its own ruin. Coleridge, having announced the "following fragment," and having insisted on the pathological nature of his text, deflects the poem still further, in a detour of 46 lines of prose. This detour involves the narrative history of the poem's "composition." Coleridge writes of himself in the third person, as if eager to disown the text or any conscious involvement with it. The Author is disturbed from his eager composition[23] and so loses the exact form of the vision. The structure has collapsed and is left in ruins.

Apparently, Coleridge had been reading from the Jacobean travelogue, *Purchas his Pilgrimage*, a twenty-plus volume account of the development of trade routes and the "discovery" of the Orient so crucial to the expansion of England's mercantile and maritime imperial power. This had served, along with the effects of opium, as the source of

———————— —▪— ————————

Confessions, *notice how the application of the adjective "English" hopefully makes safe Wordsworth's sense of place.*[19]

If the Poet has such faith in the English garden, how much more assured must the expression of that national certitude be through the medium of poetry. Wordsworth's clearest expression and celebration of his "confident and unambiguous faith in England"[20] *is given in the "Sonnets Dedicated to Liberty."*[21] *As is well known, Wordsworth's return to faith in England had come about as a result of the poet's disillusionment with the French revolutionary cause, and what he saw as France's betrayal of the ideal of English*

Coleridge's Eastern vision. Thus, albeit inadvertently, Coleridge collapses nearly 170 years of the imperial narrative in one moment. From reading to writing, via addiction, Coleridge inscribes, and is inscribed by, the history of modern England, and of English Identity as an identity performed by the insistence of voracious, insatiable desire. Yet Coleridge's strategy of displacement is also typically English, having its poetic antecedents in Edmund Spenser's *The Faerie Queene*. We can read Coleridge's introduction, not as a private and individual apologia, but, instead, as engaging with "the most public spheres of British imperial history."[24] As Spenser had displaced and deferred masculine desire and the territorial imperative through the national, mythological figure of St. George as Redcrosse in Faerie-land (thereby disowning the violence of the English towards the foreign and the female as being a violence inherent in the male project), so Coleridge disowns himself and his part as an Englishman in such stories. He does so by fictionalising himself as merely a fictive author within the narrative, rather than being the author of that narrative.

Nevertheless Coleridge cannot escape from history, from particular strands or, to put it another way, from the economic circle. The structure of economic reason is circular, argues Derrida,[28] always leading us back through the same circuits, endlessly, relentlessly; hence madness. This structural model infests Coleridge's thinking with its own madness as he writes out the poem. The madness is such, however, that the economy of economy not only posits the inevitability of the return but also, with that, a condition of forgetting as part of the economic necessity. As Derrida points out, in a remark fully pertinent to this reading of Coleridge's poem and preface, Coleridge's will to write, caught in its own double bind of forgetfulness, delay, detour and denial, is marked by both:

> reason and unreason from the inside and the outside. It is at once
> reason and unreason because it also manifests that madness of

---

Liberty;[22] hence, in part, the "Sonnets," comprising[26] poems written between 1802 and 1806.

Wordsworth's England of the sonnets contains "Earth's best hopes" (14).[25] The "Men of Kent" are the "Vanguard of Liberty" (1), the "Children of the Soil" (2).[26] Freedom is not merely freedom, but has a national character, being "British freedom,"[27] subject of the "world's praise" (3). Freedom or death are the only choices for those who speak the "tongue/That Shakespeare spake" (11-12), and whose morals are also Milton's (13); how Wordsworth knows this so confidently is a mystery; unless, of course, he is "truly English,"

the rational *logos* itself, that madness of the economic circle the calculation of which is constantly reconstituted, logically, rationally, annulling the excess.[29]

We can therefore read Coleridge's poem as fundamentally and ultimately an economic exercise, governed by the law of economic exchange, both internally, in the shaping of its fractured narratives of desire, and externally, in Coleridge's attempts to head its meanings off, before their fall into excess. Paradoxically for Coleridge, in his attempts to annul the excess—that excess which is his and yet which also exceeds him, escapes his control—logically and rationally, he only reveals all the more clearly the excess, the madness, that madness named addiction, always already inscribed in economic reason. As if to emphasize this, at the moment of writing he is interrupted, "called out by a person on business from Porlock."[31] If the establishment of English business had been the subject, in part, of Coleridge's reading matter before the vision in the dream, then it is business, a refreshingly normal, mundane activity, albeit of an unspecified nature (perhaps the "person" is a drug dealer?), that completes the circuit. If this economic fantasy should seem fanciful, notice the alliterative tying of loose ends by Coleridge. We begin with *Purchas his Pilgrimage* and end with a *per*son from *P*orlock.

The first syllables of "Purchas" and "person" are alike, while the name of the first traveller suggests commercial acquisition and transaction. Further, both "pilgrimage" and "Porlock" take up the sounds "p" and "l." Notice how Coleridge takes both his readers and himself on a detour, a pilgrimage, a journey that returns home, back to the safety of England. This recalls Coleridge to familiar surroundings apparently against his will. I say "apparently" because we are returned before we "set off" to Xanadu. Thus we are made safe, returned safely, brought home to—and by—the familiarity of business, upon which another trav-

---

and therefore in touch with the spiritual national identity manifested by the nation's canonical authors). "In everything," writes Wordsworth, "we are sprung/Of Earth's first blood" (13-14).[30] English identity, in being so decidedly rooted in the blood and the soil, eschews mere metaphysics, amounting to a self-affirmation of the nation as destiny. In retrospect, and after Auschwitz, this all seems too chillingly modern, too eagerly anticipatory of the major spiritual-political thrust of the twentieth century.

As a consequence of such an affirmation and awareness of such a privileged position, is it any wonder that the "ancient English dower" (5) is one

eller had set out almost two hundred years earlier, and upon which that traveller (and others like him) had encountered the Oriental; and, presumably, opium.

III

Coleridge's title, *Kubla Khan*, and the fragmented, unreadable structure of the subtitle, hint at the foreignness that his introduction seeks to resist. Coleridge's other is not, however, the Orient; it is not out there, geographically, but is *in* him, *of* him. Coleridge's other is Coleridge-on-drugs, Coleridge-addicted. We should not, at this juncture, think of Coleridge-addicted, as being the essence of Coleridge. To name "Coleridge-on-drugs" is to name what Avital Ronell describes as a "special mode of addiction"[37] or a "toxic drive,"[38] for which "drugs" is only one metaphor. My term, "Coleridge-addicted," names something beyond Coleridge. It names, to quote Ronell again, that "structure that is philosophically and metaphysically at the basis of our culture."[39] Coleridge's attempt to escape addiction leads back to the same structure of which Ronell speaks, for the poet "shift[s] dependency to a person, an ideal."[40] The metaphorical drug has shifted to the equally metaphorical female, another name for the desires that mobilise our cultural structures. Nevertheless, Coleridge is so addicted to the structure of detour (not realising that such a fabrication is still a part of the general economy of structure in our culture), that he desires to evade responsibility.

Coleridge's vision is not his but incorporates him. This is, at least, the story that the poet would have us believe. The vision in the dream is, strictly speaking, *unheimlich*. It is uncanny, not at home; hence the circumscribing fear remarked by the poet in his introduction. Yet tellingly, what is also being re-presented is the repressed of that which *is* most familiar. The *unheimlich* is the figure of domestic identity *par excellence*. As a necessity of the *unheimlich*, where the self has also departed from

---

of inward happiness" (6)?[32] Inevitably, of course, England, Wordsworth's "dear country" (13)[33] on which rests the Evening Star (1-2), has been populated, we are told, by "Great Men [who] have been among us" (1);[34] men such as Sidney, Marvell, Harrington and Milton (3-4).[35]

It is no surprise then, that Wordsworth chooses to return to England from France, which country "hath brought forth no such souls" as those "great men" already named (1).[36]

As Wordsworth returns to England, to Dover, returning from tyranny to Liberty, he notices a "fellow-passenger" (1).[41] This is a "Negro Woman" (2,

familiar surroundings, Coleridge writes in *Kubla Khan* of the un-remark-able, the supposed other, the silence the other side of Eurocentric ratio-nality. In effect, the poem always implies this rational discourse, although it is rendered mute and made absent by the mapping of Xanadu. Coleridge seeks to recuperate rationality.

Rationality is not available to us, however, even though the un-remarkable is given excessive enunciation. Were we to impose a ratio-nale on the fragmentary discourse, we would be denying its visionary provisionality. We would also be imposing the architecture of European reason as an overarching structure with which to recuperate otherness. Throughout the poem, we are informed of the sacred, of the sunless, the lifeless, and that which is measureless. This is a lexicon of proliferating negation, which, in a manner suitable to the historical and literary dis-course on colonial otherness, anticipates Conrad's narrator, Marlow, of *Heart of Darkness*. The text reiterates phrases, as the sunless sea is transformed into the lifeless ocean (recalling "The Rime of the Ancient Mariner"). We read also of caverns, walls, chasms, cedarn covers, enfold-ings, the "mazy motion" of the river, of sinking, shadows, and ghostly voices. Coleridge plays with the ebb and flow of associative and reflexive imagery, where each figure either anticipates or repeats, in whole or in part, every other. Everything that is, is not in this realm; or, at least, it is that which is somehow either partially or wholly absent, remarkable only in its not being solidly present. The shadows are merely signifiers of absence as the desire for presence. This is also true of the ghostly voices. Yet despite the figuring of such absence that might seem to suggest tranquility, we are, climactically, in the "presence" of the tumultuous (38-39), taken up and re-sounded, recited, in the shadowy cries of war.

The sacred—and, therefore, unknowable—river is always moving in a labyrinthine fashion before its final consumption into the death that the ocean offers. This finality is not a singular moment. It is part of the poem's unending cycle through otherness; through being-addicted

---

10), who has been "driv'n from France,/Rejected like all others of her race" (10-11). Wordsworth identifies the woman as a fellow passenger, yet main-tains her strangeness, her foreign otherness. Indeed, in beginning the poem "We," the poet has constructed an unidentified, observing and exclusive com-munity from which the woman is held by the clinical registration ("Negro Woman") of her difference.

The woman is composed of a cluster of signs which, circulating around her figure in the first nine-line sentence, do not domesticate her. She is framed, imprisoned and thereby marginalised by the doubled phrase, "Negro

that is mapped, by the figures mentioned above, as part of a "toxico-geography—an imaginary place where literature c[an] crash against its abysses and float amid fragments of residual transcendency."[42] The constructions, both of nature (chasms, caverns, covers) and the Khan's palace (the walls, the dome), belong to the toxicogeography. The constructions and their component parts perform concealment, burial, and other figural engulfings. Each of the figures and features in question dissolves absolutely fixable referents. As the sometimes visible, sometimes obscured river displaces the land, the topography becomes drawn by the poet's refusal—or inability—to accede to its mapping. Topography here is, strictly speaking, impossible, because the text acknowledges and inscribes Xanadu as *u-topos*, as non-place (as Coleridge has asserted that the poem is not a poem). The confirmation and inscription are the two sides of the poet's paradox, anticipated in the introductory note. The poet says that he cannot say. He knows that he will write what he has said he was unable to write. Nevertheless he attempts to pen it down, thereby fixing it. This is Coleridge's fixation and his fix, his addiction, also.

Nevertheless, despite—or, perhaps, because of—Coleridge's obsession with the abyssal and labyrinthine, the images of women are resolutely *there*. They reside in the poem, insisting on their presence, offering for the poet, for the Khan, for the (implicitly) male reader, who are all the same, hopelessly entrapped in the "mazy" motion of masculinity's imaginary, a disruptive meaning, itself composed of hidden pleasures, seductive abysses, and the threat of the unpredictable; for the figure of the female is the figure of unending metamorphosis within the realms of phallogocentric discourse. Its certainty is its uncertainty as a single, definable figure. Coleridge needs the image of the female to perpetuate his reliance on an "external" stimulus. The female is always already that stimulus in Western discourse, and so it is inevitable that Coleridge must have recourse to the universal addiction. Without his addiction, without partaking of his "drug," Coleridge can have no sense of subjec-

---

Woman." If domestication for Wordsworth is not possible—for this is no Abyssinian maid of some erotic, hallucinogenic dream—neither is there to be read in the cluster of signs any respect on Wordsworth's part for alterity, or any ethical attempt to comprehend the woman as capable of self-dignity, or of having an identity which is neither French nor English. The signs with which Wordsworth reads the woman partake of the discourse of the exotic female other, whilst also being drawn from a general Western, white European (implicitly, if not explicitly racist) taxonomy of African people.

The woman is "gaudy in array" (2). Although "like a Lady gay" (3),

tivity, however displaced. It is thus the female image that legitimates Coleridge's inscription of the dream. Coleridge excuses his addiction and his inability either to control his vision or to finish his poem by the inclusion of the female. Desire for the other constitutes the constantly rebuilt structure of male subjectivity, and, without which desire, such subjectivity is merely a dead shell, a memorial, a decaying architecture of Romanticism's detumescence.

Were we to discount a poetics of tumescence as a dominant discourse in *Kubla Khan*, we would do well to remember not only the humorously phallic image of the pleasure-dome itself but also the poem's "sinuous rills," its blossoms, the "mighty fountain momently . . . forced" with its "half-intermitted burst," accompanied by "fast, thick pants" (8, 9, 19, 20, 18). We should also recall the flinging up of the sacred river that, ultimately, reaches the "caverns, measureless to man," sinking into a lifeless ocean (24-27). We have approached the poem's image of war that, at this stage, can be read as another expression within the economy of male desire. Coleridge's lifeless ocean, a figure for female sexuality which, before, had been merely a sunless sea, now swallows up the masculine flow of the sacred river, into death. It is the implicitly male subject, however, who is experiencing the orgasmic moment. Interestingly, the moment is not static, not a singular instance, but a continual dissemination.

Concomitantly, the "deep romantic chasm" (12), which is also a "savage place" (14), suggests traditional art representations of female sexuality, as do other images in the poem. Notice, also, how Coleridge prefaces the chasm with the climactic "But oh!" (12). Coleridge provides an ambiguous inscription with the exclamation. "Oh" may well be the breathless remark of a subject in awe of the presence of his desire, as well as being the intimation of climax (for whom? the reader? the poet? or both, in a shared moment of masculine loss of control?). However, the sound implies the fifteenth letter of the alphabet, a symbol

---

she is not one , but merely a simulacrum. She is observed to be "meek" and "pitiably tame" (5). The latter term amplifies the former, whilst implying that she has perhaps been deprived of a "native quality" such as fierceness; that she is no longer untamed or unbroken, wild even. Thus the implication is that the French have broken her spirit, curtailed her "animality"; which of course returns us to Wordsworth's understanding of the black woman as originally savage and bestial. Wordsworth's poetry hints at more than a little quasi-anthropological interest in the woman, rather than any direct or genuine sympathy or solidarity. Furthermore, we are told that her speech is lan-

both of enclosure and teleology, yet also of absence, nullity, the abyss and, therefore, of a certain phallogocentric enunciation of the representation of female sexuality. From this moment we are led directly to the first female image.

Through this image Coleridge suggests multiple hauntings, all of which are the reiterated traces of the female figure. Multiple hauntings are implied by the line:

> As e'er beneath a waning moon was haunted (15)

which makes clear the possibility of other similar scenes. The poem presents the reader with the age-old male fear of female sexuality acquiring its own power in the vision of the savage chasm with its cedarn cover (13, suggestive possibly of pubic hair) being haunted by the wailing woman. Here the woman is merely an extension of her sexuality, a sexuality that both threatens to engulf and is also spectral. The always-returning female spectre imposes the "irrational" and "hysterical" voice,—"wailing"—such non-sense being the sign of a triple citation (the savage, the holy, the enchanted) whereby Coleridge attempts to recuperate the Other. These are the poet's translations as he seeks to fix female meaning in an effort to elide his being-caught-up, his addictive urge or toxic drive. From the figure of the woman in the chasm, the poet constructs a chiasmatic inversion of the image, through which the location is made holy and enchanted, not by the poet's application to a discourse of female sexuality, but by the wailing woman, whose presence and voice makes the site savage.

Thus Coleridge seeks to escape responsibility again. He catches himself in the lie, however, through the ostensibly antinomian binarism of "holy" and "savage," which marks the moment of deconstruction in the poet's text, being the polar extremes of conventional representations of female sexuality. Despite this, though, Coleridge is encouraging

---

guid, her eyes and face motionless (8-9); both descriptions are typical in white representations of black men and women.[43]

Thus this woman is only a symbol for Wordsworth of French tyranny; so foreign is she for him, that he is unable to transform her into a figure travelling towards England, the land of Liberty. Nor does the poet think to offer England as a refuge and home to the woman. England remains tellingly absent from this sonnet.

The compassion offered by Wordsworth is little enough; merely "proffer'd kindness" (7). Yet, because the woman responds only with languid

us to read only the metaphysical transformations (holy, enchanted) that are left in the wake of female non-rational otherness. We are enticed, by a poet already hooked, in a state of being-addicted, to disregard female presence in favour of a disturbing female trace. The disturbance, resulting supposedly out of enticement, leaves us free of guilt, of culpability, because we are unable to resist the violence that our bodies undergo when transformed by the female fix. We cannot "just say no." Yet this apparent violence, supposedly outside ourselves, supposedly induced by both the female and Oriental, is determinable as emanating from the interior of the desiring self, being a sign of the Other-within. This determines our state as always already being-on-drugs, always addicted to the figure of the female as that which fuels desire. Thus the trace of the woman is readable as that which, in any culture, is already there, *in* our discourses, as a fundamental part of the cultural unconscious, that displaces rationality and logic, calm and sensible discursive structures.

Interiority has, of course, already been predicated in the subtitle of the poem, which speaks of a vision in a dream. It is reasonable to connect the subtitle of *Kubla Khan* to the second line of the third verse that also mentions a vision (38). Whether the third verse *is* the vision is open to question. However, in the vision is the "damsel with a dulcimer" (36). The choice of the word "damsel" implies a young, unmarried woman of noble origin. That she is both young and unmarried are intimations of virginity, a reading borne out by Coleridge's choice of the word "maid." She is, then, all the more appropriate to the dream of male desire. Coleridge's choice of Abyssinia for the maid makes plain that we are still in the Orient of the white imagination, in the discourse of Orientalism as the West's Other. Coleridge displaces the desire for the African woman onto the Khan, away from himself, by the introduction of the first person pronoun. This displacement belongs to a double troping whereby, in the imaginary, the reader is, simultaneously, Kubla Khan and yet, also, not the Asian Emperor. If the Khan speaks here then it is not of our—

---

speech and motionless face, this expression of compassion in the poem seems more intended to highlight Wordsworth's sensibilities; to quote Robin Jarvis on the rhetoric of compassion in a Thatcherite context, Wordsworth's "proffer'd kindness" is ultimately "in the service of one's own self-image or self-regarding humanity."[44] *Indeed, the entire sonnet seems little more than an excuse for self-promotion, concurring in subtle ways with ideologies of Tory-liberalism in the nineteenth century, and the New Right in the Twentieth.*

Wordsworth's view of the black woman concurs with the ideology of the New Right because it is an oblique statement of nationalist self-interest. The

that is to say the English readers'—desire. Khan's desire is merely an expression of his Oriental "nature." However, "I" implicitly gathers up the reader and the poet in its community of enunciation. We may disown the "I" as that of the foreign barbarian, yet, when reading, we automatically assume the same subject position, whether or not we reject that location as disinterested readers of poetry. We are always implicated in the desire of the female other.

This second female image is at the heart of whatever displaced subjectivity we are able to comprehend. The third verse's inclusion of the first person pronoun, takes both poet and reader (and Kubla Khan), as shared subjectivity, inside; inside the text, inside the dream, inside the vision in the dream. The female is not there, not, at least, as presence. She is only remembered by the speaker/reader. She is a vision in a vision; which vision is not of the moment but in an indefinable past, as registered by the phrase, "once I saw." The male spectator desires a return to the moment of the vision, to revive the female music within the vision, which would "win" him to "deep delight" (44). The female image is constructed as infinitely deferred and, moreover, ineluctably desirable because deferred. Male desire strains after the woman's music, desiring to make the music and, therefore, the woman, his, so that he might, with the aid of the female, *erect the pleasure dome.* Read in this way the text becomes a yearning after lost masculine power represented by the expression of the male's desired return to virility. Tellingly, it is the female who makes possible male power; without the female fix the male has no power. The possibility for a recovery of such power—and, through power, a definition of subjectivity—regresses without end, into the non-place of the abyss.[45]

IV

Turn and re-turn, tour as detour, the Odyssean narrative[48] in the thrall of cravings and the premise of an imperfectly realised, always

---

woman is thus fetishised, which serves the interests and affirmation of national identity to which the return home is directed psychically. Because Wordsworth has equated Englishness with Liberty throughout the sonnets, Englishness has become sublated, made over into a transcendent nationalism. Yet as I have already mentioned, for Wordsworth it is a spiritual identity rooted in the earth and blood; to be English does not depend on "birth, nor citizenship, nor geography nor race" (to borrow from Derrida's analysis of Fichte's conception of German identity).[46]

However, not everyone can belong to this philosophical-nationalism, as the

already collapsing national identity. These are the traces that most commonly mark Coleridge's writing influenced by Wordsworth's wanderings. These traces are also those that inevitably affect any thinking about the Romantic scene of writing.

In conclusion, I shall turn back again to particular traces—the tracks of certain needles, paths leading back home—that speak of addiction throughout this essay.

Kubla Khan appears to exist outside history in mythological and imaginary space. At the same time it is a text enclosed by its own play. Relentlessly interiorised, it hides itself from the historical. This self-enclosure and exclusion are no accident on Coleridge's part. It is the very sign of the poem's historicity, its cultural moment. Coleridge's poem is a document of English identity's imaginary relationship to the Orient, expressive as the poem is of a national fear brought about by imperial and colonial incursions into the foreign.

If the imperial and colonial agendas are concerned with making other territories and other peoples English, then accompanying this is the fear that Englishness might be spread a little too thinly, its essence diluted, corrupted, lost, through being repeatedly employed as the narcotic by which foreigners lose their own identities. Wordsworth seeks to avert this fear by refusing to encounter it, by always already returning to that which is English for him; and thereby, hopefully, condensing and strengthening Englishness.

Coleridge, on the other hand, does not envision the return so clearly. In the fluidity of metaphor and metonymic figure Coleridge writes an excess that is conventionally associated with the supposed decadence and luxury of the Orient, typical, in Western narrative, of that which cannot be assimilated by the European mind. In doing so, he also unveils a condition of domestic identity, its crucial double bind.

Coleridge's "vision"—a vision he disowns—is driven by the desires, addictions and anxieties of white mythology. What the poet hides

---

sonnet makes clear; for the sonnet sequence, as the political context of the sonnet on the black woman, attempts to elevate Englishness from a mere ideology into a philosophy of spirit, claiming to represent or embody "the universal essence of man."[47] And it is at this point that the woman is left behind, excluded from a safe English home, by the poet of modern national identity. Thus Wordsworth, in returning home from France, returns himself from a position of powerlessness (being an Englishman abroad) to one of apparent power, sacrificing the black woman on the way. To borrow from Frances Ferguson, he moves from a "position of abject powerlessness"—which powerlessness is displaced onto the black

throughout his non-poem is white, masculine, English identity, peering eagerly, with a mixture of fear and fascination into the distorted mirror of its own obsessions. Coleridge obscures his national and historical identity to encompass the Oriental Other, to subjugate it to the white gaze, whilst trying to maintain the power of whiteness through invisibility.

It is precisely this gambit, though, that threatens to undermine power because if the white man—in this case Coleridge—is invisible, if he has given up responsibility, then he cannot have any claim to power. This, in turn, presents Coleridge with another problem.

For Coleridge, the problem at hand is to effect a return to a "properly" constituted subjectivity, an English bourgeois subject who can carry on business-as-usual, freed from the guilt of both addiction and desire (dealers and pushers are, after all, merely phenomena of a free market, enterprise culture); and, importantly, from desire *as* addiction. The successful completion of such a project—itself a manifestation of desire—is, strictly speaking, impossible. Coleridge, in order to locate this subjectivity, must create a place, a world of his own as Wordsworth puts it, where the subject—i.e., himself, his *self*—can exist. Coleridge's being-on-drugs, however, opens up the non-place of the unconscious or imaginary, figured as England's Orient, on which national economy depends. Coleridge is thus faced with the paradox of "this topology of a certain locatable non-place, at once necessary and undiscoverable."[50] By the very logic of the non-place, all is on the verge of the abyss, on figural-topographical borders to a site without boundaries. In such a place the subject Coleridge imagines—a "proper" subject—would be impossible. Therefore Coleridge attempts to rewrite the topology of the non-place through the inscription of the female as a point of reference, a familiar structure by which to gather his bearings. Coleridge introduces the female as stabilising, calming, familiar anodyne.

The female as domestic Other translates foreign narrative. The problem is that, as I have suggested, the discourse on the female re-

---

woman—"to one of absolute power."[49] *Wordsworth transfers abject powerlessness onto another, victimising her in the process. Such a repositioning is an effort to return to a particular truth, free of ideology; it is a return home to the supposedly value-free site of the identity called Englishness, a return from the "ideology" of being French. Yet this return is one which opens for us the lengths to which English identity will go to hide its own ideologies, and the lengths to which it will go in order to make Englishness seem "natural" and therefore unassailable by analysis, unavailable to internal critique. Wordsworth's return leads us to a necessary point of departure.*

introduces, returns to, takes the ineluctable detour of, the economy of the undiscoverable. So Coleridge finds himself again, always already, hooked, back at the point of departure. This, as Derrida has commented, is the very nature of the subject and the return of the subject.[51] In order for the subject to return to be rewritten as the reiteration of a position or place there must be that structure, figure, architecture or toxic substance that constitutes "the possibility of this kind of repetition one calls a return."[52]

No matter how much Coleridge desires escape, his escape will only lead him back to his own ruins, to his addicted self. No matter how much we may wish to dissociate our "selves" from right-wing versions of English identity, we are somehow connected. It is with this double bind that we must engage, to which we must return.

2

MATTHEW ARNOLD, ENGLISHNESS
AND A QUESTION OF SPIRIT

It has been claimed that Arnold "wrote the classic protest against Victorian anti-intellectualism." While many of his catch-phrases about fresh ideas and knowing the best that has been thought in the world may appear to support such a claim, it is still unfounded.

—Chris Baldick

While Thomas Arnold was perhaps oppressively consistent, Matthew was complicated.

—Ruth apRoberts

Arnold was both the most Wordsworthian and Classical of Victorian poets.

—William E. Buckler

I

In the first chapter, I suggested, in passing, that we can only think of Coleridge *through* Wordsworth, that the Coleridge who exists for us and whom we construct, whether as readers or as critics of whatever school, is, essentially, *Wordsworth's Coleridge.* Coleridge re-writes himself through his comprehension of Wordsworth's vision. Wordsworth's overdetermining "spirit" is of so forceful a nature that Matthew Arnold could no more escape Wordsworth than could Coleridge. Wordsworth, rightly comprehended, is a figure of Englishness *par excellence.*

The question of Arnold's Wordsworth, the "last poetic voice," ("Memorial Verses," 4) will be touched upon again, as we look at the pertinence of the question of national identity and spirit in Matthew Arnold's writing. Of course, in talking about spirit as residing "in" anything, as though it could reside in an entity such as writing, is to inherit a fundamental misrecognition of the problematic of spirit. The inheritance is not unintentional, however, it having been recalled here in order to signal the very nature of Arnold's own difficulties in his dealing with such issues.

In this chapter, I look at the issue of national identity, nationalism and Arnold's often Wordsworthian sense of spirit—of spirit as knowledge, the knowledge of a people aware of their own identity, and the immanent hollowing out of that identity, as their heritage—as expressed in poems from the 1840s to the 1870s.[1] Also given attention here is Arnold's attempt to engage with the problematic nature of Englishness, mentioned at the close of the previous chapter. The next chapter deals with Arnold's essay, "My Countrymen," in which Arnold attempts, not without some success, a transition in critical approach for philosophical purposes.

I should state at the outset, then, that this and the next chapter are not concerned with Matthew Arnold's literary criticism. I mention this because of the overwhelming debt that all Victorian scholars must feel when confronting Arnold in the wake of Chris Baldick's highly persuasive reading of Arnoldian criticism and its legacy in *The Social Mission of English Criticism 1848-1932*.[2] To attempt any reading of Arnold's writing on the categories of literature and poetry without acknowledging the breadth and cogency of Baldick's critical assessment would be foolhardy. While not looking at Arnold's criticism, I have, however, quoted Baldick for the epigraph to this essay,[3] because what will be dealt with in part here and, in more detail, in the next chapter, is the issue of Arnold's response to what is termed Victorian anti-intellectualism,[4] implicit and immanent in the poetry and, more explicitly, in "My Countrymen."

II

Perhaps the two most well-known or, at least, most frequently anthologised poems of Matthew Arnold are "Isolation. To Marguerite" and "Dover Beach" ("Stanzas from the Grande Chartreuse" and "The Scholar Gypsy" coming up close behind). Both are read as typical and yet superlative expressions of the Victorian loss of faith and the resulting crisis of cultural and spiritual identity. Such a reading is not usually related, to my knowledge, to any question of national identity. If we accept the standard reading provisionally, then the question must be raised, where is Arnold in such expressions of identity's crisis? Clearly identity's crisis is engendered for Arnold in part by the loss of Wordsworth. After Wordsworth, there is no one who has the "healing power" to resolve European crises ("Memorial Verses," 62-63). Equally, after Wordsworth's passing, Arnold's fear is that there is now no one

who "will make us feel." (*MV*, 67) But what "Matthew Arnold" is readable today, as a part of the initiation of a discourse of poetic resistance to
the current capitalisation, on the part of the Right, on the theme of
National and Cultural Identity? Is it to Arnold that we have to turn, in
the hope that he will make us feel?

Although the poems already mentioned establish, quite clearly, a
single speaker and a single addressee, the critical readings hitherto given
most credence are those which argue that Arnold's "singular voice" is
merely a filter through which a supposedly universal doubt or fear
comes to be expressed. Thus, the unique articulation and its concomitant identity, whether identifiable as Matthew Arnold or a fictive counterpart, is also, in the traditional reading, that of an Everyman. Arnold
would seem to be hiding himself, his selfhood, in giving expression to his
voice as, simultaneously, a voice *for* everyone and the voice *of* everyone.

Furthermore, this enunciation, the trace of Being-in-Crisis, is, still,
the performance of identity. What is being hidden, or glossed over, re-
written and placed under erasure through the performative voice, is
not merely a subject called "Matthew Arnold" but English identity as *the*
universal identity, as the "best" (to use an Arnoldian word) representative of universal Being. In this reading, English identity is at once the
(largely self-appointed) apotheosis of human agency, while also claiming
itself to be at the vanguard even in the moment of crisis of European
identities through the poetic referents pertaining to the Euro-Christian
tradition.

Such a manoeuvre is, of course, typical of what Derrida has called
"the self affirmation of an identity":

> Whether it takes a national form or not, a refined, hospitable or
> aggressively xenophobic form or not, the self-affirmation of an
> identity always claims to be responding to the call or assignation of
> the universal.[5]

Arnold, and subsequent constructions of "Matthew Arnold" and
"Arnold's poetry" (for which "Dover Beach" has become a virtual synecdoche) are thus involved in a project of self-affirmation in the instant of
imminent disruption; self-affirmation becomes the figure of disruption
and dissolution.

Given this paradox, of the doubling of identity and the covering up
of identity—a paradox which, incidentally, is a deliberate strategy for
identity's affirmation—what positions, to reiterate an earlier question,
does Arnold occupy politically, culturally, philosophically in relation to
Englishness, throughout some of his lesser known poems?

III

The composition of Arnold's poetry covers a period of more than forty years, connecting the Romantics to the late Victorians. During this time, Wordsworth's spirit haunts Arnold's lines to a greater or lesser degree. Despite the latter's overt Christianity and the former's always incipient pantheism, Wordsworth is never wholly absent from Arnold's writing. Arnold acknowledges this in a note to his Newdigate prize-poem, "Cromwell," composed early in 1843. In the note, Arnold states that the first stanza is an allusion to Wordsworth's "Poems Dedicated to National Liberty."

The poem is interesting inasmuch as there can be glimpsed Arnold the Republican, the supporter of democracy and revolution. Arnold's references to "sleepless waves," "buoyant sea," "exulting waves," "the waves . . . of liberty," "the solemn cadence" and "dusty plain" (ll. 1, 7, 8, 16, 19, 43) are poised between Wordsworthian echoes and intimations, which, wave-like, resound throughout this early poem, and the later figures of the "sea," "the tide," "the grating roar," "the waves," the "tremulous cadence" and "darkling plain" (ll. 1, 2, 8, 10, 13, 35), all of which inhabit "Dover Beach" in 1851, eight years after "Cromwell."

"Dover Beach," however, remarks on the "turbid ebb and flow" of the "distant Northern sea," (ll. 17, 20) in its effort to make literal the sadness associated with ebbing of the "Sea of Faith" (21). From the metaphor of the sea in "Cromwell," through the literal sea at Dover, to the Sea of Faith, Arnold moves between the secular and the metaphysical, between hope and despair, between the aspiration of revolutionary identity (the assertion of a new sense of cultural Being-in-common) and the attempts to shore up a conservative and theologically grounded sense of self which finds itself on the edge of an abyss (the zero point of loss of Being-in-common) for which the sea comes to stand. Cromwell's revolutionary army has become transformed into "ignorant armies [which] clash by night" (37).

The shift between positions is not necessarily a transitional movement of either political allegiance or intellect on Arnold's part; nor is it a change of ideological heart. This is not a question of linearity or progression. What can be read, though, is the proximity of somewhat paradoxical positions that, unconscious of the implicit contradiction, exist as necessary and culturally contingent traces of an identity grounded in a national culture during the middle years of the nineteenth century. We can go further to suggest that such traces are translatable as an exemplary mapping of mid-Victorian intellectual selfhood. So, two Arnolds at least, then, who mediate a particular version—and vision—of Englishness;

the Arnold who, with a Wordsworthian fervour reminiscent of the early *Prelude* and the employment of the equally Wordsworthian rhetorical negative remarking the passage from infancy to adulthood, demands of us:

> Say not such dreams are idle: for the man
> Still toils to perfect what the child began.

("Cromwell," 45-46)

And the other Arnold, for whom:

> . . . the world, which seems
> To lie before us like a land of dreams,
> So various, so beautiful, so new,
> Hath really neither joy, nor love, nor light,
> Nor certitude, nor peace, nor help for pain;

("Dover Beach," 30-34)

For Arnold, the dream of freedom, given its most apposite signature in the figure, actions and name of Cromwell, has turned into another, more deceptive dream, a nightmare of absence, marked by the incessant and ineluctable iteration of negation.

"Cromwell" and "Dover Beach" set the scene for the question of identity. They do so, furthermore, within a specifically national and, even, nationalist context, despite their metaphysical-theological desires. This context at once belies the universal and, at the same time, supports a certain textual, idiomatic Englishness in its always implicit claim to be the representative of universality; to be universality itself. If Wordsworth dogs Arnold's lines in "Cromwell," then the whole of poetic tradition and apparent continuity, manifested in the proper name, Sophocles, does the same in "Dover Beach"(15). This is not, though, a continuity of suffering identified by Arnold; rather, he gathers up Sophocles and, by implication, the whole pre-Christian tragic-poetic tradition and idiom, (tradition, we can suggest, as idiom) into Christianity's desire to speak (as) the universal *lingua franca* of humanity's identity.

It is important to remember, all the while, that Arnold attempts this aggregation on behalf of Christian ideology from Dover beach, the place where one sails for Europe and other lands, in various guises such as colonial force, commercial enterprise, or travelling sightseer. Dover is the place to which Wordsworth returns during his "Poems dedicated to National Independence and Liberty."[6] Dover is the place for that generation of English people who lived through the Second World War where the cliffs become the metonymic figure for English Freedom in the popular song, "The White Cliffs of Dover." Even today, as the generation of the Second World War passes away, we encounter advertisements for collections of W.W.II romantic songs which picture an RAF pilot and his sweetheart standing—perhaps in the same spot as Matthew Arnold?—with the Dover cliffs receding to a point of infinity behind them.[7] The implication is that England goes on for ever, geographically, in our imaginations, and in the commercial constructions of our nostalgic desires. Dover Beach, its chalk cliffs and the sea map out all of England, for all time, as a geo-political/psychic figure of eternal recurrence in the bid for immutable Englishness.

This suggests then that—reading the poem askance—Sophocles is, in fact, colonised as it were as a retroactive English Christian by Arnold, despite the ostensible Arnoldian/English deprecation in the text, from his vantage point; which is also the vantage point for all English peoples to survey their own land and to imagine other worlds which remain hidden beyond the curve of the earth but which are there, just waiting for colonisation, education and the chance to be little Englands. Even though the poet does deplore the distance of England spiritually from Sophocles and the Aegean, this perspective is achieved through an implied desire to rethink England in classical terms, while simultaneously gathering up the classical mode and its motifs for the purpose of Anglicising them in order that the reformation of the English spirit might go forward. From this perspective, the edge of the abyss on which Arnold stands is also the jetty or promontory from which to view one's possessions and territories; it is thus a double figure, marked by the ambiguity that is inevitable in all acts of national appropriation.

Curiously, it is Cromwell—Marvell's Cromwell, Carlyle's Cromwell, standing in a Wordsworthian landscape—who offers Arnold the hope of national identity, an identity at once radical and yet rooted firmly as an English hero; he offers a challenge to and support of Englishness. This hope, found by Arnold in Cromwell, cannot be found by Arnold in himself. This hope itself is turned, in the final couplet of "Cromwell,"

> And the wind murmured round him, and he stood
> Once more alone beside the gleaming flood

> (239-240)

into a moment of Tennysonian ambiguity[8] that anticipates Arnold's own loneliness and isolation as he overlooks the beach and the "Cliffs of

England." (*DB*, 4) The material presence of the "English Cliffs," these cliffs that have national identity in all their overwhelming and solid presence, is opposed to the ephemerality of the French coast, which vanishes with the disappearance of the light (3).[9] So we witness Arnold, before the prospect of the sea at Dover beach, and Cromwell, alone beside the gleaming flood.

There is readable a sense of oscillation between the two figures, the spirit of one eliding, inhabiting, infecting the other. And, given Arnold's resounding despair at Dover beach, *in* "Dover Beach," one cannot help but feel the echoes of a self-consciousness on the part of the younger Arnold in his choice of motto for "Cromwell":

> Schrecklich ist es, deiner Wahrheit
> Sterbliches Gefäss zu seyn[10]

Is it going too far to say that Arnold comprehends the onerous nature of believing himself to be, like Cromwell, one of the elect, one of the chosen representatives to bear the standard of all that is English? Is Arnold's self-appointed life's work to be as the teacher, translator and carrier of Englishness and the English spirit? By the 1870s, Arnold will have shifted his burden, in order to evade his doubts and to accuse, instead, the middle-classes of an absolute lack of spirit and identity. Between the 1840s and the 1870s, however there remains the question of Arnold's position on the inquest into being English.

IV

Arnold's religious despair, which is both his and, always already, more than his, (shared as it is by "mortal millions" [*M*, 4]) being something that exceeds him, threatening to engulf him, is most powerfully conjured in his verse through the image of the sea. It is the flood before which Cromwell stands alone; yet it is also the Sea of Faith. Could faith be that overwhelming for Arnold, that its tidal onslaught and roar is a simultaneous promise of its own withdrawing, a promise of the loss of faith itself?

Or are the waves, the sea, the flood, something Other?

How are we to think of the sea in terms of nationality and identity, and not merely the context of some vague or abstracted discourse circling the concept of nationality?

Arnold's other, much anthologised, short poem, "To Marguerite,"
speaks of being "in the sea of life enisled" (1; and *pace* Donne's reminder
that no man is an island) "To Marguerite" speaks also of "endless
bounds" (6) and of the "deep desire" (21) for the now lost "single continent" (16); it voices the longing that human "marges" might "meet
again" (18; the archaic form of "margins" is an evocation of its French
counterpart; Arnold unconsciously dissolves the very boundaries he
puts in place by desiring their dissolution through his inadvertent continental echo; temporally, he raises the spirit of an earlier, other, *French*
England). Finally, "To Marguerite" (the very name begins with the
promise of margins and the other beyond) closes, or opens onto, "The
unplumbed, salt, estranging sea" (24), a near perfect figuring of the
abyssal otherness which draws Arnold to its very brink.

If these figures are the expression of the fear of absolute metaphysical negation, are they not, as well, in "To Marguerite" "Dover
Beach," "Cromwell" and elsewhere, grounded in the reality of English
isolation(ism)? England and, therefore, English identity are always at
philosophical and spiritual odds with "the continent" over the question
of identity. One could go so far as to say that this provides us with a definition of English history as the history of separatist identity that is not to
be displaced onto an interrogation into metaphysics, but is a history
firmly grounded in the soil and the blood. The question is precisely historical; it is a question of—and, in Arnold's case, a quest after—temporality. It is the question and quest that haunt Arnold throughout his
life, producing and structuring the paradoxes of his discourse. And it is
this and other related concerns which are traced throughout Arnold's
writing as he concerns himself with Englishness and the question of
spirit, and with Englishness *as* the identity of the loss of spirit.

Which leads me back to my earlier question, concerning Arnold's position.

V

Arnold's position is, in part, unknowable, if only because he was
himself unsure of what position he was to take, with regard to a sense of
identity. Unable to resolve such a problem, Arnold turned, repeatedly,
outwards, in order to position himself against positions.

In his "Horatian Echo (to an Ambitious Friend)" (1847), Arnold
commands his "simple friend" (1) to ignore the struggles of political
parties. He continues by remarking that foreign affairs are "no concern
of ours" (6; three years later, in "Memorial Verses," Arnold will bemoan

the fate of a Europe in constant strife but without the power of Wordsworth's voice to heal it). The patrician tone of the first stanza, which closes the stanza with its plural possessive pronoun, authoritatively bullies both reader and addressee by the faux-democratic all-inclusiveness of "ours." We, says the poetic voice, are above politics; "we" are beyond the ideological ebb and flow of quotidian English life.

This voice, exclusive in its gesture of enclosure, moves its dismissive scorn on to specific targets in the second stanza. The masses are identified as an "invading populace" (8), and then dehumanised as a "shouldering herd" (9). Presumably, these blanket definitions cover both the lumpenproletariat and the lower-middle-classes. However, were we too quick to see Arnold as an elitist of the narrow kind, we would overlook his representation of the ruling classes:

> Ye imbeciles in present power,
> Doomed, pompous, and absurd!
>
> (11-12)

Whether government or aristocracy, the speaker reviles them in a tone of vitriolic disdain and contempt, the energy of which completely belies the impotent despair of poems such as "Dover Beach." With so much of the population defined by the social poles of the quotations in question, one cannot help but wonder where Arnold is to be found; as Ruth apRoberts has stated so succinctly, Matthew Arnold is complicated.[11] From an initial reading of the second stanza of "Horatian Echo," one is tempted to find Arnold in some Olympian place, overlooking the present day and finding comfort in echoing Horace, so as to suggest, at least to himself, a sense of poetic community and continuity (the aesthetics of universalism) untouched by the concerns of the day. Arnold, it seems, seeks to hide his own identity by attempting to distance himself from his nationality while aligning himself to an identity—that of Horace as the proper name for a "pure" poetic tradition—not tied to nationality.

Such a double act is, of course, an abnegation of ethical and political responsibility, which is given further voice in the third stanza:

> And let us bear, that they debate
> Of all the engine-work of state,
> Of commerce, laws, and policy,
> The secrets of the world's machine,
> And what the rights of man may mean,
> with readier tongue than we.
>
> (13-18)

Arnold's tone is not so clearly, unequivocally hostile here as it had been in the previous stanzas. His choice of industrial metaphors—engine-work, machine—in order to describe the political actions of the state, implies a distaste for both manufacture and the political. Such figures of speech and their concatenation to other aspects of social life locate, with machine-like precision, the period during which the poem was written.[12]

Arnold's description of the tongue that discusses human rights as "readier" (18) than his own is marked by ambiguity. "Readier" might equally suggest a tongue more fitted to the task by virtue of knowledge[13] or, merely, one more ready to talk without thought or care. This ambiguity is important because it casts doubt onto the certainty with which one can identify the politics and political identity of the speaker of the first two stanzas. The position of the speaker is mystified still further in the second half of the poem as the subject is turned to mythical poetic concerns. The speaker now considers the shared, inevitable obliteration of humanity, while directing a somewhat misogynist sneer at the fate of female beauty in the face of death. Arnold hides in universal annihilation in the double face of the political world and poetic femininity. Ironically, Arnold's turn to poetry confronts him with the political once more, in the form of the feminine. Helen (28) supposedly caused the Trojan Wars, while Juliet (29) was the indirect cause of civil strife between the Capulets and Montagues. Even for the poet, there is no escape from the political, and this is brought into focus by his own medium throughout its history.

Because there can never be an absolute retreat from the political marking of identity, Arnold turns to face this issue in two poems written the year after the "Horatian Echo." Arnold's "ambitious friend," for whom the "echo" had been written is "strictly unidentifiable," as Kenneth Allott puts it, although it "may be John Blackett."[14] All such suppositions being equal, we may speculate that the identity of the ambitious friend was Arthur Hugh Clough. In 1848, Clough was certainly the "Republican Friend" to whom the two poems were dedicated. Judging from the first of the two poems in question, it would appear that Clough's commitment to his political beliefs had turned Arnold somewhat. Gone is the sneering at both populace and rulers; gone is the fear of female mockery. In their place is an expression of solidarity with Clough:

> God knows it, I am with you. If to prize
> Those virtues, prized and practised by too few
> . . .
> Then I am yours, and what you feel, I share
>
> (1-2, 14)

Arnold arrives at his ideological affiliation indirectly, through close friendship; but he arrives at it nonetheless. His intimate feelings for Clough have turned his rancour away from those at either end of English social hierarchy and towards:

> The barren optimistic sophistries
> Of comfortable moles.
>
> (5-6)

Instead of the sea, there now flow before Arnold:

> The armies of the homeless and unfed—
>
> (12)

In this line, the dash serves a double purpose (typically of Arnold); one which is poetic, the other political. The dash allows for a break with the tumult of passionate rhetoric which had been building, clause upon clause, in the previous verses and lines. The cæsura allows Arnold to turn back to his friend, in order to re-establish and reiterate the solidarity of the first line. The dash serves a second, political function, however, and this is caught up with its poetic purpose. The dash directs us to the unspeakable; it opens out onto the abyss into which the socially marginal have been forced. In its silence, the cæsura poses the possibility of the abyss for us all, inviting us to contemplate that which is truly barbaric, whereof poetry cannot speak without a fall into barbarism itself. Encapsulated here is the problematic of Arnold's position.

Arnold's feelings do tend, though, towards a self-moderation, a new moment of imminent awareness. He shifts from despising sophistries to "sadness" (9) and a comprehension of others' "disquiet" (10) at the "long heart-wasting show." (9) Arnold's response is quiet and singular, typically liberal and humanist. The phrase "long heart-wasting show" plays curiously between interiority and exteriority; the interiority of the liberal observer's selfhood, represented in the figure of the heart, and the exteriority of the world of suffering perceived as performance, as specular occasion engendering the heart-wasting of the appalled subject.[15] Whose heart wastes? Not that of the homeless and unfed, clearly, but that of Matthew Arnold who, faced with suffering on a national scale, can only feel his own singularity wither in the face of economic and social depredations; which serves to explain for us the apparent fraternity expressed in the opening and closing lines, already quoted above.

Arnold's identity is constituted through the shared, intimate feeling between himself and Clough. It is this feeling which rescues Arnold from the contemplation of the abyss in the final lines. Clough suffers for a society at the mercy of capitalist exploitation and its social by-products, while Arnold can only feel for Clough, can only suffer in relation to his friend, and to his friend's social conscience. Through the hermeneutic gesture of circularity and enclosure, mapped by the first and last lines, with the rhetorical links of the chain being forged through the reiteration of "If"—a conditional reiteration that implies the possibility of doubt about the veracity of Clough as witness to the homeless and unfed—Arnold positions himself at a distance from the troubles of society, at the same moment that he identifies with Clough because of Clough's political identity. Once again Arnold erases identity in the act of self-affirmation.

Arnold's acts of self-affirmation lead him away from association with a greater identity. Even the prospect of a greater religious identity is problematic. In those essays of Arnold's which deal with English identity as a greater identity, we shall see him attempting to find positive terms for the expression of Englishness, rather than moving away from any identification. In "To a Republican Friend—Continued," however, we witness a further removal, a more complete erasure of engaged identity on Arnold's part.

The poem begins with "Yet," which immediately throws into question Arnold's affirmation of cautious unity with Clough in the earlier "Republican Friend" poem. Arnold's pause for critical reflection, focused in "Yet," allows him a Wordsworthian echo, calling into question (as Wordsworth had done in "Poems Dedicated to National Independence and Liberty") the then current French efforts to assert a national intellectual and spiritual identity:

> France, famed in all great arts, in none supreme;

> (4)

As Kenneth Allott points out,[16] there is also possible reference here to a similar remark of Dr. Johnson's, recalled by Boswell in his *Life*. In not declaring a cultural identity, Arnold nonetheless affiliates himself with all that is most traditionally English in literary discourse, marking in his own writing a desire to be read as one of a number of quintessential English writers, whose texts define what it means to be English and what Englishness, as a literary and cultural discourse is, in essence. In fact one could go further, to say that, for Arnold, all that is orthodox and genuine in English identity *is* "literature," its re-read traditions, its selective and canonical history, and its exclusive genealogy.

This is important because, as Arnold's verse seems to bring together the ghosts of English literary nationalism, so the next line of the second "Republican Friend" poem, although pointing thought in a different direction, invokes another English literary identity as well through two distinct, though conjoined references:

> Seeing this vale, this earth, whereon we dream.
>
> (5)

This vale, *This* Earth. If Wordsworth and Johnson are, for Arnold, the bearers of a particular model of cultural identity, who, other than Shakespeare, could be that identity's emblem? And which speech evokes the nationalistic spirit of England more than John of Gaunt's in *Richard II*?[17]

Arnold's first two clauses with their reiterated demonstrative pronouns ensure both the Shakespearean context and, through that, the unavoidable inference that the vale and Earth are read as the England belonging to an easily traceable poetic tradition. Gaunt's sustained chauvinistic diatribe even wields the image of the sea that, in its various guises, has come to stand Matthew Arnold in such good stead in all his considerations of identity and Being. Arnold's final clause in the line above also solicits the Shakespearean *geist*. The figure of the dream is common enough in Shakespeare but, in Arnold's particular context, framed by his repeated inquiries into and anxieties about his role and identity, the dream recalls Hamlet most immediately.[18]

Given this, it is easy enough to see a Matthew Arnold whose position is one in retreat. Declining to engage, or not knowing exactly how to engage, with the vicissitudes and dilemmas of everyday life; unable to reconcile poetry and poverty, verse and war, couplets and capitalism, yet also unable to bring to poetry a dissident voice that can offer up critique and scorn and an alternative vision within the native poetic tradition, Arnold withdraws further into the tradition in all its Englishness.

For all that, however, and despite Arnold's confusion over the poetic mode, he still seeks to find a socially conscious poetic voice.

VI

Arnold's critical voice is present in three lesser known poems, "Sonnet to the Hungarian Nation," "East London" and "West London."

As his poems eschew a more overtly poetic diction and syntax, so Arnold the poet becomes more easily identifiable with Arnold the essayist and critic in assuming a particular ideological identity of concerned but perplexed liberalism. In this position, Arnold gathers himself into the dominant strain of English intellectual identity in the 1860s.

The "Sonnet to the Hungarian Nation" (1849) offers a critical rebuff to the condition of all contemporary nation states, on the grounds of their respective faults. Hungary alone, of European countries, is capable, in Arnold's eyes, of achieving a semblance of heroism along the lines of "the world's dead spirit" (11). The poet's scorn is given strongest expression with regard to England, which nation the poet regards as singularly incapable of ascending to the heroic heights of classical Greek splendour:

> Nor in rich England, bent but to make pour
> The flood of the world's commerce on her shore.

> (2-3)

"Rich" is both ironic and materialistically literal. "Pour" also has a double sense. "Rich England" makes many other people poor, including the marginal and oppressed of England itself. We also have Arnold returning to one of his favourite mobile figures of speech, in the flood which pours the world's commerce on English shores: from the Sea of Faith to the flood of enterprise. There seems implicit in the movement of the Arnoldian metaphor a constantly focused criticism of those in England who have been responsible for shifting the flow away from spirituality to materialism. This is not something necessarily readable in this sonnet, but is a trace that surfaces repeatedly throughout Arnold's poetic texts.

The denigration of spirit is not merely a moment of "universal crisis" registered by Arnold; it has, for Arnold, a specific national character, and that character is Englishness. It is this national characteristic that has used up the spiritual sense of selfhood in its commercial enterprise in the coining of the materialistic, bourgeois English character. Yet I suspect that, ironically for Arnold, the usury to which he puts the metaphor of the sea and all its related figures serves only to reveal him as a typically English subject, subject to the tyrannical economy of an equally typically English discourse. This very real problem is to be found yet again in two later poems, "East London" and "West London," (1863) which are given over to apparent consideration of the social and spiritual state of England's capital.

Arnold's response to the homeless, the poor and that marginal section of the capital's population referred to by Gareth Stedman Jones as "Outcast London,"[19] is by no means unique to him. Fear of the marginalised and London's Other was present, as Stedman Jones points out, in "conservative, liberal and socialist thought alike."[20] Stedman Jones's study shows London in a state of intellectual and ideological crisis during the 1860s. In *Culture and Anarchy*, Arnold refers to East Enders as "those vast, miserable unmanageable masses of sunken people."[21] We might overlook this description as a standard registration of shock at the conditions of the working-class; except for Arnold's choice of the word, "unmanageable." Arnold's humanitarian concern is revealed in this word choice as belonging to the typically Victorian desire to police the poor. Although Arnold is not necessarily conscious of his being enmeshed in the discourses of the English bourgeoisie, this single word leads one to recall Engels's remark that "[t]he English bourgeoisie is charitable out of self-interest."[22]

This sense of self-interest surfaces in various ways in the two London poems. In 1867, the year in which Arnold's two poems were published, bread riots were frequent in the East End, the shipbuilding industry had all but ceased to exist and unemployment was at its highest levels.[23] Despite such appalling social conditions (in hindsight, only the precursors to the current levels of social depredation brought about, once again, by bourgeois self-interest), Arnold's response is one of balanced distance. Of the four verses of "East London," only the first directs the reader's attention to the East End itself, Bethnal Green and Spitalfields to be exact. For most of the poem, Arnold hides from the Real, turning away from it as he also covers up the "squalid streets" (2), effacing them from the text after having just introduced them. Arnold turns his poem to an affirmative meditation on the human soul, finding salvation from squalor in "thoughts of Christ, *the living /bread*" (8-9). Presumably, as long as the poor have the "living bread," there really is no excuse for repeated bread riots. This, at least, is one possible, disturbing reading of Arnold's use of the metaphor of bread. The reading is justified, it seems to me, by Arnold's own emphasis on the phrase, which intimates that the East End bread riots of the '60s may have been on Arnold's mind. Furthermore, it seems a typical poetic ploy for Arnold, that of displacing a figure of speech from a literal referent to a more purely figural one with a degree of violence that we have already seen in the figure of the sea.

Arnold has directed his attention away from the poverty through a meeting with "a preacher" (William Tyler, according to Kenneth Allott[24]). This serves as a convenient turning point, allowing Arnold egress from the East End and entrance to a more internalised space of contemplation. If we read through the last two verses carefully, we notice that the "human soul" (9) addressed by Arnold, who "mak'st the heaven thou hop'st indeed thy home" (14), can only be the preacher of the second verse, with whom Arnold has just spoken. As evidence of this, the preacher is, in his own words, "much cheered" (8); Arnold says that the "everlasting light" is that which "*cheer*[s] thee" (10, 12). Furthermore, the structure of the last lines of the second and the fourth verses is repeated, as "bread" and "home" are left to resonate on their own, whilst also remarking their shared metaphorical sense, the promised "home" in heaven being in the "bread" that is Christ. There is no consideration for the "pale weaver" of Spitalfields (3).[25] S/he has been forgotten. Interestingly, Arnold chooses the adjective "dispirited" to describe the look of the weaver (4); the weaver is without spirit, has had spirit taken away, and is, therefore, without hope. We get no sense whatsoever that the salvation beckoning the "human soul" and recognised by Arnold as his own implicit hope is available to the weaver. Arnold's identification with the preacher and, therefore, with Christianity, is curiously assertive in the face of the dispirited East End, given his own doubts that are expressed through poems such as "Dover Beach" and "Isolation. To Marguerite."

Ironically, for Arnold, his one reference to the life without the living bread comes in the form of a tidal metaphor: "the howling senses' ebb and flow" (11). This apostrophe remarks all those other figures of the sea (especially the Sea of Faith), providing a telling counter-reading of Arnold's favourite poetic figure. Those unmanageable masses loom large for Matthew Arnold, promising to engulf both the poet and the everlasting light. For Arnold, there is no avoiding this gathering up into the vast mass. Arnold's search for a sense of identity attempts to retreat into a purely and wholly metaphysical realm in the face of the East End. He is unable to connect himself with these Other English who, despite Arnold's every effort, impinge upon his sensibility.

Spiritual salvation is also the promise on offer in "West London" the companion poem to "East London," although it is a salvation rooted, albeit precariously, in a spirit of community, rather than the more orthodox spirit of Christian discourse. From Bethnal Green, Arnold has travelled westward and finds himself in Belgrave Square, confronted, not by a weaver, but by a female beggar with a girl and a baby:

> Crouched on the pavement, close by Belgrave Square,
> A tramp I saw, ill, moody, and tongue-tied.

A babe was in her arms, and at her side
A girl; their clothes were rags, their feet were bare.

(1-4)

The homeless and unmanageable have spread to the streets of wealthy London. They are, perhaps, unmanageable for Arnold because they have spread to West London. This grim chance encounter is, though, a horribly felicitous occasion for the Wordsworthian poet; for, if Arnold cannot avoid the poor, neither can he evade Wordsworth, and so, in order to efface partly the reality of the poor in the very struggle to come to terms with them and to see a way to find hope, Arnold returns to an image overdetermined by the hermeneutic enclosure of the poetic.

In "An Evening Walk," (1793) Wordsworth is disturbed from his meditations and the pastoral joys of the country to recall the violent image of a homeless mother and her children, starving and dying in "bitter showers" and the "torrent gale."[26] With this scene in mind, and given the great numbers of poor on the streets of London during the latter part of the Nineteenth century, Arnold appears to have arrived at an image that is indebted to Wordsworth's. This is not to say that Arnold did not encounter a female tramp; however, in one more moment of subjective recoil, the poet's unconscious may be read through this image as having released the Wordsworthian correlative in order to disarm the shock felt at the sight of the female tramp in Belgrave Square. This might seem a somewhat tenuous reading, were it not for the fact that we encounter other efforts of the text to turn aside the reader—and the poem's subject, the speaking self—from the immediacy of the encounter.

The detour—an ambiguous detour but one nevertheless—is managed in this fashion: the beggar is seen to turn to "labouring men," "sharers in a common human fate" rather than "[t]he rich" (5, 11, 8). Noticeably, the woman refrains from asking for aid from the narrator of the poem. Thus the image is of a group of like people being *managed* by the text, keeping themselves to themselves or being kept to themselves at the very least, kept in order and policed by the text while having the appearance of staying within their own order. The narrative voice excuses this action by interpreting its occurrence as happening because of the towering spirit of the tramp:

Thought I: 'Above her state this spirit towers;
She will not ask of aliens, but of friends,
Of sharers in a common human fate.

(9-11)

Mediating against this poetic distanciation, however, is the sense of
spirit and community that the third verse does evoke, even in the act of
creating distance; hence, the ambiguity of the detour of which I spoke.
As pious and condescending as the idea sounds, that the woman's spirit
"points us to a better time than ours" (14), there is still enunciated here,
however faintly, however faultily perceived by Arnold, the possibility
for hope. The balance for this hope is in the first lines of the last verse:

> She turns from that cold succour, which attends
> The unknown little from the unknowing great,

> (12-13)

which offers an imminent condemnation of the "charitable" acts of the
wealthy bourgeoisie, similar to Engels' own condemnation cited earlier.
As fragile as it is, in this instance poised so finely between the marginality expressed in "unknown" and the ignorance leading to oppression
expressed in "unknowing," Arnold comes closest to comprehending
the power of a communal identity and the desperate need for a shared
vision.

   This poem, which could so easily fall into Christian cant, caught up
as it is in the meshes of Wordsworth's spirit, is a moment of opening in
Arnold's texts, leading to the hope of a poetics of shared identity.
Ambiguity as the name for the inexpressible is everything here. For, if
Arnold is unable to find the proper enunciation of shared identity, he
does at least construct a silent space where, in the future, the inexpressible may come to find a voice.

As a poet, Arnold is caught in the interminable problem of expressing
the inexpressible. This knotty difficulty arises from the inability to determine a sense of self greater than the individual, and from never being
quite capable of escaping the prison of one's own language and tradition. David Riede, quoting Arnold, has argued that Arnold "regarded
poetry as 'more of a stay to us' than the other arts."[27] Yet, while Arnold
may have believed this to be true, (although his Preface of 1853 does
seem to call this into doubt at some stages[28]) much of his poetry does not
support such an argument; instead, we read throughout the poems of
loss, absence, the immanence of the abyss, fragmentation and a constant instability of identity, whether personal or of a broader nature.
In these and other figures of negativity, however, there still remains an
other poetic space, through which to imagine the possibility of an other
enunciation, as my reading of "West London" proposes.

Arnold does find identity partly achievable through his own interpretation of the English poetic and literary traditions. This is, of course, no new observation; but if Arnold is "defender of the literary faith," as David Riede puts it,[29] then that faith is not composed of some pan-European or Judeo-Christian *mélange*, but has a specifically national bias and identity, with all the implications of textual colonialism and plundering that such a faith carries with it. Literature is not merely something for Arnold with which to replace religion. Rather, literature is totemic for Arnold; it provides a discourse that instructs the Englishman how to be the "best" Englishman he can (there seems to be no question that women could be included in the cultural construction of Englishness). Yet Arnold's belief in the cultural efficacy and hegemony of literary discourse is continuously undercut by his own struggles to fix identity to the national mast.

It is not, as J. Hillis Miller posits, that Arnold's most significant critical terms are empty, referring to something that cannot be "named by words."[30] This formulation is too neat, too reductive, relying for its cogency on an essential, knowable and finite Arnold whose phrases circulate in a vacuum gesturing to some metaphysical beyond without reference to the Real. Because the Real is there, because social problems such as homelessness, poverty and starvation exist, (and for which poets are just as culpable as politicians, as Arnold seems to imply in his mumbled, guilty reference to "the bewildering confusion of our times"[31]) Arnold's poetry is always already involved in tripping itself over meanings, referents and connotations over which Arnold has little or no control.

Arnold's terms and phrases are complex and fragile symbols of a struggle to reconcile the fundamentally elitist practice of poetry in the nineteenth century with an ethical sense of responsibility towards a society caught in the dire effects of a philosophy of liberal individualism made manifest through human misery as the by-product of industrial capitalism in a materialist culture. So, after the 1980s and early '90s replay of the best of times and the worst of times, we can read, with a degree of tolerance, Arnold's perplexity, his desire for an other identity and, finally, his increasing tendency to move towards prose, first as an excuse and explanation for poetry, and then as criticism of "literature," and, finally as a form more suited to critical engagement with social and cultural themes.

3

ARNOLD, ENGLISHNESS AND CRITICAL AVOIDANCE: A READING OF "MY COUNTRYMEN"

We in England, in our great burst of literature during the first thirty years of the present century, had no manifestation of the modern spirit . . . And the reason is not far to seek. We had neither the German wealth of ideas, nor the French enthusiasm for applying ideas. There resided in the mass of the nation that inveterate inaccessibility to ideas . . .

—*Essays in Criticism*

There is . . . in France a sympathy with intellectual activity for its own sake, and for the sake of its inherent pleasurableness and beauty, keener than any which exists in England.

—*Essays in Criticism*

Arnold is a great and important figure in nineteenth-century thought. His recognition of "a period of transformation when it comes" was deep and active . . . Even the final breakdown in this thinking . . . is extremely important, as the mark of a continuing and genuine confusion.

—Raymond Williams

Culture . . . makes us see not only his good side, but also how much in him was *of necessity limited and transient.*

—*Culture and Anarchy* (My emphasis)

I

As the opening quotation of the previous chapter from Chris Baldick suggests, while it is generally assumed that Matthew Arnold is supposed to have written the "classic protest against Victorian anti-intellectualism," such a claim is unfounded. Perhaps the reason for the lack of substantiation lies with Arnold himself. Arnold does not merely respond to anti-intellectualism; he responds to—indeed he defines the characteristics of—English bourgeois identity as it is composed by a degree of "anti-intellectualism." To clarify: to say that the English bourgeoisie of the 1850s and 1860s were anti-intellectual would be to miss Arnold's focus. To say that the bourgeoisie were *anti*-intellectual at all would imply a conscious reaction by the English middle classes—Arnold's personal *bête noir*—against something definable as intellect. My reading of Arnold is that he did not believe the middle classes to have that high a level of consciousness! And it is this reading of Arnold's, of a particular social stratum in English life as the singular most powerful group, as, in sum, the most typical representatives of Englishness, that I want to examine, through a reading of the essay, "My Countrymen."[1]

Arnold's avoidance of the Tory-liberal model of Englishness, and his borrowing from Hegelian philosophy, is a double edged practice in "My Countryman." Arnold, like George Eliot, turns frequently to Germanic intellectual culture for inspiration and as a source of communal intellectual identity. Unlike Eliot however, Arnold is more often adulatory than perceptively critical. Despite his selective plundering of German philosophy, Arnold is still understandable as being as much an Englishman—albeit of a different order—as those against whom he directs his irony, chiefly because of what Chris Baldick describes as Arnold's "systematic suppression of theory and argument."[2] A *caveat*, however: Arnold's Englishness and his attempts to outmanœuvre the Englishness of the middle classes are not to be taken at face value. Arnold's self-conscious ploy of announcing his own philosophical feeble-mindedness may well be intended, not as a systematic suppression[3] *as such*, (that is to say as a native distrust on Arnold's part towards theory) but as a rhetorical and epistemo-ideological gesture to soothe his English readers into a sense of native empiricist and pragmatist complacency through which can be introduced an otherwise unpalatable (theoretical, continental) argument; yet it is the gesture which, initially and ultimately, turns Arnold's discourse against himself, deconstructing Matthew Arnold as the quintessential Englishman.

Furthermore, Arnold, in moving towards a half-perceived notion of the spirit of Englishness as the question at stake in any ongoing cultural critique, recognizes his own ethical responsibility in framing the enquiry in a manner suited to the subject of that investigation. Merely to criticize is an insufficient and inappropriate gesture for one seeking a newer, more profound poetics of national identity. Such traditional activity is understandable as involving the adoption of an Olympian or mandarin stance to the question at hand; such a stance requires no engagement, no deep rooted and fundamentally ontological involvement with the very forms and structures of the subject under consideration. In "My Countrymen," Arnold understands that, to paraphrase Heidegger, he has no right to dogmatic constructions.[4] Yet, inevitably, the paradox for Arnold is that, by the very nature of his comprehension of Englishness and his subsequent involvement in that comprehension, he has no recourse on occasions to anything other than dogmatic constructions.

II

Ruth apRoberts has argued, correctly, that "Arnold's eventual turn from poetry to prose is associated with a major question of the technique of the poems, and this is the important question of symbolism."[5] This is true but it does not give us the whole picture. Arnold's shift from one genre to another has to do with the quest for cultural identity, for an Englishness of style, tone and content that is not indebted directly to the spirit of long (or, in the case of Wordsworth, not so long) dead poets. It is a question of seeking an other English spirit.

William E. Buckler suggests that Arnold, in his critical verse, provides "his most penetrating sense of the psycho-cultural crisis of his time," while "deploying" the metaphor of "Classicism as a wholly appropriate corrective to the malaise of Romantic Modernism."[6] Again, this is a partial truth but one which does not read the malaise as endemic to Arnold's own verse on several occasions. Arnold's turn away from poetry is expressed as a conscious decision to rid contemporary poetry of a particular reading of Wordsworth:

More and more I feel bent against the *modern English habit* (too much encouraged by Wordsworth) of using poetry as a channel for thinking aloud, instead of making anything.[7] (my emphasis)

Arnold is speaking as much for himself as against other poets, as he sees a specifically national and cultural poetic identity too much in the ineluctable thrall of Wordsworthian expression. This quest is Arnold's personally, part of an effort to deny Wordsworth; and yet it is also bound up inextricably with a larger national quest for identity —as Arnold's letter shows—which, during the latter part of the nineteenth century, came to find itself expressed conservatively in the invention of tradition and ceremony. For Arnold, the quest involved a turn to prose as a medium in which to explore the question of Englishness.

A reading too caught up in the clichés of English identity, one that submits too readily and uncritically to the traditional structures of

such an identity, offers us a resistance to theoretical, abstract or intellectual rigour as the dominant discourse of Arnold's texts. The more
positive and probing qualities of the Arnoldian text are thus suppressed.
Chris Baldick argues that Matthew Arnold displays repeated "anti-theo-
retical tendencies."[8] Furthermore, Baldick stresses that "the conservative
argument of *Essays in Criticism* is closely tied in with Arnold's poetics:
both urge us to rely upon the harmony of an already given state of
affairs."[9] This is perfectly true, as far as the argument about *Essays in
Criticism* is concerned. Yet a more balanced analysis, such as Raymond
Williams's from *Culture and Society*,[10] (the title of which echoes Arnold,
thereby seeking to continue a tradition of socially engaged criticism
while offering a left-wing corrective to Arnold's liberal myopia) along
with a reading of essays such as "My Countrymen," suggests an Arnold
who deplores the lack of a "given state of affairs" with regard to the
spiritual identity of the English. This is no simple conservative gesture on
Arnold's part, but part of a more complicated and, as Raymond Williams
puts it, often genuinely confused[11] rejoinder to the devouring materialism of the Victorian middle-classes; for which is required a theoretical
framework if we are to comprehend both Arnold's complications and
confusions.

Certainly, Arnold is never quite as ambiguously gracious in his
estimation of the English as George Eliot who, despite her many deeply
felt reservations about English culture, offers us an interesting comparison with Arnold in remarking that:

> John Bull is open to instruction; slowly, by gentle degrees, he
> revises his opinions, his habits and his laws. It is not to be expected
> that he will ever cease to regard himself as the supreme type of
> manhood, or to think that the most unmixed truth may always be
> known by the mark "British," which prevents imposture. But he
> does modify his opinions about other nations.[12]

In the opening gambit of this essay on the German character, Eliot plays
the figure of the stereotypical Englishman through the proper name,
John Bull, whilst also opening up that stereotype to the possibility of self-
conscious critical regard and change (because of interaction with other
national identities, as the essay continues to show). At the same time as
she admits "John Bull" to be available to the discourses of difference,
Eliot manages to maintain the Englishness of the character through the
ironic act of rhetorical arrogance on behalf of the Englishman, representing him as regarding himself as the "best representative of human-

ity." Thus George Eliot at once gives and takes away, opening onto a configuration of Englishness that is mapped as malleable yet flawed, of necessity limited and transient, to borrow Arnold's phrase.[13] In George Eliot's register, Englishness is a provisional and historical category.

Here lies a principle difference between Eliot and Arnold in their comprehension of Englishness. Because of his reiterated insistence on the necessary metaphysical nature of "Culture," (necessary to his definition; Arnold cannot submit "Culture" to any form of critical analysis, it is not a category for Arnold *comme les autres*) Arnold evades the historicity and contingency in his translations of Englishness. It is this which has made Arnold subject to "continuing charges of priggishness and spiritual pride," in Raymond Williams's words;[14] it is this in Arnold which, in his most sustained arguments of *Culture and Anarchy*, leaves him open to Chris Baldick's charges of conservatism. Arnold's critical "fault"—which is not a "fault" so much as the trace and aporia of "history"—or ideological blindness is his very own cultural involvement, an involvement from which Eliot was able to create the illusion of distance more successfully (Eliot's "distance" eventually led to the suppression of history and the utopian idealism of *Daniel Deronda*: see chapter 7, below). Yet Arnold's blind spot also proves a moment with fascinating potential. As "My Countrymen" shows, a blind spot can sometimes be construed as a different focus, or a plangent vision.

III

The question is one of spirit, of *geist*, as Arnold refers to cultural identity in "Friendship's Garland."[15] For Arnold, the question is one that is difficult to approach. The difficulty lies in the fact of *geist's* political nature. "This motif," writes Derrida of *geist*, "is regularly inscribed in contexts that are highly charged politically, in the moments when thought lets itself be preoccupied more than ever by what is called history, language, the nation."[16] History, language, the nation: these are Matthew Arnold's abiding concerns and fears. History appears particularly problematic for Arnold, other than as the genealogy of literature, because it presents the poet with the more unpalatable realities of national identity. Language is the medium for Arnold through which a nation expresses, or can express, its national identity. This presents a problem for him inasmuch as while language is the vehicle of the poets, it is also the unreflective medium of jingoism and journalism, of all despirited enunciations in their basest form. The nation, in reality, does not measure up in the Arnoldian vision of Englishness to the mythic representations that the poets have performed; yet Arnold's problem is, I suggest, that he does not recognise the mythical qualities of poetic discourse, taking it instead as a collection of true, albeit lost, evocations of the national *geist* in its most noble form. As a result, the figures of history, language and the nation are mapped endlessly in their numerous reformations as the Arnoldian text wrestles with the issue of national Being as it is philosophically constituted and comprehended.

Arnold published "My Countrymen" in 1866, as a response to James Fitzjames's critical review of Arnold's *The Function of Criticism*.[17] Later appended as a supplement to "Friendship's Garland" by Arnold himself, "My Countrymen" provides us a précis of the main arguments of those sections of *Culture and Anarchy* that deal with the English middle-classes. Arnold's attack on the philistine bourgeoisie who, according to Arnold, have "not much gift for anything but making money," is unstinting throughout.[18] His essay can be saved at least partly from the charges of conservatism and elitism leveled at *Culture and Anarchy* through recognizing Arnold's own omission of any negative critique of the proletariat. This is a problem of course, because omission can mean silencing and further marginalisation (and Arnold is not wholly silent on the issue of the working class, as I shall discuss below). But, for those of us who, in the words of Raymond Williams, are "still hungry"[19] for social change, an essay such as "My Countrymen" may still be read as (the beginnings of) an intervention; a dissident text situated against the cavalier and heartless philosophy that constitutes the Tory-liberal ethos of both the high Victorian era, and of Thatcherism and the post-Thatcher years.

The dissidence of Arnold's essay is best attended to through a reading of its evasions, its vaguenesses, and its ambiguities, that are noted by Raymond Williams in his readings of other texts by Matthew Arnold.[20] Such instances effectively question the supposed steadfastness of the Arnold whose position is that of advocate for "internal perfection,"[21] and whose posture may be read as that of the dandy[22] and romantic[23] (one could argue that such an obviously assumed position, one that is clearly constructed out of a number of arch performances, is a figure designed to be politically, philosophically subversive).

"My Countrymen," however, is important because it eschews both dandy-ism and romantic posturing, whilst still remaining firmly rooted in an English context. Thus its dissidence is of a particular nature, dissenting as it does from Arnold's *oeuvre*. The essay marks both transition and break in Arnold's writing, and so comprises gestures of dissent that are not to be found in works such as *Culture and Anarchy*. Also, "My Countrymen" breaks away from the *impasse* of the poetry. Through its sustained cultural criticism of the middle class, it opens onto, and points in the direction of the Arnoldian discourse on spiritual identity, on *geist* and/as the politics of national Being-in-common, which are the figures *par excellence* of Arnoldian social aspiration. The essay's transition is one of importance to Arnold's readers today.

The essay's structure is interesting inasmuch as it may lay before us Arnold's knowledge of Hegel, mentioned in one of the letters of "Friendship's Garland."[24] Arnold opens the essay with a depiction of English middle-class comprehension of themselves as mediated through the Tory press. Arnold avoids direct criticism of this class yet, through avoidance, provides a structured revelation of the ideology of that class. From this, he moves to the continental opinion of English character as an antithetical proposition to the English people's own misrecognition. Finally, as a gesture taking us beyond the dialectic of English and continental opinion, Arnold views the potential for national spirit to be found in the American democratic structure of civic republicanism. Taken overall, Arnold's essay appears to be structured quite straightforwardly. Arnold's methods of unfolding his arguments and tracing his pattern are, however, anything but neatly delineated.

"My Countrymen": the title itself is ambiguous. One wonders whether Arnold is owning up to his countrymen *as his*, in a gesture that could be construed as one of pride, of shame or indictment; or whether there is some irony in the title , as if to say "yes, these are my countrymen, but I'd as soon they were not." And the possessive pronoun: Arnold is also admitting to his connection to a particular group of people, however ironic his tone, however broad that group may be.

With regard to the question of position that the title throws in our way, Arnold gives his hand away almost immediately in this essay. We cannot construct a sense of prevarication so easily as we could when reading the poetry. Arnold reveals himself to be a thoroughgoing Englishman:

> I am a mere dabbler in these great matters, and to grasp and hold a system of philosophy is a feat much beyond my strength.[25]

Here, Arnold owns up to an apparent inability to grasp philosophical systems, in a self-conscious disowning of intellect and a concomitant admission of intellectual weakness. He is also suggesting his own inability to think through a rigorous philosophical structure in which and through which he would be able to discuss the philosophical weaknesses of his countrymen. Thus Arnold reveals himself as unfit to advance any discourse on the subject of "Englishmen" and "Englishness" on the grounds of his own intellectual Englishness. Arnold admits himself to be guilty of that failing, which he has been charged as accusing others of by the *Saturday Review*[26] (his is an admission with a difference; for the press accuse Arnold of not being English enough, of not being the right kind of Englishman).

Yet this very gesture—one which Baldick seems to have read, without taking into account any ironic possibility—is one of Englishness itself. There is, to reiterate, the disavowal of systematic rigour; there is the writer's rhetorical device of self-disarmament; and too, his claimed hobbyist status as a "mere" amateur, a "dabbler" in difficult matters of thought. All such figures of discourse amount to a catalogue of cultural, literary identity.

This having been said, Arnold having thus announced himself through the idiomatic-national linguistic structures that "effortlessly" remark Englishness in eliding their own contexts (Arnold thereby seeming to write in an idiom-free discourse), the English writer can then proceed to talk of his countrymen, to his countrymen, with all authority and no authority whatsoever. For Arnold, authority has been authorised through those figures of speech which admit to having no authority in the first place. Arnold knows nothing and so can converse on any subject he chooses. The subject that he does choose is "British Philistines."[27]

Arnold regards "my countrymen" largely as British Philistines (not that he qualifies his definition through the national identification). He is of course talking about the middle class, a point he makes clear throughout the essay. Again though, the essayist is somewhat ambiguous. He maintains his caution and reserve as he floats seemingly nearer to and then further away from his subject at the same moment. Having noted, without any qualification or apparent ambiguity whatsoever, that he "certainly did talk about British Philistines,"[28] Arnold then goes on to say that "[e]veryone knows that the heart of the English nation is its middle class."[29] This sounds like unequivocal praise from Arnold (and as straightforward a remark as that concerning the Philistinism of the British); fulsome almost, from a man who, elsewhere, criticized at length the middle classes for their materialism, their crassness and their lack of spirit.

Arnold is, though, setting up the middle class, even in his directness, ambiguity being presented through Arnold's choice of metaphor. Although he employs the metaphor of the heart, it is not a metaphor he believes in, in this context. To believe in the heart as a symbolic figure of the human community, one has to believe also in the spirit, at least in poetical terms. As a poet, Arnold knows the laws governing figures of speech only too well. Arnold is, however, using the metaphor of the heart ironically in referring to the middle class. He figures his countrymen—whom he believes to be heartless, without a sense of spirit—in this fashion in order to introduce a longer discourse against the bourgeois representatives of the English nation, who were in the ascendant during Arnold's lifetime.

In seeming defence of his own image of the English middle class as the heart of the nation, Arnold continues by quoting from the *Non-Conformist*, specifically an article by a Mr Miall. This article states, without any Arnoldian ambiguity, that the middle class "has astonished the world by its energy, enterprise, and self-reliance."[30] Having quoted this, and having previously quoted Sir Thomas Bazley, the member for Manchester,[31] Arnold builds up the case even more strongly against himself and against his own previous arguments by quoting the *Daily News*.[32] *Pace* Arnold, the *Daily News* supports the existing stage of education for the English middle class, which class it refers to as the "the most independent, and active, and enlightened class of English society."[33] Still Arnold does not respond to this, save in a footnote later appended to that version of "My Countrymen" included at the end of "Friendship's Garland."[34] He merely, to use his own words, ranges all the evidence in black and white before himself[35] (and us; there is a sense of Arnold the schoolmaster here, who offers us comprehension tests of the unspoken, urging us to read his own aporia). Thus we read the words of Sir Thomas Bazley, Mr Miall, a journalist from the *Daily News* and, finally, that most Tory of newspapers, the *Daily Telegraph*.[36]

Still, this is no mere climax to the progression which Arnold has set as the defence against his own charges of Philistinism (a defence which is also, in part, a prosecution of Arnold's thinking on the middle class). In the culmination of this exceptionally long paragraph, Arnold returns to Sir Thomas Bazley, the Manchester MP. Bazley, a principal defender of middle-class education, that social institution which Arnold has been so foolhardy as to rail against, had made a speech which the *Telegraph* describes as being at once "grand, genial, national and distinct."[37]

Arnold says nothing about the quotation, but his choice is very telling. Notice how the terms, "grand" and "genial," "national" and "distinct," all play off against one another, so as to erect a seemingly impenetrable fortress of discourse for the English idiom. Bazley's speech is grand, yet it is genial. It has largesse, yet warmth and immediacy. It shows the mark of the true rhetorician, whilst being also the language of someone in touch, through its geniality, with the small man. It is national and it is distinct; it is, therefore, broad enough to reach the whole of the nation, (carrying with it the implication of patriotism) or that part of the nation which chooses to hear what it has to say. And yet it is distinct enough to be out of the ordinary, to be unique, the language of the liberal individual. It bears at once the marks of both national and individual identity; and that identity is, for *Telegraph* readers, Sir Thomas Bazley.

Arnold does not stop here, in putting the evidence against himself and for the middle class. He goes on to quote the *Morning Star*'s eulogy to Bazley at some length:

> He talked to his constituents as Manchester people liked to be talked to, in the language of clear, manly intelligence, which penetrates through sophisms, ignores commonplaces, and gives to conventional illusions their true value. His speech was thoroughly instinct with that earnest good sense which characterises Manchester, and which, indeed, may be fairly set down as the general characteristic of England and Englishmen everywhere.[38]

The language here is typically that of the English liberal tradition, and is worth unpacking in detail in order to understand more completely that against which Arnold levels his, at times, oblique attack (if we do not see what is at stake in this passage, we run the risk of missing Arnold's importance, and the possibility of his recuperation in the service of dissident and radical reading practices).

Arnold refrains from comment on this passage, as he had done with the quotation from the *Daily Telegraph*. He allows it to stand on its own, to resonate for his discerning readers. Obviously, it is to be inferred that his readers are the not of the same readership as that of either the *Telegraph* or the *Morning Star*. In not talking about this quotation, in not criticising or analyzing it, Arnold maintains his distance, sustaining that hobbyist approach he took up initially at the beginning of the essay. In keeping silence, Arnold allows for possible reading strategies to be developed, so as to tell more cogently against the article. In culminating the paragraph with this assessment of Sir Thomas Bazley, which is also an indirect criticism on Arnold's own position concerning the middle class, Arnold has revealed quite subtly what the heart of the middle class consists of exactly.

With its investment in the voice—and, therefore, presence—of the speaker, the newspaper report connects the (ideal example of) the English individual, a human agent produced as the result of rhetorical performance, and a specific group of English subjects who are, in turn, supposedly illustrative of the nation as a whole. Presumably, this group are representative of those English subjects spread throughout the Empire and, therefore, the world. Is this not the inference of the final words?

The *Star*'s passage has a further function for its readers. The passage defines a paradigm of bourgeois Englishness. It ranges its terms so that its readers can measure themselves against it. Are they Englishmen of the sort addressed by Bazley, or not? And, while the article parades the codes and indices of this variant of English identity, the newspaper serving to mediate social events to ideological ends, it also displays its own ideological affiliations. In ranging these articles before us, Arnold is asking that we recognise the position of and investment by the press in the question of middle class identity.

The passage moves hierarchically from individual identity as the generator of a discourse that constitutes Englishness and is suitable for all Englishmen who suppose that they share this "individual" identity, and who all speak the same language; that is to say, the same version of Englishspeak.

Bazley's constituents are talked to as they liked to be talked to. How do they like to be talked to? In the language of "clear, manly intelligence." There is inscribed in this passage the apparent willingness of the audience (both those who heard Bazley's speech and those reading the newspaper's account) to join in the continued production and dissemination of a national identity at the level of discourse. Their consent—their co-optation—is figured in the announcement that "they like to be talked to" in a specific fashion. The reader of the newspaper is also being coerced, of course, being bullied eventually by the press into accepting a normative definition of Englishness through the climactic revelation of "Englishmen everywhere").

The inference of the phrase, "clear, manly intelligence," is that what is clear is manly and vice versa; that clarity and manliness are those elements out of which is engendered intelligence. To be intelligent is to be both manly and possessing of clarity of speech. Here is a near perfect example of the way in which the rhetoric of the Right works; what can be implied is that obfuscation, the opposite of clarity, equates with femininity, effeminateness, effeteness and, in the context of the last line, the foreign as well. We are meant to infer that Masculinity is a prime quality of a national identity founded on and shored up by an equally national language. That which is effete produces sophisms and commonplaces. Tellingly, the verb used by the *Morning Star* to describe the action of "clear, manly intelligence" is "penetration." The implication is too obvious to require further elucidation (except, perhaps, for those on the Right).

It is not going too far, I think, to read here that the masculine sexual metaphor is meant to "undo" the foreignness and unmanliness of sophistry. John Bull (Sir Thomas Bazley, his Manchester constituents *and* Englishmen everywhere) is not *sophisti*cated. He does not indulge in fallacious reasoning; neither is he subtle or devious. Instead, he appeals to his countrymen (who are also "my countrymen"; Arnold's title never lets us forget our connection and, thus, our responsibility to others, despite the ironic distances he installs in his writing) in the way that they enjoy being appealed to. Or, at least, so the newspaper tells us.

The article moves on to describe how the speech was "thoroughly instinct with that earnest good sense which characterizes Manchester." Of interest is the term "instinct" (although the idea that good sense is that sense which is earnest, with no time for either equivocation or humour is indeed fascinating). We can gather from this term that "clear, manly" speech comes as from a wellhead; it is just there, "naturally," waiting to spring up instinctively. Bazley's language needs neither construction, nor any recourse to rhetoric; it is as natural as sunlight or the bleating of sheep.

The speech, belonging peculiarly to Manchester, characterizes Manchester, or so a London newspaper informs us. Coming from it, it is itself also that which defines "Manchesterness." The language is not that of southern intellectuals such as Matthew Arnold. Despite this very local quality which defines the speech as Mancunian, however, the *Morning Star* continues, ignoring its own claims for the language of locality, of idiomatic self-definition, to state that the speech "may be fairly set down as the general characteristic of England and Englishmen everywhere" (as always in Tory journalism, Englishwomen are silent and silenced; they are otherwise simpering or shrill). We have now moved from the local and specific to the national and the general. What was peculiar to Manchester, is peculiar to Manchester no longer, because its very peculiarity is what defines true Englishmen. Cleverly enough, Arnold's choice of passage is concerned with a city that lies roughly at the heart of England, to recall his earlier metaphor. Yet Arnold has nothing to say about this, or about the piece.

We are told that the language of the politician is not bedecked by needless rhetorical frippery; nor does it stoop to the other extreme, choosing not to rely on the hackneyed or clichéd phrase. The penetration of which the article speaks, serves to find a middle ground in discourse, which is the ideal language of consensus politics, of the middle class (which, to all intents and purposes in 1866, means those who have the vote). "True value" is thus discerned in such speech. The economic figure used by the *Morning Star* offers a telling trace of the complicity between liberal language and free market practice, where the bottom line in both is "true value," the value of the speech is defined by its "good sense," an apparently determinate quality that can be agreed on, like the colour and taste of roast beef and ale.

This "good sense" is also a characteristic of the people of Manchester, if the *Star* is to be believed. It is these people, the article would have us understand, who are the best representatives of Englishmen. The passage traces in a circular and circumscribing manner, those attributes which are at once peculiar to the exemplary individual and to the majority for whom and to whom that individual speaks. The "body politic" is also the "body national." "Englishness" is represented in both, and mediated through the Tory press, from the atomistic to the universal and back again (leaving out the social sphere, of course).

Thus the speech of the Englishman is that which hides its rhetorical devices through insisting that it has none. So, Sir Thomas Bazley; and so, Matthew Arnold, as at the beginning of "My Countrymen." The question that remains is whether Arnold is wholly conscious of his own actions and devices. This cannot be answered with any certainty; but the problem raised is whether Arnold, in working from within, in effecting the internal, sustained critique through parody, shadow-play and mimetic tracing (all instances of deconstruction), has not in fact deconstructed himself; has not in effect recuperated himself into the English identity that he seeks to solicit.

The Englishness at stake here is what Arnold describes as "characteristic of the representative part of the British nation, the part by which the British nation is what it is, and does all its best things, the middle class"[39] (the language of journalism so couched as to imply that the representative part is in fact the whole). Ingeniously, Arnold has chosen to re-figure the middle class not through his own (admittedly biased) descriptions of them, nor through their own self-descriptions (in fiction, biography or other predominantly middle-class media), but through the middle classes' principle discursive organ, the newspaper. This organ of generation, Arnold makes plain, is both in the service of the middle class, while also being the shepherd of that class. Without stating overtly that this is his intent, Arnold unfolds before his readers the image of Tory press complicit with a Tory bourgeoisie, and both enmeshed in a liberal-capitalist hegemony which they perpetuate.

Upon demystifying middle-class identity, Arnold deflects any criticism of himself immediately by reverting back to a very English defence. This is done through Arnold's admission that the newspapers know more than Matthew Arnold of the "Truth" and that he was "suffering deservedly" at their hands for "meddling with practice" through theoretical work, what Arnold calls "the slow and obscure work of trying to understand things."[40] This disclaimer unveils Arnold as writing within an English identity through its style and tone; it reveals him as English as those about whom he is writing. Yet he is also displayed as a very different Englishman. Again, the theoretical Arnold has appeared, through a glass darkly as it were. In his juxtaposition of his own slow and obscure work—too much an Englishman, Arnold finds the most "natural" terms for what he does, thereby attempting to efface his own critical activity—against the "practice" (with the denial and erasure of theory and discourse, mediation and ideology, which this word evokes) of the dominant class, Arnold parries the native tendency towards empiricism.

Arnold continues, remarking that the newspapers have a "trenchant, authoritative style for communicating"[41] the "truth" of the middle classes to themselves; which truth is, in Arnold's own words, that they are "enlightened."[42] Arnold goes so far as to draw on the *Morning Star*'s description of Bazley's speech, in order to define the newspaper's ability to "penetrate through sophisms, ignore commonplaces and give conventional illusions their true value." Arnold is, of course, being ironic in turning the words of the report against the newspaper, those who are being described and those who read the newspaper. In the first clause of the very next sentence the irony multiplies, and we catch Arnold's own laughter as he writes "[e]vidently it is nonsense. . . ."[43] Yes, evidently the *Star* is perpetuating nonsense of a specifically political kind, although Arnold does not in fact say this outright. Yet we can interpret the clause against the evident and ostensible meaning, given the Arnoldian play of ambiguity, interpretative aporia and charged pauses.

Arnold's playfulness throughout is delightful. He keeps himself moving, guarding himself from attack through his apparent openness, flitting from one place to another before an irate reader might have a chance to pin him down. He alights at various seemingly inconsequential points in order to exploit their weaknesses by opening himself to them, running the risk apparently of drawing critical fire. Presumably, such situational opportunism is designed precisely to irritate a certain kind of reader, that kind of reader, for example, for whom jingoistic ejaculations are merely "comon sense." Arnold draws on the discourse of those he is seeking to open to criticism, in order to unpick before his reader the various strands of the text-ile weave of Tory-liberal belief. In doing this, Arnold disarms his critics by meeting them head on, anticipating their arguments, and parodying those arguments through the opportunities afforded by crass journalistic rhetoric.

In yet another climax of Arnold's rhetorical dalliance, it is written that Arnold "resolved to offend no more"[44] In the next paragraph, Arnold says with all the self-conscious effacement he can muster that he makes such a statement as a "sincere penitent."[45] The mock-humble genuflection before the altar of the fourth estate's authority is precisely this: mock. It mocks the conventions and contexts on which such a statement draws and by which it is framed. Constantly, Arnold undercuts himself, tugs at his liberal-English forelock, and backs himself into a corner of his own making. Having said that he is a sincere penitent, having resolved to offend no more, having said that he does not belong in the sphere of argument surrounding the question of education that his essay has taken up—with which in previous essays Arnold has chosen to engage—Arnold then returns to the *Saturday Review* and the *Morning Star*, doing so with yet another twist, one all the more finely tuned for having been hitherto forestalled so relentlessly by his use of a very English style. As Arnold puts it:

> When the *Saturday Review* tells me that no nation in the world is so logical as the English nation, and the *Morning Star*, that our grand national characteristic is a clear intelligence which penetrates through sophisms, ignores commonplaces and gives to conventional illusions their true value, do I feel myself compelled to receive these propositions with absolute submission transcending reason; indeed this would be transcendentalism, which the *Saturday Review* condemns.[46]

Arnold turns the newspapers' philosophical assumptions against themselves and their attacks on himself (employing a degree of Hegelian logic in the process). Having reiterated once more the Englishspeak of the *Star*, he displays that discourse at the moment of its own paradox.

One cannot help but recall as one reads "My Countrymen" that Arnold, in layering, again and again, the remarks about penetration of sophisms and so on, echoes that same gesture made by Shakespeare in *Julius Caesar* when Mark Anthony returns constantly to Brutus' own assertion, that he is an honourable man. Reiteration produces a meaning opposite to that which the words are meant to bear with them. Arnold repeats the article of faith *ad nauseam* so as to hollow out the import of the journalese, thereby undermining its pretensions to ideologically-free true value in its assertions for the true English discourse and the identity which that supposedly promotes.

One cannot help but feel, indeed one is forced to understand that Arnold means the opposite exactly of what he is saying or inferring; that, despite his "uncritical" quotation of the *Star*'s article, he feels very critically about it and what it represents. He wants us to feel in the same manner, not only towards the newspaper, and by extension towards Sir Thomas Bazley and the readers of the paper, but also—and this is the crucial import of Arnold's discourse—that transcendental Englishness, that metaphysics of Englishness of which the *Morning Star* (amongst other newspapers) partakes. This metaphysics involves a statement of "articles of faith" not open to criticism or question. Such articles just *are;* they constitute the condition of Being for national identity, being nebulous by having clarity, while simultaneously being all-enclosing, all surrounding. They are impervious to reason and available only to believers, as though Englishness were somehow purely metaphysical, and as though The Englishman were, in fact and inferentially, God.

In performing his oblique criticisms without criticising, Arnold has thus far partaken of a politics of critique described by Derrida as "those modalities of 'avoiding' which come down to saying without saying, writing without writing, using words without using them."[47] In engaging in the politics of avoidance, Arnold has rigorously taken on his opponents through choosing not to resist them and without falling into the trap of being wholly recuperated by the dominant modes of configuration in arguing in the manner of the opposition. In this way, Arnold has exhibited the functioning, framework and fabric of bourgeois identity. Having thus initiated his dismantling of middle-class discourses and the image the middle classes have of themselves, Arnold moves beyond this inaugural critique.

IV

Arnold has told us that everyone knows that the heart of the English nation is the middle class; he has revealed to us the newspapers as the representatives of that class, to itself and others; he has shown us how the representatives understand themselves as all the English and how they are at pains to perpetuate this illusion. Having done all this, and having thus reached a point of Absolute Truth and Absolute Knowledge (not his own but that of the middle class), he makes the bourgeois English position relative, denying its absolutism by discussing "foreign opinion."[48]

Arnold starts the next paragraph with the comment, "I must say that the foreign opinion about us is not at all like that of the *Saturday Review* and the *Morning Star.*"[49] "I must say" is another of those typically English gestures. This phrase hides the author's own position in a figure of ineluctability against which he seemingly cannot struggle; indeed, he is compelled to utterance by the very difference of "the foreign opinion" In the next sentence, Arnold says "I know how madly the foreigners envy us, and that this must warp their judgement."[50] We can now see how readily, how wittily, he plays the helpless, somewhat perplexed Englishman, in order to make possible the act of criticism.

His discourse is not xenophobic, of course. He is not showing foreigners up for their envy of the English; anything but that, in fact.
By saying that the foreign judgement is warped in this oh-so-English, bemused yet
faintly indignant manner; having just ranged before us the evidence of
the press and then recalling the essay's recent past in the proper names of
the papers, thereby providing a context for the remark about foreign opinion; Arnold manages to imply precisely the opposite of what he is saying. In
sum, what the foreigners have to say is accurate, far more accurate than the
English opinion as disseminated and mediated by the English press. He
goes so far as to dismiss foreign opinion on the grounds that it can "never
be decisive" and that he is "only tak[ing] it for what it is worth."[51] Both these
ploys, partaking as they do of the strategies of self-effacement and avoidance, effect an ideological countervailance against the ostensibly English
tone in which Arnold performs the voice of "My Countrymen."

Arnold then provides his reader with a catalogue of German and
French assessments of the English. In doing so without any irony whatsoever, he constructs for us a frame into which we can place his own
"humble," "untheoretical," "repentant" essay. When Arnold says he is no
politician,[52] we know that, though this statement is literally true, yet it is
not the truth of Matthew Arnold's discourse, which invokes a politics of
national identity through the games that are played with the poetics of
that identity.

Furthermore, when Arnold positions a French newspaper's
remark, that, in the face of cholera (so prevalent in Paris during the
early nineteenth century) the only "language" the English can understand is the discourse of trade,[53] it is not necessary that he should make
transparent his own position on the condition of the English character
or spirit. His response is to adopt a glib tone, which he turns immediately from the foreign accusations against the English obsession with
trade at any cost (even human), to the English themselves, talking of
their "happy unconsciousness" and "imperturbable self-satisfaction."[54]
Such manoeuvring and politicking finds itself summed up self-reflex-
ively in Arnold's comment on the *realpolitik* of English self-interest in
matters of commerce:

For never, surely, was such a game of cross-purposes played.[55]

Whether it is Arnold's intention or not, this commentary serves to define
for us the author's strategy throughout this essay. The essay is nothing
short of a subtle polemic; it is, in effect, a very English political essay.

Arnold moves through his catalogue of foreign impressions to discussion of prominent English politicians such as Pitt and Palmerston. In

doing so, he lays before us all our responsibility in any act that the English Government takes. For no minister's policy is his alone, anymore than it is a particular Government's only. As citizens of a democracy, all policy is our policy and our policy is "the policy of England."[56] Arnold is urging on us our civic duties which we cannot and must not avoid. This is the Arnoldian imperative that so much of the essay has been used by Arnold to move towards: our individual responsibility is towards our national identity, and those we elect are merely our best, most typical representatives. It therefore follows that if there is a failure of Government, if there is an error of judgement on the part of an elected member, that fault lies not with that person but with us all as members of a community.

So Palmerston, who is invoked by Arnold as the most typical, if not the best representative of national identity.[57] Yet, there are those who consider Palmerston as a great man and Arnold is not going to disagree with this, if only for his own purposes. Palmerston's greatness, writes Arnold, lay in "our all 'acknowledging him as our best impersonation.'"[58] It is important to note at this juncture that Arnold puts the remark in quotations. We should, following Derrida, know that such a device is not to be trusted; that this is anything but the simple truth; that this is to be regarded cautiously, guardedly. The quotation marks close off the comment from the text, foregrounding it as something to be read in a different light, to be resounded in a different register, and not necessarily one that rings true. Thus, Palmerston is our best impersonation. An impersonation is, though, a simulacrum, a fake or fraud even. And, if Lord Palmerston is *our* best impersonation, it follows according to Arnoldian logic that "we," the English nation and English identity itself, are comprised of simulacra; Englishness of the kind reviled by Arnold is a counterfeit Being. No sooner have we read this than we notice, in the following sentence, that Arnold returns, once again, to those by now tedious and ridiculous lines from the *Morning Star* about "clear, manly intelligence" and so on.

The line about Palmerston can be taken further: Arnold's point is that Palmerston's impersonation is merely an individual representation of the middle class, the "redoubtable phalanx" as Arnold calls it; "our great middle class" he says, which, as he points out "makes Parliament, and which supplies the mind, the will, and the power requisite for all the great and good things that have to be done."[59] Arnold is telling us what we all know: that Parliament is comprised of members of the middle class, and Parliament, through men such as Palmerston, "our best impersonation," who have brought England "to the third place in the world's estimation, instead of the first."[60]

Thus from Bazley to Palmerston; from one minor politician to a major figure in the sphere of Victorian politics; from the local to the national, and then to the international scene, where England is put in its relative place by Arnold, standing in ridicule because of its own representatives, the middle class. And as Arnold's timely return to the *Morning Star*'s purple prose reminds us, the difference between Bazley and Palmerston is one of degree rather than kind. Arnold has acted as a tour guide of Englishness, taking us via the apotheosis of bourgeois identity, Lord Palmerston, and all which that identity represents and impersonates, back to our point of departure, the tour having afforded us an "other" perspective.

So how, exactly, is one to define this middle class? Arnold has indicated it, giving us signposts towards it. He has displayed for us its main organs; yet, for all that, he has done little more than this. We can feel smug in siding with Arnold as politically impoverished and impotent liberal/left intellectuals against the thoughtless and crass middle classes in their "happy unconsciousness." We need to do more, however. Arnold needs to do more; and, indeed, he does so, by separating out the identifiable faults of the middle class from those of the aristocracy, to ensure that the two are not confused.

As Arnold points out, the faults with which foreigners accuse us are not those of the aristocracy, for whom he reserves praise, albeit faint. Instead he qualifies these faults, faults defined by others and not himself, faults which he merely admits to, as being the following:

> rash engagement, intemperate threatening, undignified retreat, ill-timed cordiality . . . testy, absolute, ill-acquainted with foreign matters, a little ignoble, very dull to perceive when it is making itself ridiculous.[61]

These, we can take it, are essential components in the structure of identity for Arnold. The criticisms of others confirm a suspicion of that part of the English national character as being parochial, authoritarian and unreflective to the point of being obtuse.

In this critique though, Arnold is not without some praise for the English, or particular characteristics of native identity as he sees it. Once again, Arnold avoids identifying these himself, referring back to foreign opinion. Arnold's continental companions speak of "energy with honesty," a formulation which Arnold admits to admiring, with the provision that there also should be added intelligence (though not of the clear manly variety).[62] This energy with honesty is England's great positive force for Arnold, the force which had caused England to rise as a nation. The phrase which Arnold quotes so approvingly is somewhat idealistic, a little too vague in its definition. Arnold therefore tries to qualify the description of identity by providing us with a social and historical structure, supposedly offered by a French acquaintance. Talking of an England of the recent past, it is said that:

> The lower class worked and fought, the middle class found the money, and the aristocracy wielded the whole.[63]

This single sentence is an accurate description of English social structure and the interrelation of the classes in the manifestation of what Heidegger terms its "everydayness." Yet, because it is so precise and also so stark, it posits the potential for a comprehension beyond that of its merely descriptive nature. Thus Arnold opens up Englishness in itself and to itself, without imposing a criticism or analysis from outside. What we read in this sentence is very much a question of what we want to read there. Is this only descriptive, merely a sketch of hierarchical relations, or do we not find the evidence for a critique of class structure, given the evidence which Arnold has so far presented us with?

Arnold accords the working class with a fundamental and crucial rôle in the construction of a modern England, perhaps despite himself. This, although a slight moment, is important for the re-reading of Arnold. From this, Arnold moves, inevitably for him, to literature.

Though again supposedly paraphrasing his continental friends, Arnold identifies two political poles of English literature in the names of Byron and Scott.[64] Scott expresses a "robust, genial conservatism," while Byron represents "defiant force and indomitable pride."[65] Genial conservatism, defiant force and indomitable pride are the terms in which Arnold himself, I feel, would like us to understand Englishness, even though ironically, for this discourse of identity, Scott is Scottish, as we know; he remarks the otherness within national identity whilst also sustaining the ambiguity of identity in being a conservative figure. Interestingly enough, Arnold describes these literary voices as "voices of the great aristocratical spirit."[66] This mention of spirit marks another turning point in Arnold's essay.

The failure of England according to the anonymous foreign voices, is due to shifting hegemonies, where the balance of power has shifted away from the aristocracy to the middle class.[67] This failure, this fall into bourgeois materialism has caused the hollowing out of English identity and the negation of spirit. One feels that Arnold uses the words "aristocratic" and "aristocratical" as vague synonyms for the idea of spirit rather than as reference to a particular class, even though he has referred to that class itself. This is a problematic moment of confusion in Arnold's essay, the terms being heavily overdetermined by their class and social implications. Yet we sense an Arnold who, in moving through his engagement with the malaise of Englishness, is struggling to find another voice, a voice both for himself and for Englishness.

V

Arnold, having been careful to identify himself as an Englishman through his rhetorical signposts, and having introduced the multiple voice of the foreign, unspecified other—that voice which first raised the spectre of the toiling, fighting working class—wields those voices of alterity to map out the absolute degradation of the proletariat; which degradation, Arnold insists implicitly, is a direct corollary of the middle-class will to power:

> Without insisting too much on the stories of misery and degradation which are perpetually reaching us, we will say that no one can mix with a great crowd in your country, no one can walk with his eyes and ears open through the poor quarters of your large towns, and not feel that your common people, as it meets one's eyes, is at present more raw, to say the very least, less enviable-looking, further removed from civilized and humane life, than the common people almost everywhere. Well, then, you are not a success, according to the modern standard, with your common people.[68]

Immediately, insistently, *intimately*, we are confronted with the fact that "my countrymen" are also, always, more than just the middle class, despite the efforts of that class to insist on itself as the only class (thereby giving ground to the lie of the 1980s that we live in a classless society). "My countrymen" are "your common people," "your" being not only the possessive pronoun directed at Arnold—he thereby implicates himself in social responsibility—but also the possessive with which Arnold forces recognition on his readers; for "yours" is ours, is mine.

"Without insisting too much" and "to say the very least": the voice of the other, of the foreign and the foreign within opens to us in reasoned, measured phrases, the phrases of English liberal discourse, the horror of the poor and the social context for their poverty. The connection drawn by Arnold is that the material poverty of the working class has come about as a direct result of the spiritual "poverty" of the middle class.[69] Arnold is careful to avoid making the analogy one of equivalence. He argues instead for a causal relationship, which harkens back to the French newspaper comment on the English love of trade and the nation's concomitant lack of care about the spread of cholera. The middle classes are shown to have a drastic material negative effect on both foreigners and the domestic working class through their own greed and social short-sightedness.

Arnold also makes plain that it is the English middle class on whom he is commenting, rather than some vague notion of a middle class, inimical to healthy social relations. Unlike their English counterparts, the European bourgeoisie exhibit and enjoy "the growth of a love of things of the mind; and the growth of a love of beautiful things."[70] These are the requisite qualities for the modern "spirit," according to Arnold. Middle-class English identity is so in thrall to materialism that it has oppressed others while suppressing its own spiritual needs.[71] It is also argued, in a comment partly foreshadowing Walter Benjamin, that the

> capital pressing danger of England, is the barbarism of the middle class; the civilisation of her middle class is England's capital, pressing want.[72]

One hundred and thirty years later, after the cynical manipulation of national identity by Tory-liberal ideology, we comprehend the urgent truth of this commentary. We understand also how, through the cumulative effects of critique, self-reflection and condemnation, Arnold has raised the necessity of the question of spirit to any consideration of national identity. Perhaps we also begin to recognise the necessity for avoidance: of speed in the critical process, of dogmatic constructions, and of maintaining a purely disinterested and external position in the act of criticism.

Once the discourse surrounding the question of spirit has been thus effectively signalled, Arnold is able to move to the next level of necessary critique: the criticism of the aristocracy and, through that, the issue of class:

> The *English system* of a great landed aristocracy keeps your lower class a lower class for ever, and materialises and vulgarises your whole middle class.[73] (my emphasis)

Arnold's ventriloquism is scintillating in its economy and precision as he identifies the essential structure of oppression. One reads in Arnold's text a way through to a radical democratization of Englishness founded in an ongoing internal critique. Arnold's thought is subtle enough to identify the problem of English society as inhabiting a system that is, in and of itself, English; hence, the economy of the problematic of national identity, revealed in its circularity and perpetuation.

Arnold sees the problem in specifically national terms. At this moment, his use of the foreign voice, allied to the use of quotation marks, works to powerful effect. Here, instead of equivocating, the quotation marks frame and foreground the commentary all the more lucidly. So strong is the performance that Arnold's Englishman, the mere dabbler, is made to seem all the more barbaric and ignorant, his sole riposte being blurted "clap-trap."[74]

From the position such a criticism serves to put in place, Arnold, despite being "no arguer,"[75] exhorts his readers (in echoes of Hamlet) to:

> . . . all persist in it who can, and steadily set their desires on introducing, with time, a little more soul and spirit into the too, too solid flesh of English society.[76]

No one can shirk their social duty and responsibility to "their countrymen." Arnold encompasses everyone. He desires that we channel *our desires* into introducing soul and spirit, recognizing that the answer to social problems is not only in material abundance. Arnold's view of Englishness is essentially a social one, constructed out of a shared identity with a national context, as the final words of the quotation above show. Arnold invokes duty in order, to paraphrase Derrida, to recall what has been promised in the name England.[77]

VI

Arnold's essay "My Countrymen," is readable as initiating a potentially dissident discourse of affirmative resistance to bourgeois identity and the closure of critical thought. Yet, in order for that resistance to be more powerfully affirmative, it needs to be recast in alternative terms, an *other voice*, if it is not to be recuperated into the Englishness from which it seeks to distance itself. The problem for Arnold is in the term "English" and other related names.

Finally, in this essay, Arnold steps back again. This, he says, is due to "all the rebuke" his original speculations had brought him.[78] Arnold says that finds himself more and more in the position of a "mere listener."[79] But if Arnold is only a mere listener to others' voices—first to the voices of the newspapers and other critics of "Matthew Arnold," secondly to his foreign associates—he is a listener who "calls himself Anglo-Saxon rather than English."[80] This is an important distinction in

Arnold's terms. For the term "Anglo-Saxon" defines an identity not overdetermined by the qualities of Englishness that Arnold has set out to trace in "My Countrymen." In defining himself as Anglo-Saxon rather than as English, Arnold has drawn upon an old term for a new purpose. Through the name, he can define that quality of identity which he seeks to preserve, to engender and to encourage in others. It is a name that calls upon us to recall our duty to think again beyond the authority of reason that "England" and its associated terms impose.[81]

The name "Anglo-Saxon" invites us to re-write Englishness in others' terms, in terms that are not subject to recuperation through and by middle-class values and ideology. As a way of giving this new/old name a firm grounding in cultural identity, and as a means of escaping England imaginatively, Arnold turns to America. In America, Arnold suggests, although the people are of the same race as the English, "Anglo-Saxonism triumphs."[82] Acknowledging that the Americans have faults of their own, along with those inherited from the English middle class, the Americans have, according to Arnold, "a vivacity and play of mind . . . which comes . . . from their democratic life, with its ardent hope, its forward stride, its gaze fixed on the future."[83]

Thus Arnold turns to an other "Englishness" an "Englishness" that is not one; he turns to an other Anglo-Saxonism, that of America. With this turn, he turns towards democracy as the hope for us all. It is specifically to democracy as the manifestation of Anglo-Saxon *geist* that Arnold looks, in the hopes of domestic reform within and by the middle class. With this hope comes the *caveat* that, for "want of any eminent gift for telling on the world spiritually," the English may be doomed.[84] For Arnold, even the American working class has attained a culture not available to their English counterparts.[85] Somewhat idealistically, Arnold seems to view the model of America and its democratic republicanism as the unquestioned answer to England's fast diminishing world status. To America, Arnold looks for the answer to the question of Englishness. He finds as part of that answer a literate culture.

Arnold cannot give up England altogether, however. His idealism—which is not his, but that of his "friend"—is given short shrift. In the moment that he envisions his alternative Anglo-Saxonism, he underplays it by stating that he is not satisfied with "plans of vicarious greatness."[86] In the final sentences, Arnold reverts to a favoured metaphor from his poetry, that of waves, to describe the movement of history, and to envision also the ebb and flow of nations.[87] The figure of the sea is in the last lines a figure for historical flow, of competing hegemonies; it is also a figure of limitlessness through which Arnold can inscribe the endless activity of the questions he has sought to raise. In having recourse to this figure, Arnold resists closure, yet motions to the figure of the abyss in a last instance of doubt and ambiguity.

Given figures such as the one immediately above, it is easy enough to glimpse a recurrent "gesture of postponement"[88] in Arnold's writing. However, the gesture of postponement may be more a gesture of political avoidance, part of a strategy to ward off the violence of speed; especially when that speed collapses the space wherein critical thought can take place and is applied to the political and social life of people. Arnold is not beyond the seduction of such speed. Yet in "My Countrymen" speed is held off, avoided with a conscientious dexterity and faithfulness to the matters at hand.

Raymond Williams effectively translates Arnold's own moments of acceleration, arguing that, at such moments, Arnold's responses to the vulgarities of his age—vulgarities which are all too often recognizable as being similar to those of our historical moment—fall into the structures of the stock riposte of the Victorian liberal intellectual. In such instances, Williams contends, Arnold's criticisms are equally as vulgar, as "Victorian" in the middle-class sense.[89] There is a humbling lesson in this for us as critics.

Arnold's writing is at its most even-handed when abstaining from a fully committed polemical attack. In such abstention, there is traceable another commitment which I have tried to illuminate; a commitment on Arnold's part to the thinking through of a philosophical discourse on the politics of identity. Arnold recognizes the impossibility of Englishness in its cultural guise of liberal-materialism. The dominant Englishness of the Victorian era is marked by the absence of a national spirit; hence a return to this "Englishness" in recent years, as part of the systematic suppression of spirit and communal identity. "My Countrymen" is not without its faults. Yet, in almost every line, we read Arnold working with Englishness, with its identity as his identity, whilst resisting the temptation to posit facile answers. Arnold cannot wholly escape his own entanglement in middle-class identity; he knows escape is impossible, as is the escape from metaphysics. He does, however, attempt to see this identity from beyond itself, beyond its reflection of itself and in doing so, Arnold engages in a dialogue with this identity, opening it to us, showing us the possibility for revision.

4

CRITICAL NATIONALISM AND THE
"TRUTH" OF (IDENTITY IN) ELIZABETH GASKELL

I

It is difficult to say anything about Elizabeth Gaskell's writing.

This is a truth, more or less, about the fictions of Elizabeth Gaskell, a truth because of the truths "of" Elizabeth Gaskell; which truths are nothing short of acts of radical mimesis (the reiteration of a scene faithful only to the instance of that scene and not to a general economy or theory of Mimesis) that deconstructs Truth, *Logos* and all other stable categories. These truths—which are provisionally definitions of identity and are not The Truth—unsettle certainty and "any guarantee of critical, theoretical, or hermeneutic reappropriation."[1]

For the reader of Elizabeth Gaskell today intent on a singular political reading, the definition of a single, coherent, political position might prove a problem. This interpretative difficulty is due to Gaskell's anticipation, and inclusion, of several differing, often contradictory, ideological voices in the space of a single text. Gaskell gathers into her writing many positions and situations that are broadly political, often mutually contradictory; and she does so not through an active gesture of gathering but through the act of desistance. She desists from critique, from the sounding of an authoritative voice, so as to leave the possibility of silence in which there can be heard various political discourses. Gaskell's texts do not attempt to avoid the snares of traditional modes of thought; such evasion, she realizes is impossible (this is one of the truths of Elizabeth Gaskell). However, in the face of formal structures of thinking, Gaskell's desistance opens gaps through which dissidence is enunciated.

The problematic of the single reading is therefore further compounded by Gaskell's refusal to allow a particular voice either hierarchical or hegemonic primacy. It is all but impossible, for example, to identify a single site for the narratorial voice of *North And South*, because the voice—if we can assume such an unproblematised, monolithic presence—neither assumes nor assures a transcendent locale incorporating "its" narrative.

Depending on which character is speaking in the novel, Gaskell's metalanguage is usually sympathetic to that speaker. Thus, at different moments, the text appears Tory, Whig or radical in its polemical undercurrent. No simple or full identity is more than partially established, without that structure being, in some fashion, critically solicited at another textual instance. The narratorial voice is never absolutely identifiable with one ideology. Such obscurity is not, again, equivalent to the assumption of superiority, but is, instead, part of Gaskell's recognition of political identity's paradoxical nature within a national context. Furthermore, such recognition incorporates a true democratization of narratorial enunciation. Gaskell's writing foregrounds the inscription of the "truths" of cultural identity and reality in all their fragmented complexity.

I will focus, in this chapter, on three of Gaskell's shorter, less read texts, "Round the Sofa," "An Accursed Race," and *Cousin Phillis*. I have chosen these, rather than longer works, because I comprehend Gaskell's writing primarily to be episodic and exemplary, rather than narrative and linear. This structural condition is important to Gaskell's carefully controlled revelation of the truth(s) of national identity. Such identity is always culturally specific and provisional. Gaskell's truths are local and, hence, *fundamentally national* truths. They avoid the universal and metaphysical, being specific to the condition of Englishness mediated in Gaskell's writing. Identities are rooted in the intellectual and social context; they are predicated on the idea of community. Gaskell understands the details (to use her word) of English culture's "heterogeneous nature."[1] From this understanding comes the author's enunciation of the communal self with its multivalent voices. Because Elizabeth Gaskell recognizes such heterogeneity (and because, readable in Gaskell's text there is the implicit understanding that the Other demands that I respect its alterity) to be ethical she must "write them [the details] down as they arise in my memory."[3] Thus Mrs. Gaskell constructs a narratorial voice expressing a "Being-for-others," as part of a literary communism.

II

In seeking to define a "literary communism," Jean-Luc Nancy remarks that "the singular voice of interruption is not a voice without courage."[4] The voice of which Nancy speaks is neither necessarily that of the author nor that of the narratorial or narrative voice,[5] nor any character or group of characters. The voice in question finds its expression between these situations and the reader's interpretation. Nancy's courage of interruption often consists in the ability to dare to be silent, a silence always already in being between specifically identifiable singular voices. Such a silence, such courage "*allow*[s] *to be said* something that no one—no individual, no representative—could ever say."[6] The voice in question announces community, incorporating and anticipating, without co-optation, several—though not all—positions, which are frequently contradictory or paradoxical.

The courageous voice of which Nancy speaks, that voice which sounds between statements and resounds in the silences between the political positions of characters, author, narratorial voice and reader, is nowhere more in evidence than in Elizabeth Gaskell's writing. Gaskell, refusing to adopt a singular voice for her texts and refusing to choose the limitations of party-political line or specific ideology, offers the possibility of a true and ethical communication. This communication comes at the very limit, "at which all politics stop and begin."[7] Such limits are, according to Nancy, those constituting the possibility of communication itself, which, in turn, is the means by which we determine ourselves as community and exercise an internal—and, therefore, implicitly political—critique of our cultures.[8]

"An Accursed Race" performs such an internal critique of English prejudice, albeit in a seemingly oblique manner. In order to approach this story, we need to take into account, briefly, the story's context. As one of a number of stories, published in a "chain," beginning with "My Lady Ludlow," "An Accursed Race" is connected to the other tales by an unidentified narrator, who re-tells the stories that have been told in Mrs Dawson's literary salon, in Edinburgh. Supposedly, then, each of the stories from the collection entitled "Round the Sofa" have been told, originally, by different narrators and are now reshaped by the anonymous narratorial voice who makes the links between the tales. As Edgar Wright points out, Gaskell makes only a "minimal gesture of developing individual personalities,"[9] even though the characters of the story tellers are appropriate to the stories that they tell. Gaskell, in keeping the definition of individual character to a minimum, is better able to form a structure that eschews the singular voice in favour of the plural vocation of both community and communication. Through such a voice, the writer expresses differing political and philosophical beliefs that, nevertheless, carry an immanence: of collective spirit and collective identity, finding possible, other, expressions, through a form of Nancy's literary communism.

The characters in question, although barely delineated, are interesting. There is Mr Dawson, a surgeon, "who had obtained a reputation for the cure of a particular class of diseases";[10] Mr Sperano is an Italian exile, "banished *even* from France."[11] (my emphasis) Presumably, Mr Sperano finds himself doubly exiled yet accepted into Edinburgh literary society because of his politics. There is Mr Preston, an independent landowner from Westmoreland, and Mrs Dawson herself, whose "broad tongue"[12] identifies her as being from Liverpool. Of this accent, the narrator comments, significantly, "I hear something different to other people, but I like it because it is just you."[13] The narrator cannot be precise in what she he hears, referring to "something." This quality is important politically because of its indefineability. Something that is of the accent, yet not wholly identifiable as such, resists definition and therefore containment. The accent affirms and announces a difference of cultural identity that has resisted a linguistic standardization attempted by the upper classes, through their representative in these stories, Lady Ludlow.[14] It is worth noting also that all the characters gathered together speak an accented English. This suggests a community of identity founded on difference and a respect for, and enunciation of, that difference.

As the implied accents and the salon structure make plain, there is no one, homogeneous, national identity being expressed through the oral performance of "literature," even though there is a shared tongue making communication and, therefore, community possible. This, in turn, does seem to bring into question what the identity of literature is in a positive yet resistant fashion. One cannot say that the stories collected together express a single vision or ideology, beyond the desire to share and communicate tales that illuminate social injustices and iniquities, as in "The Poor Clare," a historical tale telling of Protestant intolerance towards Catholicism in mid-eighteenth century England.[15]

"An Accursed Race"[16] is also a historical narrative of racism in Western Europe directed towards an obscure group, the Cagots. A "true" story, not a fiction, this tale is told by Mr Dawson. For the modern reader, "An Accursed Race" is most disturbing when the narrator reports of the comparison of the Cagots to "vermin."[17] Popular lore tells of them being "born with tails."[18] They are said to smell,[19] have thick lips,[20] no ear lobes;[21] surgeons were ordered by the King of Navarre to examine the Cagots' blood for genetic differences;[22] and, "in the greater number of towns, it was decreed that the outward sign of a Cagot should be a piece of red cloth sewed conspicuously on the front of his dress."[23] Although this narrative is concerned with people who were Catholics, and although Gaskell's story is based on historical incident, we

cannot help but read this text today, after Nazi Germany's treatment of
Jews and Slavic Catholics, and with the recent re-emergence of neo-Nazi
groups in Europe and England, as anything other than an indictment of
what we now term fascism. Indeed, Gaskell's story reveals the already
powerful phenomenon in the 17- and 1800s of racist, religious and biologically determinist forms of brutality, for which Elizabeth Gaskell had
no specific name, but, against which she was compelled to narrate.

Remembering the concomitant rise of industrial capitalism during
the author's lifetime, we can read Gaskell's text tracing the transition
from feudal to bourgeois society, in a historical, cultural and economic
trajectory from the early modern period ("[e]ven at the close of that
period which we call the Middle Ages"[24]) to the "great French revolution."[25] Gaskell recognizes that, in the words of Nicos Poulantzas,

> [i]t was fascist ideology that was to reunite the power bloc . . . The
> rise of fascism . . . represents an *offensive step* and an *offensive strat-
> egy* on the part of the power bloc, and of big capital in particular.[26]

Gaskell maps this double offensive, of ideology and economic structure, not only historically but also through the mobilization of the dominant powers and discourses in Western European society that were
employed to form a hegemonic consensus against the Cagots. We read
of the doctors, the Law, of government and state apparatuses, and the
Church, operating, concertedly and insistently, in their desire first to
marginalise and then destroy the Cagots.[27]

There is much more about "Euro-Fascism" in this tale, especially
pertinent in the context of stories of "ethnic cleansing" in Bosnia and
the systematic victimisation of Turks and other foreign nationals in
Germany; but the question I want to ask at this stage is what about
England? Where is England in this tale of an oppressed race?

The answer, roughly speaking, is (at) the beginning and end of
the narrative. We start from England and return to it, as will be shown
(this recalls the "law of economy" governing Coleridge's imagined ram-
ble in the preface to *Kubla Khan*; see Chapter I, above). England is not
used, however, as a structural frame or paradigm of social moderation
(one of several conventional definitions of Englishness that Gaskell
ignores). Nor is England given ethical autonomy from Europe. Gaskell's
history insists, albeit tacitly, that England be compared with and considered part of Europe; Gaskell's insists that England cannot be allowed
the luxury of thinking itself as isolated. Gaskell thinks through the issue
of Englishness as one complicit in a general European attitude of racism,
that transcends national borders, and is directed towards a non-

European other. In reading "An Accursed Race" in this way—this being in keeping with my reading of progressive, cosmopolitan tolerance expressed by the existence of the salon, and through its tales—I am suggesting that we comprehend the narrative as belonging to Gaskell's general economy of the "inscription of our infinite resistance"[28] to varieties of oppression (one can extend such an interpretation to novels such as *North and South*, *Sylvia's Lovers*, and even, although in more curtailed fashion, to *Cranford*). This resistance is not some misguided democratic impulse towards correcting whatever we perceive as the "faults" of other cultures and countries; the resistance is already immanent within our own culture, operating against the attempted suppression of differences that construct a heterogeneous national identity. The suppression of which I speak is figured as the suppression of the spirit of that identity which inaugurates difference, engendering change and the possibility to "live on,"[29] to live beyond the individual or singular voice (or that vocal consensus which attempts through the forms of racial purity or particular models of democracy to impress homogeneity on minorities). This is, in essence, that which is being enunciated in the writing of communal story-telling.

"An Accursed Race" begins:

> We have our prejudices in England. Or, if that assertion offends any of my readers, I will modify it: we have had our prejudices in England. We have tortured Jews; we have burnt Catholics and Protestants, to say nothing of a few witches and wizards. We have satirised Puritans, and we have dressed up Guys. But, after all, I do not think we have been so bad as our Continental friends. To be sure, our insular position has kept us free, to a certain degree, from the inroads of alien races.[30]

Notice the mock modification of opinion which leads to a catalogue of native atrocities; notice also the ironic relativisation in the fifth sentence of this passage; notice finally the registration of ambiguity in term "insular position," which leaves the echo of the resounding fact that, frequently, the first victims of English prejudice were the English themselves. The story ends with the following tomb-stone epitaph, from the grave of a Mrs Mary Hand of Stratford-on-Avon:

> What faults you saw in me,
> Pray strive to shun;
> And look at home; there's
> Something to be done.[31]

The two passages connect clearly enough in ways that do not require explication. If the narrator, in the first passage, means to imply by the expression "we have [not] been so bad" that torture and burning are somehow "better," "more acceptable" forms of punishment, hatred and intolerance—better because immediate and physical, more acceptable because of their being open manifestations of brutality and ignorance—than the juridical-doctrinal-medical discourses incorporating surveillance, marginalisation and silencing which the story proceeds to catalogue, there are those who would find this reassuring.

Yet those readers would also miss the irony of this passage, which makes apparent the fact that, as a paper supposedly intended originally for presentation by Mr Dawson at the Philosophical Society,[32] "An Accursed Race" acknowledges implicitly that there are certain protocols of polite institutional address to be followed. This is especially true when the subject under critique is the national identity of one's audience (whether Mr Dawson's or Mrs Gaskell's). Such acknowledgment, such deferral and modification of tone is a very *English* gesture (similar in effect and kind to Arnold's rhetoric of apology that admits to a lack of theoretical rigour, discussed in the previous chapter). In the gesture, glib humour is almost indistinguishable from convention. And it is precisely that glibness, and the irony accompanying it, which allows the political point to be scored all the more effectively. Gaskell deploys the English idiom with fine precision, underlabouring[33] the structures of right-wing national identity.

This kind of "Englishness" allows the comparison in the excerpt by making analogous torture and immolation with satire. English fascism—notice that Dawson/the anonymous narrator/Gaskell chooses, twice, to insist on England rather than Britain as the site of victimisation — knows no sectarian boundaries in this opening paragraph. The reader cannot help but recall this startling introduction throughout the tale of the Cagot. So, "not having been so bad" really amounts to an admission of having been much worse. What is clear is that the "English" are, and have been, consistently culpable in victimizing other Englishnesses.

Thus we should read the distinctions of Englishness to which *Round the Sofa* alerts us. That kind of English identity to which the members of the salon do not belong is defined by Dawson's choice of the word "insular." The word has a double resonance, referring both to geographical insularity (again, the choice of "England" over "Britain" is an ironic indication of this) and to mental and ideological insularity, amounting to a political unthinkingness. It is precisely this English inability to open itself to self-enquiry and internal criticism onto which the story opens, at beginning and end.

Gaskell's presentation of the epitaph offers the reader a figural re-marking of the tombstone from which the inscription comes. Standing alone at the close of the story, this figure stands as the potential epitaph and headstone of English identity. We read our own imminent demise, our death coming as a result of our own intolerance. Yet in this Dickensian prescription of annihilation as the result of our politics of racism, as though we were all chauvinistic Scrooges, we read also a faint hope for change and so for living on. At the final moment of the story, the presentation of the epitaph demands of all readers an ongoing deconstruction of the structures, institutions, practices and discourses of insular national identity, insisting that there is "something to be done" at home, in England itself. There is in this gesture what Jean-Luc Nancy calls "that [which] we call a politics, the way of opening community to itself."[34]

At this limit of narration, at its "final" border—the "end" of the story—Gaskell opens the border by resisting the completion or closure of thought, refusing to admit to a "last word" on racism.[35] In doing so, she makes possible an understanding of the continuance of both literature and community—of literature *as* community—through the signification in the final lines of the epitaph and in the indeterminability of the word "something," whilst also announcing that there is an "irrepressible political exigency"[36] which must be addressed. Thus it is particularly after the story, in silence (or at the provisional limits that I have quoted) that the courageous voice speaks a truth of national identity, speaking of and with an alternative voice for that identity, by which enunciation identity can reform itself in order to dismantle the politics of insularity.[37]

III

Dismantling the insularity of English identity while seeking to preserve that which is positive in the spirit of the past's identity can be understood as a principal concern in the *nouvelle Cousin Phillis.*[38] The text reveals a critical comprehension of what is most beneficial for the future of the nation in its readings of cultural being, transforming, *translating* Englishness without discarding or demolishing it.

In this story, Gaskell remarks a generational transition within England (as she does in *Cranford*)[39] for the purposes of maintaining the vitality of the positive aspects of identity's spirit at a moment of broad cultural change. In tracing transition and also breaking away from dead elements of the past, such as an unquestioning faith in the law of the patriarch, we read that what knowledge a younger generation has to offer is not necessarily of the order of a positive or fruitful "progression"; such movement may be "tainted" by a shallow appropriation of the foreign inimical to the health of Englishness. This does of course raise another problem; that of a resistance to the foreign simply because it is foreign.

But Gaskell avoids the problem—she does not actively avoid it but encounters it through desistance, knowing the problem to be unavoidable—focusing on the issue from another angle, moving to an other situation not complicit with identity's sense of power over the foreign. Gaskell chooses to think through the relationship of the domestic self and the foreign other. She does not attempt to re-present the foreign *as such* (such a mode being, of course, impossible without the violence of mastery). The author focuses instead on the appropriation of a certain style in clothing, taste and thought by Mr Holdsworth, who is Gaskell's figure for an English type. Holdsworth appropriates without thought, and without thinking through whether a spirit of an other national identity can be said to exist (not in the sense of being, but in the sense of being other, of being unappropriable).

Thus Mr Holdsworth's "European affectation" is not necessarily readable as a rejection on the part of the author of the continental in favour of "good" Englishness. Rather, we can read a critique by Gaskell of the Englishman whose appropriation of the foreign is merely one more form of colonisation. This colonisation on Holdsworth's part is effected with a carelessness for cultures, both his own and others, and is reiterated in his carelessness towards Phillis. She is always merely attractive frippery for Holdsworth, much like his continental reading. Should this should seem too judgmental, too reductive, Gaskell is careful to complicate the figure of Holdsworth by making him charming and attractive to the reader also.

Paul Manning, the narrator of *Cousin Phillis*, tells us that Mr Holdsworth, "had travelled on the continent, and wore mustachios and whiskers of a somewhat foreign fashion."[40] The second clause of this sentence is indicative not so much of a condemnation on Gaskell's part of the continental *per se*, as being a criticism and revelation of Holdsworth's lack of seriousness, involvement with and rootedness in a particular cultural identity. The clause remarks a lack of attachment also to any sense of domestic identity. Out of this "lack," Gaskell has Holdsworth leave England for "French"—as opposed to "English"—Canada,[41] where he will eventually marry a woman "of French descent";[42] so Holdsworth is mapped as a figure for a tribe of English people seeking an alternative identity in the new but drawing extensively on the old European sense of Being.

The whiskers, a metonymic figure for Holdsworth's lack of intrinsic native "character," are of a part with "his tone of badinage (as the French call it)."[43] It is ironic that Paul, in remarking Phillis' ingenuousness and her misrecognition of Holdsworth's irony at her expense, should be the one to identify the tone in this way, applying to it the foreign term. This alerts us in a somewhat self-reflexive manner to Holdsworth's other cultural traces, through the parenthetical advertisement of the national and linguistic origins of the term.

The question is raised, whose pen is it that slips in the parentheses? Whose marks are these that trip us and give us pause? Paul? Elizabeth Gaskell? The question is unanswerable, if only because the silent marks of the written trace are silent and remain so, there to be read but unreadable, unidentifiable, untranslatable. Paul may well slip in the phrase, "as the French call it," but how are we to understand the remark, given its being cordoned off within the paired parenthetical signs? If the remark is Paul's, as we may speculate it is, then surely he has learned the term from his mentor Holdsworth.

There is a doubling of irony here, for those of us who, like Phillis, are a little too parochial. Paul's appropriation —if we accept the appropriation as his, provisionally—of the foreign at this point has a double edge. While Holdsworth's frivolous playfulness is being commented on by his friend and subordinate, Gaskell, the narratorial voice or the text may be understood as revealing Paul's "contamination" by Holdsworth's European traces. Paul is correct to define Holdsworth's speech as badinage, of course; but his definition can only be effected by the literary inscription of the "foreign" into "English prose." We can therefore ask what is "proper English"? English and, especially, literary English is itself contaminated by French, amongst other languages, and has always already been so. English itself contaminates itself, even in its acts of linguistic colonisation and appropriation, rewriting its identity through its desire to fill its gaps with the appropriate "bon mots" taken untranslated from other languages; it is thus that the "Englishness" of the language lives on, surviving and adapting. A certain foreignness is a condition of English identity. Gaskell's act of writing, a necessity of the scene of narration, is the pretext and prescription of the "impurity" of identity as a condition of its own Being. This impurity of identity is, as the example shows, precisely textual; whereby the trace of the other—in this case, the foreign tongue—is remarked as a writing which articulates and is articulated by difference and cultural heterogeneity. Thus it is that Gaskell makes the reader aware that there is no fault in the foreign as such; thus it is that there is invoked a community of the literary and a literary communism.

Whatever fault does lie here is not one of (a question of the right) national identity, but rather a fault belonging to Holdsworth; a fault which he himself admits to when confiding to Paul that he has given Phillis a novel by Manzoni.[44] Paul's fear of Holman's displeasure over Holdsworth's gift is dismissed by Holdsworth, who asks:

why make a bugbear of a word?[45]

For one who is so careless of cultural contexts, Holdsworth chooses his words very carefully.

This linguistic awareness on Gaskell's part, the seeming precision with which she chooses certain words (and certain names) for certain characters, should lead us to consider for a moment a gramophony; an oral, aural and written trace, sounded in three of the male characters' names: Holman, Holdsworth and Manning. There is readable a shared economy in these which we can relate to their cultural functions.

Holman, as preacher and bearer of the Word, represents the authority of God. He is not open to speculation or skepticism and so figures the "whole man," the wholeness or unity that supposedly accompanies unquestioned and unquestioning belief. Yet his inability to question skeptically and his desire to accept without question the fact that, as he puts it, we do not know who "invented the alphabet,"[46] as a sign of the truth of God, is a sign of a hole, a hollow or a blank page in his knowledge, which he refuses to examine. In being the representative of *Logos*, of Truth, he gives away the paradox of Truth, which paradox is Truth's untruth or, to put it another way, the truth of Truth.

If Holman is the representative of the "whole man," Holman is also the hollow man. As "whole man," Holman's ambiguous name is composed of two syllables, the first of which sounds the paradoxical ambiguity; thus "w/hole-man." Each of the syllables are partly re-written and partly re-write the names of both *Hol*dsworth and *Man*ning. The former connects wholeness and absence with value or economic "worth." the implication is that economy (in the restricted sense) both accrues and wears away value. Paul's surname, on the other hand, suggests a masculine empowerment or engendering, and is itself a re-mapping—in a Freudian or Lacanian reading—of the symbolic economy of the railway and its phallic penetrations and disruption of the "virgin" English countryside.

It is of course the younger Manning who introduces Holdsworth into the Holman household, causing albeit indirectly the disruption of Phillis. There is then a powerful connection between the masculine forces of this story that is both brought together and pulled apart in their signatures, signatures indicative of the phallogocentric economy.

The signatures alert us to the power of the word, which power equates, for some, with Truth itself. Holman's belief in the Word of God and the Letter of the Law amounts to a powerful proscriptive tool with which to police those less knowledgeable: in short, Holman holds to the absolute or metaphysical Truth or *Logos* as a cultural bugbear, a spirit to frighten children. Phillis is the child of Holman and it is to her that Holdsworth gives the book, thereby flaunting Holman's authority which is rooted in the Word-as-bugbear. So Holdsworth's dismissive, off-the-cuff remark is wholly to the point; through it, Gaskell scores a palpable hit against those who observe the letter while disregarding the spirit.

Principally, it is Holman against whom the point is made. If Holdsworth takes words, and the Word, too lightly, there is a very real sense that Gaskell wants us to understand Holman as adhering too strictly to the letter of the law. Holman is the man for whom Virgil has a timeless quality; this is no mere aesthetic judgement, however. Virgil's timelessness, his elevation to metaphysical status, comes from the fact that, according to Holman, the poet is able to describe:

> *to a T* what is now lying before us in the parish of Heathbridge, county–,England. (my emphasis)[47]

Holman's faithful adherence to the Truth of the Letter is made clear in the commonplace phrase I have emphasized, while his pedantry is expressed in the postal precision he uses to name his view of the countryside.

Obviously, Holman is unaware of the irony in his appropriation of Virgilian tags for the purposes of defining the English landscape. In rendering Virgil's epithets as supposedly eternal or "enduring,"[48] Holman is culpable in the colonisation of literature for a nationalistic purpose. But in being so, in unconsciously defining his own sense of Englishness in a manner that is so politically problematic, he is used by Gaskell to unveil a typical gesture of liberal humanist thought. Holman's mis-reading of Virgil is a more fundamentally serious political act than Holdsworth's imitation of foreign whisker styles, even though Holdsworth is the ostensible "villain of the piece." Holman's act of mis-reading is more serious because it is informed by education and intellect in the service of cultural definition and the maintenance of English parochialism.

Thus in thinking through the figure of Holdsworth and his foreignness, we have also to take into account that which Gaskell weighs in

Holdsworth's favour. In favour of Holdsworth, albeit indirectly, and against a too parochial and closed-minded Englishness, Gaskell offers us the early scene of Miss Hannah Dawson berating France, "all who had ever set foot therein,"[49] and by illogical extension Holdsworth himself, as Paul Manning points out. If we do not remember the narrow bigotry of Miss Hannah's diatribe, then we miss Gaskell's critique of closed Englishness and her not uncritical sympathies towards Holdsworth.

A parochial mentality in general is commented on by Gaskell when she remarks that there was a vague dislike on the part of the villagers towards Holdsworth because of his southern accent which, the villagers assume, Holdsworth employs to give himself airs.[50] A conventional New Critical reading of this attitude would misrecognise the point here, interpreting the villagers' reaction to Holdsworth as an foreshadowing on Gaskell's part of Holdsworth's betrayal of Phillis. The fallacious logic used by such a reading serves to reproduce the parochialism of the villagers at an aesthetic level by making a narrative connection where none exists.

Yet whatever positive qualities Holdsworth does possess, he is not entirely trustworthy, as Gaskell has us understand through Holdsworth's dealings with Phillis. Because of this, we should not be too trusting of the ideology that informs Holdsworth's praise of Mr Manning:

> [He is a] . . . Birmingham workman, self educated . . . having never associated with stimulating minds, or had what advantages travel and contact with the world may afford . . . working out his own thoughts, into steel and iron . . . a fortune, if it pleases him . . . it's evidently good blood.[51]

Holdsworth, who prefaces this eulogy to the self-made individual with the disarming comment, "I am only speaking the truth,"[52] (as though such a thing were possible; this phrase alone should alert the reader immediately to some kind of Tory-liberal legerdemain) is an advocate clearly of the economic and ethical doctrine of the Manchester School, favoured by Samuel Smiles (who might well be considered as one of the architects of Thatcherism). Holdsworth's discourse is an expression of individualism as "a pretty pure ideology of the market," to quote Roy Bhaskar.[53]

The description of Manning could easily have been extracted from Smiles's own biographical illustrations from his popular *Self-Help*,[54] published just four years earlier than *Cousin Phillis*, in 1859.[55] Consider, for the purposes of comparison, these passages from Smiles's nauseating homily to right-wing selfhood:

The instances of men . . . who, by dint of persevering application and energy, have raised themselves from the humblest ranks of industry to eminent positions of usefulness and influence in society, are . . . so numerous[56]

Inventors have set in motion some of the greatest industries of the world . . . our means of locomotion . . . have been the result of the labour and ingenuity of many men and many minds.

Mankind at large are all the happier for such inventions . . . The steam-engine was nothing . . . until it . . . was taken in hand by practical mechanics . . . Watt was one of the most industrious of men; and the story of his life proves, what all experience confirms, that it is not the man of the greatest natural vigour and capacity who achieves the highest results, but he who employs his powers with the greatest industry and the most carefully disciplined skill—the skill that comes by labour, application, and experience.[57]

From this "biography" of Watt we find ourselves back at the description of Manning, whose own "labour, application, and experience" have made him what he is, despite "having never associated with stimulating minds." The language of Holdsworth's biographical sketch is carefully considered so as to dovetail into Smilesian ideology, even to the point of the qualifying negatives which insist we see Manning as a truly isolated individual whose "success" is due only to himself.

The problem with Holdsworth is, therefore, carefully set up by Gaskell, in order to make all the more effective the revelation of his moral condition, with regard to his treatment of Phillis. For we are to see beyond Holdsworth, in order that we might comprehend the nature of men who adhere to a similar political, ideological and philosophical affiliation. Holdsworth's "flaw" is not his supposed contamination by the foreign other; Holdsworth's infection comes from within. We read that he is mapped by the discourses of an obviously domestic Tory-liberalism that marks him as a particular kind of Englishman. His voice is at its clearest when in support of right-wing ideology, as in the example above. It is for this reason that he is sent away by Gaskell, banished from Gaskell's vision of England. Gaskell rids her England of, what is to her, the wrong type of Englishman, as she seeks to reform the old England of Holman around notions of care and community which can benefit from the new technology; and it is through the figure and narrative of Paul Manning that caring and technology come together.

IV

Gaskell's radical mimesis is figured most thoroughly through the character of Holdsworth; he is always more than the stereotypical villain in a stock tale of dalliance, seduction and betrayal. Of course, this is the thread of a plot that Gaskell plays with and plays out. She does so in order to move beyond the limitations of this structure; she shows the limits or horizons that mark such a narrative structure, reforming the structure by her momentary and sometimes contradictory adherence to and mimicry of discourses not traditionally associated with stock narrative figures. If we are to understand the possible reasons for this, we need to comprehend Gaskell's own investment in the idea of spirit as the expression of identity in a community.

Gaskell recognizes the very nature of spirit through her efforts to keep it vital. She is not concerned with the idea of a single or transcendental Spirit as part of a metaphysics of Englishness. Thus when dealing in *Cousin Phillis* with the older generation, Gaskell gives the narrator's father praise, while offering gentle criticism of Phillis's father for not being sufficiently "progressive," for not comprehending the need for development and change in England through the discourses and activities of science. Gaskell understands that spirit as cultural identity is what cannot be objectified. Nor can it be given absolute uncritical reverence when evoked through forms such as "the past." Spirit in a communal sense, and being crucial to a notion of Being, of Being-in-common, which is not an absolute, "forms part of the series of non-things, of what in general one claims to oppose to the thing."[58]

This is why it can be difficult to say anything about Elizabeth Gaskell's writing. Because Gaskell's writing is not concerned with "the thing" as Derrida refers to the Absolute, to Truth, *Logos* or the Metaphysical. Gaskell's concerns are with "non-things," with those cultural traces which form the textile weave of our communal identity. Gaskell's text evinces a concern with reiterating, re-presenting, performing those traces, faithfully, comprehensively and with rigorous attention to all the moments and movements of paradox, contradiction and dialectic tussle. Thus, in Gaskell's writing communal identity as the outcome of a critical nationalism lives on through strategies of refusal, resistance and affirmation: the refusal of and resistance to reification and homogeneity and, therefore, the death of the spirit of identity; the affirmation of that spirit's survival. This is why, once again it is so difficult to write about Gaskell's writing, without critical reduction. Gaskell partakes of a relativism of spirit.

Such relativism is situated from the first by the highly partial and unreliable narratorial voice of *Cousin Phillis*. Paul Manning is written

by both blindness and insight. These allow him to narrate, whilst autho-
rizing his own errors in dealing with and talking of others (even in the
distance between the moment of narration and the moment of event,
the blindnesses persist as part of the narrative mode). While Paul's blindnesses and insights are personal to him, they are also particular to his
historical moment as well.[59] Paul is identified as remarking on—re-mapping—his own historicity with his references to branch lines and the
penny-post reform. Thus Gaskell writes Paul not only as the observer of
these changes in the cultural life of England but also as an active partic-
ipant, an agent written by such events other than and different from
himself as narrator.

It is necessary therefore to understand Paul as doubled, not only as
a discrete, whole being. To comment on his remarks about his own historical moment is not only to suggest that Paul is "within time" and at a
moment in history simply or unproblematically. Paul is "in" the 1830s
and '40s. But we can also read him as the narrative articulation of what
Heidegger has called *Innerzeitigkeit*. "Paul" as narratorial voice awaiting
the translation of the reader is a trace of what can only be interpreted
somewhat crudely as the enunciation of "inner-time-ness." His articulations, whether informed or ignorant, whether locally "true" or "incorrect," partake of the radical temporality of Being's movement, whereby
Paul's "Being" is informed by community; his is a being-there-for-others.

In giving Paul the "authoritative" standpoint of this story and yet
having him make errors whilst also expressing his "unknowingness" (he
knows that he does not know), Gaskell's writing unfolds the condition of
Being as *always already communal in its identity*. In being thus structured,
the text may once again be read as rejecting metaphysical fixation and
Absolute Truth (such is the truth of [identity in] Elizabeth Gaskell).
Furthermore, Gaskell's writing unfixes the illusory autonomy of individualism (as represented in Holdsworth) and, therefore, free-market,
capitalist manifestations of the liberal impulse, of which the notion of
individualism is just one more articulation. Through his partiality, Paul
is written as tracing a partiality shared by others. Such a trace when
read figures the shared temporality of identity's enunciations.

There is also remarked by (and in) Paul a loosening of the holds of
the authority of textual truth. While both Mr Manning and Mr Holman
have a reliance on the written word,[60] Paul does not remember exactly
what is written, or where he has read it. His is a blindness to the exact
form of the written word, (explainable in part as a difference in the cultural priorities of generations) his insights into other forms of knowledge
being of a different order. Even Holdsworth is caught up with writing,
this explaining some of his affectations; these are manifestations of

Holdsworth's comprehension of the letter, rather than the spirit of the foreign other. Paul resists the letter, however, and is written by Gaskell in order to resist dead bookishness. Indeed this resistance in itself allows Paul a more tentative and "felt" —spiritual—relationship to knowledge; he is not bowed down by the weight of Absolute Knowledge, he is not made subject to it. Such resistance is not necessarily a conscious act on Paul's part but is readable as yet another instance of Gaskell's foregrounding of her agent's historicity and culturally contingent location.

Through Paul, Gaskell writes the untruth of Truth. Through Paul, through his partial vision and the relative blindnesses of the other male readers, Gaskell motions towards the provisional status of all epistemological verity being contingent on the intersection of technological and social forces; and this indication of Gaskell's always directs us to images of England and Englishness in transition. Thus *Cousin Phillis* is engaged with a radical relativisation—and revitalization of historical movement, while simultaneously keeping the spirit of past discourses alive.

V

But what of Cousin Phillis herself? This is, after all, her story supposedly, a story named for her. Silent, passive, acquiescent even, she appears to inhabit a space, to be a centre to which men are drawn, about which they revolve, and over which they contest, at least implicitly. In being the articulation of this other, desired locus, does Phillis, *can* Phillis speak to us about Englishness, its relationship to gender and its preservation through gender?

For her father, Phillis is there to provide mute expressions of "sympathetic appreciation."[61] She is also the receptacle for her father's knowledge and "dead-and-gone languages."[62] She even seeks to please him through reading Dante in the original, although she does not speak Italian.[63] To others, she seems equally subservient. Holdsworth observes of her that she is a "quiet girl, full of household work."[64] Typically, Phillis is one who says "nothing," but keeps "her head bent down over her work."[65] These are of course standard, even clichéd performances of the ideal domestic female, caught between the proscriptive parameters of the middle-class masculine discourse on women.

Paul observes all this in Phillis; but he also observes something else more disturbing, not so in keeping with this model of the demure rural maid, and to which I shall come in a moment. Phillis' first appearance in the story is to Paul. To him, as he tells the story, she is still present, as she was initially: " I see her now—cousin Phillis."[66] This statement of Paul's would seem to fix Phillis as being, in some manner,

eternal and unchanging. And, to an extent, she is. Phillis is comprehended initially and throughout the narrative as a combination of stillness, silence and colour. For example, when Paul first sees her, he
notices her blonde hair, white skin and blue dress. Yet the very qualities
which constantly draw Paul's—and through Paul, the reader's—attention
to Phillis seem also to diminish her; as Paul observes towards the end of
the text, "She seemed always the same, gentle, quiet and sad."[67]

And what we come to notice is the way in which Paul's frequent
descriptions of Phillis—descriptions which take on the resonance of a
series of stylised portraits—halt the narrative flow. Indeed, they do more;
they break quite violently with the narrative impulse. They take to themselves, and the stasis with which they are inscribed, a space and place
(the female as space/place) quite removed from the historical/mate-
rial contexts and conditions that mark this text elsewhere. This removal,
this desistance, is in itself a disturbing hiatus, a suspension of social life
which narrative records and mediates. But there is also something else
which can be read as disturbing.

We can read this as a female interruption of a male impulse to
narrate. And in this interruption—which is also an eruption—is enunciated the gaze of the male observer as manifestation of his desire. For, if
colour, stasis and silence are always the key elements of Paul's descriptions, they are also those elements which perform Phillis, and which
remark an impulse to toy with a coy, indirect eroticism, as in the following passage:

> She must have been half-undressed; but she had covered herself
> with a dark winter cloak, which fell in long folds to her white,
> naked, noiseless feet.[68]

In painterly fashion, the folds of the cloak and its darkness direct us
to, while being juxtaposed with, the white, naked, noiseless feet. The foot
serves a double synecdochic purpose. It signifies Phillis and all the other
constructions of Phillis by Paul; and it also returns us to the idea of
Phillis just before this scene, intimated in the first line of the above passage; we are returned to that moment in which, as Paul puts it, she *must
have been* half-undressed. This insistence on Paul's part is merely part of
the powerful erotic charge, and is typical of the resonances surrounding
Phillis throughout the *nouvelle*.

Phillis's picturesque eroticism points us to a general economy of
desire of which she is the unwitting focus. She attracts unsolicited attention in the streets;[69] even her father's desire to endow her with knowledge seems an attempt to engender himself within her. The question

raised by such eroticism and its contexts is a double one: does the eroticism belong to Phillis, or is the eroticism constructed through the narrative memory of Paul Manning, who still sees Phillis as she first was (he
does not merely see her as she was, but sees her *now*, unchanged, an
apparent verity)? This double question is, strictly speaking, unanswerable; we cannot read in favour of either answer without imposing our
own ideological predilections onto the text.

But this very ambiguity with which Gaskell mediates the figure of
Phillis does suggest an attempt to engender (a space for) desire beyond
the economy of narrative, while simultaneously keeping Phillis as a figure of ideality at a permanent remove from the fulfilment of the reader's
desire. This speaks of an integrity of identity belonging perhaps to the
radical mimesis of which I spoke at the beginning of the chapter. In
maintaining a space to herself, Phillis suggests the unchangeable, *but
with a difference.* She implies a continuity of a feminine and spiritual
identity (registered iconically by the glow she seems to generate) which,
though in stasis, is neither static nor statuesque (which is to say not
phallic, not merely belonging to and objectified by a festishizing male
discourse), but perpetuated, regenerated by an eroticism outside the
circuits of masculine narrative, masculine economy, masculine history.
Thus she figures the feminine as the spiritual in national identity, as
genius loci, outside history, outside the intrusive penetrations of rail-
ways, and outside the material, social changes which *Cousin Phillis* reg-
isters.

Such a reading does of course leave itself open to charges that
the traditional binarisms of Man/Woman, Culture/Nature,
Society/Country are being reintroduced, thereby marginalising women
by ignoring their lived, material existences. This is true, and it is a construct by which Gaskell's narrative is partially recuperated. However,
this does not dismiss the power which Gaskell assembles around Phillis.
Phillis does connect learning to the land; she bridges the gap between
dead and gone languages and seasonal, organic renewal in a manner
unavailable to Paul, Holdsworth or Mr Manning, none of whom have
any real sense of the continuity of place offered by the country. And
Gaskell attempts to write herself out of her own double bind by mediating Phillis through an eroticism which suggests a power beyond masculine control, thereby positing the possibility for an other Englishness
which is essentially female, and which is written with an ethical respect of
otherness.

This sense of otherness, predicated on an inner, recuperative
power is expressed in the final line of the text, which is Phillis's own:
"We will go back to the peace of the old days. I know we shall; I can, and

I will."[70] Phillis has the last word, and it is a strangely ambiguous utterance; for it articulates the double bind that Gaskell's writing of Phillis embodies. At once, this line is a recuperative, conservative gesture, problematised politically by the will to renew being located in the individual psyche; yet at the same time, the line suggests an opening out, a new start based on old ways, based on a sense of continuity. Phillis's final words thus intimate closure, whilst also refusing it by opening onto the expression of a desire connecting past and future in the eternal present tense of Phillis's reported speech. Her words are always being uttered; the statement never finishes. And it is perhaps significant that Paul, who had been the narrator, has been displaced, as Phillis assumes a centrality at the limits of the text, at the limit of narration. Thus Phillis comes to speak in her own right finally, as the voice of an other identity, never fixed, never definable; and offering hope for identity because of that.

VI

Behind and through the discussions of Phillis and Paul Manning, the Letter of the Law and the authority of the word there lies another question which concerns us directly; the question of exegesis and its relation to identity, which I want to turn to briefly, in conclusion.

The question of exegesis is frequently made into a question of asserting the meaning of meaning. Interpretation is enlisted in the hunt for origins and final causes. Thus the exegetical drive is one towards pinning down identity. The question of exegesis is the question of fixing limits. Or, to put it another way, the answer to the question of exegesis is "the limit" itself, which is one more way of saying that identity can be finally, ultimately, confidently asserted. This is achieved in an ideological context all too frequently through nationalism and its signs. Yet, as George Eliot reminds us, at what we take to be (the beginning of) the "end" of *Middlemarch*, "[e]very limit is a beginning as well as an ending. Who can quit young lives after being long in company with them, and not desire to know what befell them in after years? For the fragment of a life, however typical, is not the sample of an even web."[71]

This announcement highlights, as an argument which may be turned to in the consideration of *Cousin Phillis*, Gaskell's anti-methodological methodology. Gaskell presents and mediates the fragments of lives, such as Phillis's, not insisting on the whole, not predicating the immanence of full identity. Instead, she lays before us the fragments of identity *as* fragments, touched and affected by the material contexts of the social, cultural, historical weave: hence Paul Manning's fragmentary and fragmented grasp on a reality he calls Cousin Phillis, and which his narrative can only attempt to grasp finally through what amount to aesthetic-erotic clichés. Gaskell succeeds in miming the limits of (the search for) identity and (the search for) the Truth (of identity) through the highly partial quality of Manning's narrative. Gaskell's writing apprehends in its every fibre the knowledge of the provisionality of limits and the limitation of interpretation as absolute comprehension. Gaskell's silences on identity enunciate and affirm the thinking of the duality of the limit, as both beginning and ending and, yet, as neither solely.

This comprehension of Gaskell's, an understanding put into practice far more successfully than anywhere in Eliot, despite the latter's aphoristic sharp-shooting, is not merely a strategy of writing. If it were, we would be witness only to one more question of style. Gaskell's practice has traced in its delineations of the fragmentary issues of identity implications for reading and criticism. Gaskell invites, cajoles, coerces and seduces us into thinking about the possibilities of reading and interpreting differently, from other positions within Englishness. Gaskell's mode—that which resists the Truth—insists on an internal critique of the contexts of our own identities. As the end of the story concerning the Cagots makes clear, without having to spell it out, the criticism, the condemnation of others' political acts is easy enough. What is harder, but all the more necessary, all the more urgent—there's something to be done—is the inversion of such questioning in order that it might foreground our own political acts as they serve in the constitution of identity.

If, therefore, we are to be faithful to the politics, ethics and economy of Gaskell's writing, we have to acknowledge that the problem of criticism itself is a problem, *the* problem, of the limits of the political positions of identity (to echo Nancy), and a problem also of not acknowledging those limits, of not understanding what is articulated by and at such limits. The texts of Elizabeth Gaskell apprehend the appropriation of identity through textual interpretation by miming, incorporating or parodying such situations (as in Holdsworth's free-market liberalism re-figured in his attitude towards Phillis). Thus, producing a single reading—which is to say a single position—on Gaskell is itself a problematic exercise that, in any attempt to be true to Gaskell's truths, has to be acknowledged.

However, the implications we can draw from Gaskell's texts for a sense of national identity are important. Gaskell displays a repeated understanding of and tolerance towards a number of varying political positions. Indeed, the positions are, in turn, defined by the discourses of English society which mediate the social structure and cultural identity of the English middle class during the mid-nineteenth century, which

Gaskell cannot avoid. Here is the double bind, of which Gaskell's writing shows an implicit understanding. Each discourse, each position, is given voice within Gaskell's writing. Gaskell thereby acknowledges her engagement with both the positions in question and the limits and possibilities of a critical narrative involved in the practice of identity's fashioning.

While Gaskell's tolerance is not given in response to all political positions (certainly not to the Right, as I have tried to show in my reading of "An Accursed Race"), none of those that are tolerated are accorded an absolutely valorized hierarchical position. Gaskell's writing acknowledges that such a Truth is just not possible; we live in a world, and in societies, figured by competing hegemonies. It is with these that we have to work, to ask questions of, and to reform for the benefit of all; these are the truths of (responsibility to identity in) Elizabeth Gaskell.

5

WILKIE COLLINS AND THE
(SECRET) HEART OF ENGLISH CULTURE

There is a question of identity at the heart of every one of his novels.

—Catherine Peters

He emphasises play, doubling, and duplicity. His labyrinthine narratives . . . involve . . . the shaping of social identity, above all within that simultaneously psychic and economic institution the family.

—Jenny Bourne Taylor

In political and intellectual life, in the movement of ideas, in the code of behaviour that prevailed in society, the middle classes . . . could easily weigh their growing influence and measure the advance of their two darling children, liberalism and individualism . . . In a society as dynamic and creative as mid-Victorian Britain, what gave the bourgeoisie such confidence was the certainty of having on their side both history and the moral law.

—François Bédarida

We have an inveterately false and vicious system of society in England. If you want to trace one of the causes, look back to the little organized insincerities of English life.

—Wilkie Collins, *The Fallen Leaves*

I

Like Elizabeth Gaskell, Wilkie Collins writes with a critical eye on the shaping of national identity. Again like Gaskell, Collins's focus is on the little things, the seemingly insignificant details of everyday, middle class life in mid-Victorian England. Such details form the network of the English way of life for both writers. Out of such details, they mediate their own singular visions of England and its dominant classes.

To draw a comparison, a distinction even, between the two novelists, Gaskell can be read as showing a repeated interest in the external relations of people and things from a more clearly defined "sociological" perspective. Collins, on the other hand, performs a densely imbricated textuality caught in the very fabric of Englishness, self-consciously aware of its own nature while also teetering on the brink of a collective cultural unconscious. Collins's writing can be read as opening the unconscious to us while also lapsing into that very same unconsciousness. In sum, Gaskell finds a degree of distance from the Englishness she interrogates; that is to her advantage. Wilkie Collins, on the other hand, embroils himself in the labyrinth of the national subject; this is to his. Through attention to the "little things," Collins unfolds the troubles, contradictions, hypocrisy and corruptions that are as much a part of the architecture of the heart of English culture as are the positive values. In the words of Jenny Bourne Taylor, Collins simultaneously assimilates and resists "a contradictory set of contemporary discourses."[1] Before looking at the ways in which the heart is laid bare in some of Collins's novels, let us take some brief examples of "the little things."

Collins's writing is structured and informed by "deep" figures of Englishness, where in the structures of the text we read ideas become evident truths, to paraphrase François Bédarida;[2] figures informed by the double certainties of history and moral law,[3] where ideology has passed into a communal unconscious, to surface again at the individual level as the currency of opinion, as Victorian *doxa*, or as writerly traits, as the marks of what we recognise mistakenly as "style."[4] Because such figures do make overt reference to the English subject, however, their appearance leads to the mapping of "character" or identity beyond that of the writer, or any single subject. We comprehend, behind the individual lives, a "national character" moving in and out of the shadows. When Collins has one of his characters say, "[w]hen trifles make themselves habits of yours or of mine, they become part of your character or mine,"[5] he is providing a valuable insight into the drift from the ideological to the "natural," and of the hiding of the ideological in the "natural." Such figures which do make the transition to become sedimented in our cultural unconscious are often what we refer to as "figures of speech." In using such a term, we gloss over the cultural and national context of these commonplaces. In doing so, we remain within the economy of the unconscious from which we can never wholly escape. Collins's language typifies this paradox, making it a paradox because of his repeated shifts from arch self-consciousness to absolute unawareness, and back again.

Any writer does this, of course, only ever having recourse to the medium of the language in which s/he writes, and by which s/he is determined. Yet this in itself is a critical commonplace which cannot be left as the iteration of the unthought. Collins shows up the problem of the fall into un-reflection on his characters' parts. Collins's own moments of writerly self-referentiality seem more deliberately posed (and poised), his moments of unawareness more completely void of insight, than those of other writers. Such extremities of position are, in themselves, fascinating indices of a national identity rooted in its historically con-tingent moment. Reading the extremities, the inconsequentialities, and reading what Collins has himself referred to so tellingly as the "little organized insincerities of English life,"[6] can lead us to the secret heart of English culture (if only to see the heartlessness of the middle class). It is precisely because the insincerities *are* organised, because they comprise in a systematic fashion both structure and genealogy readable as the philosophy of "Being-English," that we can discern the cultural con-struct of national identity.

II

Part of any such identity is a somewhat necessary lack of awareness. A certain "native" unawareness on Collins's part can be understood to stem from a confidence in a sense of national identity (though not an uncritical confidence). It is due to this confidence, a confidence some-what typical of English middle class culture,[7] that Wilkie Collins can write in *The Law and the Lady*, without any pause whatsoever, of the "vileness" of Scottish law in comparison with the "honesty" of the *English* legal system. He glosses over completely the reductive nature of the "guilty/not guilty" binarism, which the latter system holds as a crucial fig-ure of its identity, while, in Scotland, at least defendants have the possi-bility of achieving the verdict of "not proven." Furthermore, it is the same confidence that authorises Collins to follow these judgements on the relative merits of English and Scottish law by having his heroine cite Ogilvie's *Imperial* Dictionary, as proof of such an asservation.[8] Collins has Valeria Macallan cite a dictionary the very name of which invokes English authority and the expansion of English territories (and, in the imagination, the growth of England itself[9]). Authority, thus wielded, suppresses absolutely any recourse to reason, thought or analysis.

Valeria is, however, structured by Collins as a somewhat "flawed" and unseeing, unaware narrator. In this way, Collins makes her more English. Like the Englishmen of the novel, Valeria is constructed as being limited in ability and intellect, although this has more to do with her being English than with her being a woman or having a second rate mind. Her unawareness is merely part of the fall into native unconsciousness that we can read as part of Collins's understanding of Englishness. But the solution of the novel's mystery depends on being aware, being able to see from a non-English perspective. *The Law and the Lady* revolves around small details which are crucial to interpretation and the question of national identity, often having "self-conscious recourse to Gothic conventions."[10] This self-conscious recourse is involved with the disclosure of identity's constitution.

Like many of Wilkie Collins's books, *The Law and the Lady* is littered with papers and torn-up letters, contradictory legal documents, written confessions and diaries. The English middle class of Wilkie Collins's narratives are copious writers; many reveal their secret or other selves through hidden texts. Such texts are at the heart of the bourgeois world that Collins unfolds. It is as if, while Collins has no trouble in interposing blatantly unrealistic authorial interventions into his narratives for moral, didactic or polemical purposes, it best serves his political and ethical interests at crucial narrative moments to allow the middle class—Arnold's heart of England—to reveal their own hearts; to admit to their own part in the organised insincerities that constitute the condition of England and English subjectivity; to show what lies at the heart of the ideology of Englishness. Hence the profusion of documents. Crucial to *The Law and the Lady* and to the distinction it makes between Scottish and English identity is a missing letter.

The letter is a small but crucial detail necessary for Valeria Macallan in establishing her husband Eustace's innocence. Having been accused of killing his previous wife and taken to trial, Eustace is given a verdict of "not proven" which casts a cloud over his marriage to Valeria, a cloud she is determined to disperse by proving the truth of her husband's innocence. That piece of evidence which is missing, and which is necessary, is a letter from the late Mrs. Macallan which clearly shows the dead woman as taking her own life.

When Valeria visits her husband's Scottish estate, Gleninch, where the death took place, she observes that the park of the house "was, *to an English eye*, wild and badly kept . . . it was as bare of all ornament as a factory, and as gloomily heavy in effect as a prison" (my emphasis).[11] Valeria's comment, typical of her chauvinism towards the Scots and Scotland, reveals more about English identity than she is aware (here being an acute example of Collins playing self-consciously between unawareness and insight). The English eye can, in effect see only what is proper to the English eye. The park has none of the ornate propriety of manufactured English country estates. Yet tellingly, and with great irony, the two comparisons which Valeria draws are with two of the most significant and socially reprehensible institutions of English Victorian society, the factory and the prison. Thus Valeria's discourse, in being limited to those cultural analogies which are available to it, resounds inadvertently with judgmental social echoes that speak to us of a less palatable aspect of national identity on which much of the Victorian bourgeois world is founded.

Whilst looking around the park, Valeria notices the dust heap, in one part of which she observes scattered fragments of waste paper.[12] Noticing her reaction to the dust heap, the Scots Lawyer, Mr Playmore remarks (in a tone which must be read as mocking), "In *tidy England*, I suppose you would have all that carted away, out of sight . . . We don"t mind in Scotland . . . some of it comes in usefully. . . ."[13] Playmore's remarks pointedly oppose national practices and habits, revealing the Scots in a generally more utilitarian, if not practical light. And as it turns out, Playmore's comment is prophetic. For the dust heap contains the fragments of the letter for which Valeria is searching; which fragments are eventually unearthed and pieced together by Playmore and Benjamin, Valeria's father's clerk.[14] Had the letter been lost in England, torn up on an English estate, it would have been lost forever. Thus it is a minor characteristic or detail of Scottish and not English identity—a detail of habitual practice which should be understood as having ideological significance in the context of the narrative—which ultimately makes possible acts of reading and interpretation, which in turn determine the innocence of Eustace Macallan, thereby rectifying the ambiguities of the Scottish Law, which Valeria had described as vile.

III

The Law, its unquestioned authority and its gaps are a constant concern to Collins. If Collins's view of English Law is favourable in *The Law and the Lady*, in another novel, *Man and Wife*, Collins raises the question of the very unsatisfactory nature of the English laws surrounding the institution of marriage, with regard to the woman's total lack of power or access to the law over the matters of property and personal abuse. Collins's criticisms of the law reveal him as no unquestioning admirer of the system. We can read, then, a disparity in ideological positions between the two texts, while both also serve to raise the issue of the relation of gender to national identity (a question it is necessary to raise, even though it cannot be gone into in more detail here). Throughout Collins's novels, there is always an implicit connection drawn between the social and psychic aspects of femininity and the national context within which the author embeds his narratives of female victimisation and female helplessness before the Law.

This would in turn raise other questions about a certain, seemingly violent yoking together of national identity and the female, which itself may speak of a desire within the constitution of Englishness that needs to incorporate "woman" with its self-realization. But two questions raised by this are: Can national identity have a gender? or is gender overdetermined by Englishness? In *No Name*, Collins writes, "the personal attractions of Mrs. Vanstone . . . had depended solely on her *native English charms*" (my emphasis).[15] The novelist's remark would seem to have it both ways, indicating that identity can have gendered attributes, whilst also bearing the implication that gender is itself written by national characteristics. To any reader today, such a remark sounds faintly absurd; the idea that a woman's charms are native to her country of origin is ridiculous. Or is it? The problem is that such a way of thinking is so remote to most of us, that we cannot recover the faith invested in such a remark so as to make its ideological "truth" seem second nature. Thus we are amused and pass over what can be read as a fundamental revelation of the ways in which national identity is complexly structured. Collins is apparently unaware of this particular sign of his own cultural overdetermination.

In another novel, *The Guilty River*, however, Collins shows himself as being closely attentive to national axio-idiomatic utterances. Speaking of Cristel, Gerard Royle, the narrator of the novel, comments that her "father was 'well-connected,' *as we say in England*" (my emphasis).[16] Collins places his narrator's comment within quotation marks in order to foreground the euphemism and so allow the reader the possibility for thinking through the context of such a statement. Going further, Collins affixes a national identity to the statement itself in the final clause, the possessive pronoun gathering narrator, author and reader inside the Englishness that is identified through self-conscious articulation.

This device, by which Collins roots language in its national, cultural and, at times, historical contexts, is used by the author repeatedly throughout *Man and Wife*.[17] Although this novel has no first-person narratorial voice, Collins will often have Sir Patrick Lundie—who, we are meant to understand, is apparently another kind of Englishman, one from a less materialistic, more thoughtful era—comment disparagingly on the younger male generation's liking for slang and other types of colloquial speech (Collins often uses figures from a previous generation as representatives of an "older" Englishness, such as Benjamin in *The Law and the Lady*; this is not idealism on Collins's part, but serves as part of the construction of a generational dialectic on the subject of identity). The point being made is a conservative one; that Englishness is being altered through the debasement of its prime currency, the English language; and that men of the upper middle classes, from the mid-Victorian period with university educations, are chiefly responsible for this degradation. Of course, the quasi-Dickensian Sir Patrick is speaking as though an ideal state for the English language could exist. Collins gives Sir Patrick no self-consciousness, but filters his own self-reflexivity through the character, thereby creating a tension between awareness and unconsciousness. Collins mediates this by external, narratorial comment on Sir Patrick, mapping this figure as belonging to an older fictional typology. Sir Patrick belongs in and to an eighteenth-century text, yet inhabits the nineteenth century, mostly unaware of his own anachronistic nature. Through the tension this creates, Collins is able partly to play out the cultural problematic of bourgeois culture's identity in *Man and Wife*.

If the problem is one of language and its relation to native identity, the problem is revealed further in *The Moonstone*, where Collins unmasks more directly still the everyday myopia of Victorian identity:

The effort of writing a few sentences, *in plain English*, completely cleared my mind of . . . cloudy nonsense.[18]

The statement is that of Franklin Blake, and its tenor is close to that of the journalists shown up by Matthew Arnold in "My Countrymen." Blake's remark positions plain English directly counter to the obfuscating tendencies that affect the mind, referred to elsewhere by Blake as the "labyrinth of useless speculations" and the "mist of my own metaphysics."[19] Interestingly enough, these are no abstract metaphysics; they too have a national identity: German. So Collins uses Blake to juxtapose foreign learning (that to which Arnold turns in opposition to plain English) and native common sense, which dialectic is only resolved in the act of writing, where Englishness gets the upper hand.

What does emerge from the reading of such fragments is that Collins eludes a single position (as does Elizabeth Gaskell) in his recourse to the play of tropes that are most lucidly comprehensible as figures of Englishness. His attention and fidelity to them, as belonging to the details of everyday life, are such that it is hard to know to what degree the element of parody is present, and whether the parody is intentional. Such a strategy fragments the consolidated surface of any cohesive identity, allowing us beneath the skin and closer to the heart of mid-Victorian identity.

IV

In order to see the native heart, it is sometimes necessary to see it from another perspective, another vantage point in order to peel back the ideological skin. At home, the English are not always easily displayed. The middle classes hide themselves in an ideology of universality. So, the English have to be taken abroad. In *The Haunted Hotel*,[20] Collins tells a gothic tale of the English abroad, raising, as he does so, the spectre of an older literary convention and, with that, the figures of other xenophobic fictions which promote Englishness at the cost of other identities. In doing so, he constructs an ambiguous narrative around the English presence overseas, raising for us another spectre, the troubling *zeitgeist* of colonialism as a psychic impulse necessary to the constant recuperation of identity. In order to understand this impulse, it is necessary to draw on arguments concerning the structure and condition of colonialism's more openly aggressive sibling, imperialism.

In a summary of Hannah Arendt and Joseph Schumpeter's analyses of imperialism,[21] Daniel Bivona talks of the "psychic appeal" of imperialism.[22] Schumpeter's argument is that imperialism is merely the irrational and inefficient supplement to capitalism. The same is also true of the colonial urge. Schumpeter suggests that imperialism and colonialism answer to "no [strictly logical] need within capitalism," while yet being the "essential motive force[s] of modern history."[23] Accepting Schumpeter's argument, it would appear that imperialism and colonialism are of the Freudian order of things, figuring a working out of the return of the repressed, whereby, according to Schumpeter, the "dead always rule the living."[24]

The dead therefore are not strictly dead, to paraphrase Bivona.[25] They live on, haunting our social structures, haunting the philosophical and ideological forms behind our institutions; hence imperialism and colonialism's psychic appeal. Imperialism and colonialism call an uneasy truce between our ghosts and our selves, whilst making manifest the appeal to re-figure ourselves in as many places as possible; they offer the possibility to re-form others in our own image, to suppress alterity in the name of our fathers. Imperialism and colonialism also appeal perhaps because their imperatives run directly counter to the *frisson* of the gothic. In gothic fiction, the Englishman and, especially, the Englishwoman abroad were subject to nameless terrors at the hands of foreigners, frequently Italians. In the Imperial, colonial age of Victoria, however, the English middle class rule the world with their clear common sense and their technological superiority. Their ideology, liberal humanism, generates a universalising shadow, erasing difference; difference of class, of culture and of gender. So, if what frightens the English subject is the foreign other, conquer the other, make it part of the self by subjugating it to domestic identity (although the other will always erupt, threatening the stability, propriety and limits—the national boundaries—of identity).

Yet, if there is a psychic appeal to colonial activity, there must also be the chimerical presence of guilt that lies repressed and is all the more troubling for being so. To return to Schumpeter's suggestions, there is the imminent idea, always troubling to national identity, that colonialism is morally and ethically wrong. And, if colonialism is untenable and repulsive as both a political impulse and the geo-political remapping of desire, what better way to colonise, whilst not seeming to do so, than to buy property abroad, rather than just take it by "main force," as the Victorian phrase had it? Why not have a holiday in the sun?

To buy property is to make it one's own, to make it proper to one's self, legally and morally (at least within the parameters of middle class belief). For purchase is not robbery. The villa, the land, the hotel which are purchased become English. Although abroad, they are no longer foreign.

A hotel, furthermore, offers the chance to recoup some, or all, of one's expenditure, whilst also offering a place abroad for the travelling English (Collins tells us at one point that the Palace Hotel appealed mainly to English and American customers for its clientele[26]). The suggestion of colonialism is diverted, as the property becomes inserted into the circuits of capitalism, which in turn is whitewashed with the appearance of benevolence (at a cost). The hotel offers a home away from home, a place for all the family, a little corner of some foreign city that is, forever, England.[27] At the same time, the idea of the hotel satisfies the imperatives of liberal humanism's universality. Middle-class ideology reframes itself rationally, suppressing its own otherness, while simultaneously erasing the foreign other.

The irrational supplement will always return, however, its gothic excesses dismantling rationality and identity. What we find is that this supplement comes from nearer home than we would like to imagine; it comes from within us, from the very heart of our identity.

In *The Haunted Hotel*, Agnes Lockwood is jilted by her fiancé, Lord Montbarry, who chooses to marry instead the Countess Narona, a woman of obscured middle European origin.[28] Lord Montbarry, having moved to Venice with his wife and her brother, Baron Rivar, (whose exact relationship with the Countess is ambiguous) is taken ill and dies.

Henry Westwick, the youngest member of the Montbarry family, loves Agnes but is discouraged by her. When Montbarry dies and his property is dispersed, Agnes's servant, an old nurse originally in service with the Montbarrys, is bequeathed a small sum, which she asks Henry to invest for her. This he does by buying shares in a project of his own, the Venetian Hotel Company.[29] The property which the company purchases to convert into a hotel is the palace that had been rented by the late Lord Montbarry, the place he had died. At the same time, Agnes, a long time friend of the Montbarry family, is taken on as governess by Stephen Westwick, the new Lord Montbarry. From this moment in the narrative, all the family, including Agnes, visit the Palace Hotel. And as the visit to the hotel makes plain, it is not a foreign ghost come to plague innocent English travellers; neither is the spirit of the palace a vengeful English spectre returned from the grave to plague his suspect foreign widow. The author ignores such banal textual figures, in order to write the haunting of the English aristocracy by one of their own. The visceral manifestations of Lord Montbarry are solely for the senses of his own family, as if to bring before them their psychic culpability in the victimisation of women such as Agnes and the Countess, both at home and abroad.

In this almost incestuous narrative, Collins reduces English Victorian society to its hallowed nucleus, the family (including the servants). Even the first Montbarry's courier, Ferrari, is married to Emily Bidwell, an old pupil of Agnes's.[30] The investment of the nurse's windfall by Henry keeps even the economic affairs of the story in the family (as is only etymologically "proper" to the term "economy").[31] Thus, in this claustrophobic and, one feels, unhealthy atmosphere, (the dis-ease comes implicitly from the family, rather than from what they encounter) the question of Englishness is clearly turned over as one belonging with all propriety to a thinking of the concept of the family; Englishness becomes a question of whether one can identify oneself as belonging to the family, and whether one can discern the outlines of that structure, along with the attendant discourses of property and propriety.

The nurse's trust in Henry because he is a Westwick—that is to say, a typical representative of the typical English upper-middle-class family—ties the classes together, whilst re-telling the narrative of class dependency and unquestioning faith on the part of the working class in its masters (a narrative figure already played out in Emily's request to Agnes to help secure her husband's position with Montbarry). This conservative tale of "simple minded" faith and class subservience is borne out by the "success" of the hotel.

Collins sets up this familial structure, along with all its attendant conservative impulses however, in order to shake the structure all the more thoroughly. To do this, he needs to pay attention to the minutiae of English life.

English servants, we are told, dislike the Continent and, on being taken abroad, leave service promptly.[32] The suggestion is that the working classes are less cosmopolitan and, therefore, less at ease in unfamiliar contexts. This seems a somewhat judgmental attitude that ignores the access to—and, so, familiarity with—the foreign that accompanies financial independence. However, another reading might be that the working classes have a "native common sense," lost by their masters. Whichever reading we choose, Collins seems to be confirming a parochial vision of Englishness brought into sharper relief by the Continental perspective.

Such narrow-mindedness is given further support in the presentation of Dr Bruno, "an eminent physician in Venice," whose eminence is authorised by his having both resided in England and his being familiar with "English forms of medical practice."[33] These qualifications, from the Commissioners' report on the death of Lord Montbarry, clarify the extent to which the ideology of Englishness pervades any narrative account. It is but one of several examples Collins offers us of how "the ignorant English mind," to use the Countess Narona's words, "is apt to be insolent in the exercise of unrestrained English liberty."[34] "Ignorance" and "insolence" support a pejorative reading of "liberty" counter to its more frequent sense, "freedom." The English "take liberties" with foreigners as a direct result of their ideological attitude concerning their place in the world.

Of course, in his constant attention to the little details of English life,[35] Collins does make the English abroad appear faintly absurd, even though his tone is not ostensibly one of mockery, parody or satire. He has his characters do the mocking, and in a manner that is telling with regard to the English. When Francis Westwick smells an unpleasantly pungent odour in Room 14, (the room in which Montbarry had died) he opens the window. The French proprietor comments, "you English people are perfectly mad on the subject of fresh air!"[36] Another Montbarry, Mrs Norbury's experience of the room is also enigmatic. Her insistence on being moved to another room is remarked by the Italian porter as yet one more example of "English eccentricity."[37] So, Collins employs his minor characters' voices to judge this family critically as typical and yet ridiculous representatives of national identity. The Montbarry family stand in for "the English." Collins thus fixes Englishness in such a way that the Countess's remark given above does not really come as anything of a shock, and we even feel the veracity of its judgement.

A simple reading of *The Haunted Hotel* (that reading which Henry Westwick pushes for, almost driving himself to a nervous breakdown) would understand the Countess as the apparent "villain" of this text. Yet, unlike other stock foreigners in gothic narrative, the Countess's villainy is highly ambiguous. Her comment on the English is disturbing for its truth, and not because it delivers the cheap thrill of the pantomime villain's utterance (even though Collins does engage playfully with such expectations). There are three main details in this text which count in the Countess Narona's favour.

First, Agnes Lockwood herself defends the Countess in the face of English accusations that she is a mere foreign opportunist.[38] There is a slight implication in this that Agnes, as a woman, comprehends the readiness for opprobrium in the commentary of the male members of the English middle class, when a woman's virtue and intentions are at stake. Second, there is the evidence of Ferrari's letter, in which he admits, "I like her. She has the nice, easy foreign manners—*she* talks to me as if I was a human being like herself."[39] Foreign manners equate with a refusal to act out the impositions of class between master and servant which are so much part of the English class system. The evidence thus far against the Countess Narona, along with the prejudicial gossip that attends her reputation in the English clubs, is reducible to the facts of her gender and country of origin, those factors determining her identity as *other* than English national identity.

Finally in the Countess's favour is the strange narrative *non sequitur* with which Collins opens his novel, where the Countess, as yet unjudged in the text, visits Dr Wybrow, to enquire after her mental health.[40] The reader is given an estranging and subjective view of the Countess which cannot be discounted. The first two chapters have little enough to do with the main narrative of *The Haunted Hotel*; yet we are presented with a largely sympathetic interpretation of the foreign female, which should not be wholly dismissed afterwards and which serves to frame the English attitude towards the foreign as female, the female other and both in traditional narrative convention as the sites of the perceived threat to national identity. At the same time, this presentation of the female as enigma before the masculine authority of medical/psychological discourse gathers to it some of the principal concerns of that discourse in the latter half of the Victorian era, revealing self-consciously a particular fetish at the heart of psycho-medical enquiry, whilst also anticipating Freud's question, what do women want? Collins's bravura opening decentres his own central narrative, announcing all that comes after as—of necessity—banal and clichéd narratives outmoded by the new scientific investigation into identity.

Thus Wilkie Collins has effectively derailed the nationalistic gothic premise before this particular Orient express has even left the station. And he has done so, let us not forget, by having that figure, who is read by the English to represent the threat to English identity, apply to the authority of an eminent English physician (whose reputation was at its highest point[41]); whose professional opinion is that the Countess's intellect is not deranged.[42] Collins thereby offers his readers the only kind of incontestable proof which they themselves understand: the word of a professional Englishman at the top of his profession, with the authority of English science and "English forms of medical practice" to back his diagnosis. Nationality, science and the middle-class deity, profession, are deployed as Collins's holy trinity of middle-class identity. The gothic is thereby deconstructed through recourse to authority which Collins opposes against the bigotries of English *doxa*, out of which narrative comes.

The question which is raised by the Countess's innocence is a multiple one: of reading, of interpretation and translation; of that which gets omitted and corrupted in its passage into English.

While staying at the Palace Hotel, Francis is approached by the Countess Narona. Knowing Francis to be a theatrical backer, the Countess asks him to produce a play which she proposes to write about an English lord, his foreign wife and her enigmatic brother who are staying in an old Venetian palace, where the action of the play occurs. Francis, having experienced the inexplicable odours, and having already been informed by Henry of his own strange experience with room 14, is interested in the proposition, especially since Henry's ordeal had put in Francis's mind the idea for a "ghost-drama" entitled, predictably enough, "The Haunted Hotel."[43] If the reader experiences a *frisson* or a sense of *déjà vu* at this moment, it is not due to any ghostly presence, other than that of the spectre of the text in its own doubling. Collins enfolds us in the meshes of what seem today to be post-modern coincidences, structuring a labyrinthine figure appropriate to the Venetian setting. The text is folded, doubled and re-traced, its narrative *parages*,[44] its meanderings, becoming inextricably linked as its boundaries and limits are dissolved. And this, inferentially, strikes at the heart of any certainty of or for identity. The English family becomes shaken through the questioning of empirical assurances that the world is stable and there to be owned as part of English property and what is proper to the English. Ghosts and narratives erupt to unhinge the stability that any single narrative strand always promises as support for the polite limits of bourgeois self-identification.

The most obvious point being raised by Collins is, of course, that there is always another story to tell; there is always some ghostly figure of alterity which haunts our most confidently structured national narratives. In this case, that figure and voice of the other is a double voice, a doubled image, that of the foreign female. For Coleridge, this had been a source of fear and doubt; poetic endeavour could not be separated from national identity. For Collins however, separation or, at least, distanciation is possible; so that the image which had been in *Kubla Khan* the threat to Englishness (and yet the promise of a return to Englishness) is now a figure to be used in the self-conscious dislocation of national identity.

The Countess, who has been suspected without ground by the Montbarry family (as she had been held in suspicion by English society generally), knows precisely what is at stake in presenting her own narrative, a narrative which may or may not be her story. In a moment of arch-reflexivity, upon introducing Francis to the idea of the play, she says:

> I am a living enigma—and you want to know the right reading of me. . . . Here is the reading, as your English phrase goes, in a nutshell.[45]

Self-consciously, the otherness of foreign and female identity is foregrounded, and directly in relation to the question of reading. The Countess turns the screw on the issue one final notch, by indicating pointedly the English idiom she is borrowing—taking back for the other— in order to re-work the tale of the Haunted Hotel.

This would not be so disturbing a moment—and I think it important that we attempt to register in full the disturbance that the Countess's remark is designed to cause—were it an isolated instance. However, as the Countess comes to narrate her fictionalised version of events (let us not make the mistake of supposing unequivocally that her melodrama is a true statement of facts), other arch-references are made.

The Countess, in a moment of panic, after having met with Henry and Agnes, despairs of finishing her play. She implores Henry to read her draft.[46] Too weak and overcome to continue, the Countess returns to her room, leaving Henry with the manuscript. On beginning to read, he "changed colour as he read—and looked up from the manuscript like a man bewildered. 'Good God! what does this mean?' he said to himself."[47] What confronts Henry is a challenge to the certainty with which he surrounds himself throughout the novel in the form of his own speculations. The Countess's manuscript is thus a direct challenge to the epistemological structures that shore up Henry's—and, for that matter, the rest of the family's; also, by inference, the English middle classes' sense of identity. Henry's question is about meaning and the unknowable; it is about the limen of the self, and the challenge posed by the other to the ideological constructs that constantly perform the liminal nature of identity through the medium of narrative. On completion of the text, Henry considers its meaning and its resistances to rendering up meaning further:

> Was the monstrous plot, revealed in the lines which he had just read, the offspring of the Countess's morbid imagination? or had she, in this case also, deluded herself with the idea that she was inventing when she was really writing under the influence of her own guilty remembrances of the past? If the latter interpretation were the true one, he had just read the narrative of the contemplated murder of his brother . . .[48]

The point here is an obvious one, but must be made nonetheless. The story is truly, literally *monstrous*, without definition, without ending, having no closure. The passage unravels through what amounts to a declension of conditional clauses, so that what Henry is left with in a final interpretation is the fantastic story-book plot of planned murder.

Thus certainty and identity are seen to revolve around final access to stock plot developments, which foreclose on continuing self-analysis and critique. Without stock plots, the English cannot position themselves in the world psychically. Henry's reliance on the obvious narrative as paradigm for existence allows us a glimpse into the logic of nationalism and the colonial supplement. Neither nationalism nor colonialism's excesses can be logically justified, their continual supplementation relying on the non-logical re-iteration of tried and tested stories. What is monstrous for Henry is the threat of continuous deferral of closure which threatens his sanity. The certainty required by Henry is that the threat of the foreign is always already there as a constant threat to English life and identity, and therefore must be suppressed. This is of course the economic structure of English colonialism. The English abroad have, by going abroad, placed themselves at danger in the face of the unknown; so it is only reasonable (the argument can be read) that they assert their own national identity, through colonisation, through the purchase of hotels catering primarily for English tourists, through staging narrative dramas telling their—authorised, if melodramatic (if ultimately unbelievable, at least psychically reassuring)—version of events. Thus, discursively and practically, at home and abroad, the English need to be told stories about the danger to their Being, in order that they might re-establish their right to their identity.

Collins is, therefore, estranging the ideological text of identity and its narrative logic, by toying with and refusing closure; and he does so through the palimpsest that is the Countess Narona's unfinished manuscript. Her death, which comes as Henry reaches the last pages of the Countess's melodrama, means also that no end can be found for the story of the Montbarrys and Agnes Lockwood. Victorian Englishness, for all its apparent self-confidence and self-assurance, is reliant inescapably on both the foreign and the female, both of which seemingly seduce English identity in promising to tell a sordidly English tale, only to withhold any guarantees of certainty, and thereby having the final laugh.

The end of *The Haunted Hotel* is somewhat problematic. While the author's pre-"post-modern" oscillations are suitably jarring to the stability of identity, there is still the inescapable "historical" fact of the text's moment of production. A middle-class mid-Victorian readership could not be left without some resolution, however hurriedly cobbled together, and Collins's ending positions the psychic and national identity of his readership for us. Despite the fact that Collins brings in a verdict of "not proven" on the Countess, her death, along with the earlier death of the courier, Ferrari, does purge the novel of miscegenation. Death stalls the circulation of the foreign. It then remains to the English to make tidy endings.

The new Lord Montbarry[49] consigns the Countess Narona's manuscript to the fire, calling it "rubbish,"[50] the author thereby displaying—through another of those attentions to native detail—the operation of the conservative pragmatism of the English subject. Lord Montbarry is obtuse to possible meanings and nuances of interpretation, too common-sensically English to bother with the unsettling effects of plural readings and foreign texts. He even dismisses the spectral events at the hotel, describing them as "sheer delusions."[51] The problem is that Lord Montbarry's intrusion into events in such a definitive manner is readable as an attempt on the author's part to close any distance between reader, narratorial voice and characters, closing the book on the story in such an authoritative and unquestioned fashion that this appears a somewhat unsubtle and coercive attempt at conservative closure. Furthermore, Montbarry's pragmatism is underwritten by a desire to close off the present from the past, to forget a ghostly family reminder of the "un-English" behaviour of his elder brother towards Agnes.

This coercive attempt at closure is part of the assertion of the solidity of English identity, a crude re-mapping of identity's outlines, backed up by the predictable revelation of Henry's and Agnes's impending marriage. Agnes is gathered up into the folds of the family as a means, perhaps, by which the family seek to absolve themselves from their share of guilt belonging to the dead Montbarry's conduct towards Agnes; it is not, after all the Countess who commits an act of faithlessness. Collins connects his traditional narrative ending—traditional, that is, in an *English* narrative context—of the wedding with a more psychically orientated twist, also aimed at the re-assurance for the reader of the stability of Englishness. No foreign travel for them, Henry and Agnes honeymoon on the banks of the Thames.[52] The single domestic waterway, symbolic figure of the imperialist and mercantile enterprise of the English nation, and that river which leads to and from the heart of England, its capital city, stands in resolute opposition to the labyrinthine and sinister multiple waterways of Venice, with their western "history" as the margins of the Oriental.

Yet if the Thames is there as a final reminder of national identity, as instrumental to the construction of identity, we should also remember that waterways, far from being merely marginal, are both frames and moving figures that institute the dissolution of solidity. Collins's promise of the domestic resurrection of the English family, at home and content with itself, is ironically undercut. The waters of the Thames flow ineluctably into, and are flowed into by, the canals of Venice. English identity can never stand alone, but is always, already, contaminated and dispersed, displaced by the foreign. The English can never be at home completely. There is always a sense in which they are abroad; this and the responsibility accompanying it, the ghost in the text seems to be saying, must be acknowledged. The dead always rule the living.

V

Is no protest needed, in the interests of civilization, against a revival of barbarism . . . ?

—Wilkie Collins

Man and Wife is arguably Wilkie Collins's least self-conscious, self-reflexive novel.[53] It is not ostensibly a book about books, papers, writing and texts (although all these elements are somehow integral to the novel's structure). However, *Man and Wife* is one of Collins's most relentlessly engaged fictive polemics. It is the novel most obviously concerned with the condition of England, national identity and the ideologies that inform the male English subject. The novel's critique is ranged against those amongst whom power—economic, legislative, political power—circulates in England as a result, more or less, of a university education. Thus *Man and Wife* is not a "political" novel in the sense that Disraeli's or certain of Trollope's novels can be said to be political; it does reach, however, into the "deeper" politics of cultural discourse and circulation within the lives of the upper middle classes.[54]

Despite its seriously flawed and ideologically reductive depiction of the working class in the figures of the mute servant Hester Dethridge and Geoffrey Delamayn's trainer, Perry, *Man and Wife* is doubly important in its unfolding of the layers of brutality that mark the English class system and its connection of that violence to gender. A dominant narrative strand (one which Collins explores more playfully in *The Law and the Lady* and *The Woman in White*) is the helplessness of women before both socially constructed and physical manifestations of male power, and the mediation of that power through the written and practiced authority of the Law. In the narrative triptych of female victimization and suffering figured through the two Anne Silvesters (mother and daughter) and Hester Dethridge, Collins reads the generational and class based nature of male power. The historical and cultural continuity of male violence, both metaphorical and literal, is mapped out in this fashion, providing for the reader a reiterated ideological counterbalance which gives the lie to Sir Patrick's conservative assertions that things were better when he was a young man.

The question here is one of the cultural marginalisation of women which is imaginatively played out in the novel in such a manner as to make a connection with the issue of national identity. The main action first occurs in Scotland, working into the narrative the problematic status of the marriage laws in Scotland. The problem of the law is clearly defined as a national problem that leaves Anne Silvester's social status in doubt. Yet clearly the marginality of women relates, inferentially at least, to the marginality of Scotland in relation to England. The problems are gradually brought home, as it were, as the narrative transfers events from the margins of England to its heart, London.

Also unbalanced through the figure of women's cultural marginalization is the idea that the novel presents its readers with a "current" state of social degeneration, manifested through the national fascination with sport. Sir Patrick reads the current social state of England as a condition of steady decline from his own youth. Yet the very term "degeneration" as it is used by Sir Patrick is in itself typical of a deep conservatism, desirous of a mythologised past, of which Sir Patrick is, in part, the representative. "Degeneration" for Sir Patrick implies a steady, unbroken decline, a continuous linear slide. Collins's narrative of victimised women contests against any such simple readings through its deconstructive logic that dismantles the neatness of social boundaries and historical moments.

The narrative of the women is formed out of doubling, supplement and dis/continuity. While the younger Ann Silvester posits the non-logical theory that her fate has something to do with a biologically determined inheritance of "victim status" from her mother, this is mis-recognition on Ann's part because of culturally determined thinking that leaves her unaware of the material conditions which determine women's social existence. Yet the material, historical nature of her mistreatment is made very apparent by Collins's yoking together of this narrative strand with that of the widespread brutality of the middle-class male character, as that is socially determined. In fact, Collins teases his readers to accept the argument that favours biological determinism through the non-logical supplement of the reiterated name "Ann Silvester." Such a narrative device suggests we suspend rational under-standing, in favour of a more mystical approach to understanding Ann's story. Thus Collins is able to trace the metaphysical tatters that adhere to the pseudo-scientism of the Victorian popular discourse based on Darwinian theory.

At the same time however, Hester's presence breaks down this Victorian intellectual cul-de-sac. Her age (roughly equivalent with Sir Patrick's) spans the two generations of Ann Silvester. Her class forces other understandings on the reader; her inability to speak, the psycho-somatic result of physical violence, is a crude, though powerful symbol of all women's relatively marginal and silenced position. Beyond and, perhaps, before the immediate acts of violence which caused Hester's silence, there is another metaphysical and totalitarian presence; that of the Law itself. The Law, which constitutes Hester's Being-property as wife, brings to bear the inevitable force of the Law which guarantees her silence. Law, as the "founding act" (as Derrida puts it) of marriage is, in its necessary connection to force, might and violence, the agency ensur-ing women's silence.[55] Women are subject to "cruel abuses," victims of the "*national* eccentricity" of "grossness and brutality," to borrow from the author's preface (my emphasis).[56]

In his preface, Collins is at pains to make clear the specifically national context of male brutality on a widespread scale. Collins dislo-cates the Victorian term "rough" from its working-class orientation, to turn it against its originators; the middle and upper classes. For Collins, "roughs" can also have "clear skin and [a] . . . good coat."[57] Such roughs are

easily traced through the various grades of English society, in the middle and upper classes.[58]

The author thereby effects the estrangement of culturally and historically specific class-terminology. Such terminology is part of the means by which one class seeks to maintain its hegemonic position over another, through the use of pejorative nomenclature as social/anthropological taxonomy. And, furthermore, if the working-class is in conventional discourse, the "roughs," then the implication for those who use such a term is that they—the middle and upper classes of English society—are the "smooths." Thus naming the social other turns upon unspoken self-definition. Collins's attempted overturning of the implied binarism must have had a degree of power, albeit limited, which is today irrecoverable. Yet his efforts at polemical estrangement are necessary strategies from which we can learn and thereby grasp the structures of national identity, when hidden within the "natural" and everyday.[59]

For, as Collins says (and this is as true today, as it was for Collins), "[w]e have become so shamelessly familiar with violence and outrage,"

> that we recognize them as a necessary ingredient in our social system.[60]

Collins's efforts are directed against the embedded and customary, domesticated forms of violence, both verbal and physical, which English male identity perpetuates in the name of its own identity's continuance. Hence the author's insistence on protest through the medium of narrative.[61] Protest is the necessary precondition and preface for critique and reformation. Protest leads to the potential for overturning of established structures and normative models. Such overturning for Collins takes the practical form of constant estrangements of the familiar and domestic, making them seem unnatural in order that the English might see the English at home, but with a difference.

This can be read as the guiding principle of *Man and Wife*, a principle at its most encapsulated, condensed form in the 50th chapter. If *The Haunted Hotel* had been a model for unveiling Englishness through the device of taking the English abroad, then in *Man and Wife* the author reverses the process, bringing a foreigner in to England,[62] in order to witness the English at a national event such as a sports gathering.

Chapter 50, "The Foot-Race," begins, apparently, with a three page digression from what have been the main strands of the narrative up to this moment. The apparent digression concerns a "solitary foreigner" who "drifting about London, drifted towards Fulham on the day of the Foot-Race."[63] The Foot-Race in question is that in which Geoffrey Delamayn, the representative of upper middle-class brutality, is to take part, running for the South of England against the North.

The author's introduction of this unnamed "foreigner" of no specific origin is a little disconcerting, if not startling. While the Foot-Race had been expected, the intrusion of the foreigner has no ostensible connection with the narrative development; he can only be there in order to have some possible bearing on directing the reader's interpretation of events. The abruptness with which he is introduced hints at mystery and implies some of the stock conventions of the sensation novel. It is only as we read, that we realise that Collins has strategically deployed this anonymous figure as a device with which to unpack the Englishness of social, sporting occasion systematically and in anthropological-documentary fashion.

Collins draws his foreigner into the "current of a throng of impetuous English people."[64] Collins's emphasis on the collective national identity of the crowd is unnecessary, strictly speaking, in narrative terms. The definition does, however, juxtapose foreign individuality with a lemming or herd-like national quality. The foreigner is not lost in the crowd, but kept in view throughout the passage, as he traces for the reader—because of his foreignness—the Englishness of the social scene, thereby displacing its "natural" occurrence. And, as the narratorial voice is traditionally to assume or create the illusion of omniscience over narrative events in the classic realist text, so Collins's foreigner is written so as to assume an omniscience over Englishness through a distanced, somewhat comic observation of events.

Once in the sports-ground, the stranger observes:

> . . . thousands of people assembled; composed almost exclusively of the middle and upper classes of society.[65]

The stranger is used to add support to the author's remarks in the preface, concerning the attraction to brutality that is characteristic of the English middle classes. Collins's punctuation slows the reader's eye, inviting the reader to ponder on the spectacle of the massed middle classes, a narrative scene usually reserved for the working class. The term "composed" is carefully measured, and is suggestive of a concertedness on part of the classes mapped in the final clause. "Assembled" also suggests the gathering of a congregation, as though the thousands were at church or a concert. What is going on here is a subtle interconnection of discourses and social event for ideological effect; Collins has drawn terms from a specifically middle-class context, in order to re-enforce at the linguistic level the class of the majority of the spectators. Yet in doing so, in using such calm, orderly and polite terms (terms which speak of bourgeois identity) in relation to a sporting event, Collins has effectively shaken the boundaries of middle-class definition through the very medium of definition itself. Language itself is foregrounded in its estrangement as a medium for identity's mediation and construction.

Yet authority is not that easily removed. The stranger turns for explanation of the scene to a policeman, whose presence offers to the reader the psychic authorization of the crowd, while at the same time policing the gathering. Such a gesture on the author's part would seem initially to suggest ideological reassurance, bringing to the scene a sense of order and control, and thus re-establishing and re-mapping the parameters of English identity.

The foreigner asks the policeman about the events taking place.[66] This singular moment is made all the more strange, as the policeman, declining to "waste words" on the foreigner, merely, yet significantly, points to a poster advertising the day's events. Collins forces the oddity of the scene to its limits, replacing the symbolic figure of authority with his own finger, "a large purple forefinger, with a broad, white nail,"[67] which indicates the advertisement. *Gravitas* and absurdity collapse in on each other, as the Law (manifesting its long arm, presumably) is foregrounded through the ludicrous synecdoche which prohibits interpretation more than offering a means to translation. The policeman's finger effectively renders all meaning incommunicable, while also showing that the Law does not encourage communication, It is, instead, inimical to communication and meaning, seeking to impose its brute, mute presence.

However, even such a violent manifestation of English authority—which, admittedly, is undone by the preposterous mediation given it in the narrative—cannot prohibit the foreign quest for knowledge (a quest foreign to English identity).

The absurdity of the description of the policeman's finger is continued in the description of the sporting event. The foreigner receives this explanation from a "polite private individual."[68] The three terms of this phrase serve in conjunction as a paradigmatic and ideal model for the aspirations of the bourgeois Victorian psyche. The phrase encapsulates all that the English middle classes of the mid-nineteenth century desired. And, at the same instance that we register this encapsulation, we can also remark on the limits of the Victorian will and national identity, for which the phrase can be taken as a euphemism or metaphor.

Understanding the absurdity of the individual's description is facilitated by the presence of the foreigner. Because of his foreignness, details such as knowledge of the teams' respective colors, which are otherwise taken for granted as a result of native familiarity, have to be explained. Through description, the mundane and everyday are made peculiar. This in turn effects the ridiculing of the domestic indulgence and, thereby, the domestic character.

In re-telling the explanation, Collins moves from a pair of connected phrases, "national importance" and "national passion" as part of the critique of national identity.[69] The explanation revolves around the colours of the teams and the insistence on the "solemnity" of the occasion.[70] As the shift from "importance" to "passion" suggests, the pitch of the narrative is raised as it moves generally away from the rational, until the climax, when "Muscular England" is invoked, as a place immune to logic and criticism.[71] A constant inescapable nationalistic trace is unraveled throughout this passage, showing the inevitability of the assertion of nationalism as the result of any self-exulting spectacle. The national(istic), *nationalism itself,* is mapped in its transcendent and overdetermining importance as a philosophy of identity, despite the ostensible, local focus on the explanation of the sports meeting. We can therefore comprehend the level at which the critique of nationalism and national(istic) culture is being pitched.

This is not the final or only climax of the critique, however. If it were, there would still be the possibility of a misrecognition of the degree to which the English are being put on view (and, in some respects, on trial) before themselves; it would still be possible to misunderstand that the criticism as being drawn not against English middle-class culture as a whole, but only against those who attend sporting meetings, or indulge in sports (which can be read as the general tenor of the novel). Collins's endeavours in the opening of this chapter are of a broader, more strictly philosophical and ideological nature than the delivery of a mere polemic against a certain crass and mindless indulgence in vicarious pleasures found through the spectacle of organised physical exertions.

In its tracing of the national character then, the explanatory passage allows for a move from the narrower themes to more broad based issues. These are foregrounded as the foreigner's reflections on all English middle class social gatherings. Pausing to consider all that he has seen and heard, it crosses the foreign stranger's mind that:

> He had met with these people before. He had seen them (for instance) at the theatre, and had observed their manners with considerable curiosity and surprise.[72]

"These people" does not mean, of course, the same individuals, but groups of people all of whom are essentially ideologically similar, all of whom share the same identity. And that they and their type are to be found everywhere is indicated by the parenthetical remark in the passage quoted. What the foreigner has encountered is the prevalent, collective social identity of the middle classes. What he observes about this shared identity, this particular dominant manifestation of Englishness, is that it shows little interest or little spirit for intellectual pursuits;[73] it has no "sympathy with any of the higher and nobler emotions of humanity."[74]

In the analysis of the English at the theatre which follows, Collins terms them ironically "the countrymen of Shakespeare."[75] This is, of course, the standard yardstick of English identity, and Collins is inevitably invoking the cultural icon of Englishness for the purposes of elitism (as do Wordsworth, Arnold, Ruskin and countless others). Importantly, however, this yardstick is not being used as a measure of the shortcomings of the poor and the working class, but is directed against those who themselves deify Shakespeare and who constitute the hegemonic power-base of authorised, unified national identity.

This long paragraph continues its polemical invective against the powerful middle class, the heart of England, by exposing the "genteel English brains" and "genteel English hearts'" cultural predilection for "bosoms," "legs," "jokes," "scandal," "rank and money."[76]

Here is a cogent indictment of middle-class identity which is still relevant to the culture and identity of England in the 1990s. What the criticism serves to unmask is the direct collective culpability of the bourgeoisie in the betrayal (to use Collins's word) of the more positive aspects of national identity, and of those who have been exploited and marginalised in the name of Englishness. This passage, with its symbolic concatenation of what are today readable as tabloid concerns—bosoms, legs, jokes, scandals, rank and money—unveils that it is not some mythical lower class figure (such as "Essex Man") who is at fault *per se*. Such a figure is merely the privileged agent of a prurient and sensationalist discourse, and a symptom of a conservative national identity resolute in its refusal to open itself to internal critique. Those who are to blame for the narrow unthinking construction and perpetuation of a Tory-liberal ideology, expressed through what Collins calls so aptly the "stolid languor" of the middle class,[77] are those who maintain their power by hiding away in/as the secret heart of Englishness.

VI

The anonymous foreigner's presence in England makes clear the difficulty involved in trying to comprehend English middle-class identity. The presence of the Countess Narona in *The Haunted Hotel* also makes problematic the nature and conditions of Englishness. Both foreigners show the necessity of considering the structures of Englishness from different and estranged perspectives. And as these characters help us comprehend, the problem of Being-English is a problem of self-awareness and self-questioning. This problem highlights an essential difference of bourgeois identity in England from other national cultural and spiritual identities.

Terry Eagleton has said that the "metaphysics of nationalism speak of the entry into full self-realization of a unitary subject known as the people."[78] Generally speaking, this analysis is accurate. However, in terms of English middle class identity, a crucial element in the unitary self-realization of national Being is the self-forgetting of the conditions which allow access to that identity. Englishness buries itself in the natural, the inevitable, as a means of attempting to ensure its continued existence and hegemonic and colonial success, whilst also supporting such activity with the letter of the Law. So unreflective is Englishness that it shields itself from any but the most determined attempts at analysis. Such shielding through unawareness effectively deflects comprehension because it hides its structures within the appearance of being natural and also in a mute quotidian materiality, mapped out in part by the beginning of the 50th chapter of *Man and Wife*. To the foreigner, the nation is a mystery, only the thieves being understandable.[79] In these few pages, Collins ranges his criticism across broad and deep ground. It is the intensity of the passage and its attention to detail which makes available the deep and sedimented layers of Englishness. Collins writing is involved in what Derrida describes elsewhere as a "desedimentation of the superstructures of Law that both hide and reflect the economic and political interests of the dominant forces of society."[80] The rest of the novel can only hope to focus on one or two issues and discourses in English cultural life. Yet Collins's momentarily intense unmasking of the English at home provides devastating insights, relevant to any cultural critique of the nationalistic side of national identity. It is only through attention to detail, to such detail, and only by being faithful to Collins's own understanding of the "little things," that we can measure his importance as a mediator of everyday English life.

Finally, what Collins opens for us across the range of his novels is the degree of reliance on gender hierarchies in the deep structuring of English life and national identity. One of the most politically significant meanings we can construct for ourselves from our reading of Wilkie Collins concerns the questions each novel raises about the social and psychic links between the victimization of English women in society, and the struggle for expression of an arrogant certainty in the masculine character of Victorian identity. Victimisation occurs as a result of the constant failure of that will-to-identity as a will-to-power. If this is the truth of gender relations that Collins explores, then perhaps it is a truth to be explored with regard to questions of class relations.

If today, we hear the frequently uttered dogmatism that we live in a classless society, perhaps this is because the failure of the will-to-identity is at a moment of unprecedented crisis. In many ways, Collins's writing is understandable for its inauguration of disturbances which can, in paying attention to detail, lead to the conditions wherein crisis occurs as a political effect of dissident and oppositional critique. Attention to detail and the politics of disturbance belong properly to a materialist methodology of calling attention, directing the gaze to the historicity of culture, of a culture; to give precedence, contra liberal humanism, to the material over the metaphysical, in order to detail the rootedness, specificity and provisionality of Englishness; and to imply, by necessary and logical inference, the possibility of change, if only the analytical tool can be put into operation against the banal structures of repetition and simulation which maintain oppressive narratives such as the inevitability of social oppression and the victimisation of women. Collins reiterates such narratives in order to draw our critical attention to the social, psychic and cultural contexts of such stories, and to show that they are not fixed and eternal but merely the effects and performances of other secret discourses. The politics at/of the heart of Englishness is a politics of secrecy. Collins can show us how a counterpolitics, of disturbance and estrangement, can bring such secrecy out into the open, thereby calling it into question as the necessary condition of national identity.

6

THE IDEOLOGY OF ENGLISHNESS:
THE PARADOXES OF TORY-LIBERAL CULTURE
AND NATIONAL IDENTITY IN *DANIEL DERONDA*[1]

There is a sense in which the worthy child of a nation that has brought
forth illustrious prophets, high and unique among the poets of the world,
is bound by their visions.
    Is bound?
    Yes for the effective bond of human action is feeling, and the wor-
thy child of a people owning the triple name of Hebrew, Israelite, and Jew,
feels his kinship with the glories and the sorrows, the degradation and the
possible renovation of *his national family*.

—George Eliot, *Impressions of Theophrastus Such*
(my emphasis)

Wie kann jedoch «das Sein» überhaupt darauf verfallen, sich als «der
Gedanke» darzustellen?[2]

—Martin Heidegger

For Eliot, as for so many Victorians, the most problematic trope was that
of synecdoche. What was the relationship of the part to the whole?

—Daniel Cottom

I

Daniel Deronda is a story about national Being and the dialectic
between "national families"[3] felt by the eponymous hero. But, in order
to evade for the moment the point made by Eliot that "men can do
nothing without the make-believe of a beginning,"[4] I shall start somewhere near the end of *Daniel Deronda* with a remark made by Daniel to
Gwendolen Harleth:

The *idea* that I am possessed with is that of restoring a political
existence to my people, making them a nation again, giving them a
national centre, *such as the English have*, though they too are scattered over the globe. (my emphasis)[5]

This critical position of Deronda's, a position that is also a re-position-
ing of him by Eliot within the political unspoken of the novel, is important to bear in mind in the reading that I am proposing. The position is
one that seeks a negotiation between power and powerlessness, specifically in terms of the "national family." Daniel attempts to empower
himself. Yet, in this one statement of Daniel's cited above, it would
appear that Deronda writes himself back into the structures of a particular area of English culture and identity precisely because of his
active efforts at self-empowerment through the acquisition of another
identity. The particular English identity, definable as Tory-liberal,[6] is
one that Daniel Deronda—and *Daniel Deronda* also—seemingly questions, analyses and rejects from Book 2 onwards.[7] Hugo Mallinger is a
typical historical agent of the Tory-liberal ethos, as much caught up
and affected by the outcome of parliamentary economic policy from
the 1820s onwards, as he is, on speculation, a parliamentary mover of
the liberal compromise. Against the structures of Tory-liberalism, as
represented by Eliot in the figure of Mallinger, Deronda had shown a
resistance to his own identity being shaped "too definitely"[8] by the "system"[9] of Englishness into which he had been placed. Daniel's re-writing
of himself at the end of the novel focuses the paradox in English cultural politics that is traced in (the question of) the narration of an identity that is implicitly caught up in the narration of nation.[10] It is because
Daniel acts against the ideology of Englishness that he is read—and
written by Eliot—as caught by the paradoxes of identity. Eliot writes
Deronda as seeking to express the condition of national Being through
conscious thought and thereby exposes the problematic nature of such
an enterprise.

I shall return to the quotation I have introduced as I attempt to follow this thread. First, however, in order to comprehend how activity
and consciousness constitute the grounds for failure and recuperation,
let us look at some Eliot protagonists who do nothing and are, therefore,
not caught by paradox, as is Deronda.

II

That Daniel is such an active and privileged subject within the
novel is perhaps symptomatic of the political problematic of identity

for Eliot. Daniel, more than any other Eliot "hero," takes matters in his own hands.

George Eliot's fictive use of the figure of the artisan offers a significantly different perspective on identity from that provided by Daniel Deronda. Eliot's artisanal figures speak to the reader about the concerns of community and the preservation of its identity. Each artisan is contrasted to members of the aristocracy or gentry, whose traditional roles have been involved with the maintenance of the community, yet who no longer fulfill that purpose adequately. The artisans of Eliot's novels, however, do not engage directly in effecting the attempted preservation or re-definition of their societies. Silas Marner, like Adam Bede, does nothing in the novel that is named for him. In saying that they "do nothing," I mean that neither Silas nor Adam appears to be responsible directly for the development of their respective narratives through any direct action taken by either man. Principal characters such as Marner and Bede have a degree of autonomy from the narrative. While they are involved, both in their communities and in the stories that George Eliot weaves, their activities cannot be wholly described as either integral or heroic in any broad sense.

Both Adam and Silas have a sedentary energy that is not discernible in terms of the narrative construct. Both figures, however, possessing a small fund of knowledge, are re-figured as the *loci* of the narrative strands within which they are read. Eliot positions them in relation to their worlds in such a way that, in reading, we comprehend these artisans as having been somehow transformed or translated by their experiences, even while they foreground a transformation of the community. With Daniel Deronda, there is always the sense that the idea of community and communal identity is somehow exhausted.

The received wisdom of both Marner and Bede constitutes an epistemology older than the immediate cultural context of the novels in question. In being older, such knowledge proves that it is resistant to cultural flux. Thus, there is an anachronistic discursive pattern woven by Eliot in Bede and Marner. Of course any character in a novel is traced by social "languages" and ideologies that are neither particular nor essential to that character. These belong, instead, to a cultural and/or historical instance. Thus both the actions and language of a character may be read as determined by historical formation. Frequently, if not constantly, a character's "internal" discourses may be contradictory among themselves. One the one hand this marks the human agent *qua* human. On the other hand, however, the contradiction or paradox serves as an index of human agency's historicity or materiality, of being in a world of social interaction at a specific place and time.

For example, in *Adam Bede*, Arthur Donnithorne behaves "immorally" because Eliot writes him as the stereotypical callous and cynical young country squire; however, Eliot also endows Donnithorne with a small degree of conscience and self-consciousness. He comprehends, albeit dimly, that his actions are a form of outmoded—and, to some extent, fictional—behaviour. Such behaviour is the stuff of eighteenth-century life and novels. Donnithorne's slight pangs of guilt determine his own moment in history, while also being a single indicator of Eliot as a nineteenth-century writer, working against the grain of fictive convention. Thus Eliot develops such tensions to leave behind what she comprehends as the negative legacy of the past, while preserving what she discerns as the past's positive aspects; an activity on Eliot's part entirely in keeping with her readings in Comtian positivism.

George Eliot uses characters such as Silas Marner and Adam Bede and their class-position as a medium for the philosophical enunciation of a spirit of the past. Through the evocation of this spirit in such men, and through the foregrounding of their artisanal activity as the everyday manifestation of spirit, Eliot reforms community along more expressly bourgeois lines, while jettisoning worn-out external social relations, such as feudal, manorial, aristocratic and—in the case of Casaubon—clerical hegemony. As Eliot banishes Donnithorne from his home, so, in *Silas Marner*, she either kills the Casses or makes them barren. That which Eliot seeks to preserve from the past is not outward structure or societal institution. Instead she attempts to re-write spiritual values and beliefs made secular through the figure of a broad-based provincial middle class, all of whom pull together, more or less.

This class group—that of Eliot's own father—is given singular voice in the forms of Silas and Adam. Even though they do nothing, they express a consensus opinion involved with and coming out of the best interests of the community. Thus, through Marner's and Bede's "central" presence in their novels, George Eliot foregrounds the enfranchisement of bourgeois ideology through the corrective lens of an older spirituality.

Eliot constitutes her artisans' Being as a Being-for-others, a Being-in-the-world. They exist, not for themselves, but to aid others. Their being is determined as they have responsibility to others as a general mode of existence. Eliot's conceptualization of subjectivity is foregrounded in the artisanal presence as the presentation of an ethical responsibility or duty to the world. To be is always to work, to produce and to be involved in reciprocal exchange, no matter how isolated that work is. Whether Silas weaves in his cottage or Adam's carpentry is performed in a workshop adjacent to his home, both men produce for their communities, and are maintained in turn by those communities. Silas is not only the weaver; he is, as the subtitle of the novel informs us, the weaver of Raveloe. This may of course seem like an obvious point, but it is so obvious that we tend to overlook the import of the subtitle. Silas cannot exist without his community. Furthermore he does not have any being for the reader unless it is in relation to Raveloe. He is implicated inextricably (there is even a work-related pun in the name of the village, which suggests a textile mesh and undoing; Eliot requires of us that we unravel her narrative thread).

Bede and Marner, having received an education of sorts, being aware of discourse circulating outside the immediate context of their communities, are produced by what Peter de Bolla calls a "discursive analytic."[11] The discursive analytic is not merely one discourse amongst others. It is not thinkable as an utterance belonging either to Silas or Adam; nor is it a distinguishing feature of their utterances. To define their positions in such a way would still constitute a New Critical and humanist gesture rooted in the notion of essentialism or individual autonomy. The discursive analytic is the gathering of disparate discourses from which Eliot weaves her characters in their complex entirety, and from which Eliot's writing is woven. More than this, the discursive analytic is a function of Eliot's discursive hierarchy within the text. It moves in, out and through a single character, groups of characters, and is readable also in the narrative voice. This voice is, itself, a mesh of languages, a text-ile construct, the purpose of which, for Eliot, is to resist the dehumanization or alienation of the English subject.

Eliot polices her stories in the effort to resist dehumanization, and she does so by mediating the internal and external levels of the text through the paradigmatic figure of the artisan. Importantly, Eliot centres her artisans by naming her fictions for them, and for her re-creation of artisanal activity, whereby the duty to work is manifested in an ethical responsibility to the life of others. But the use of the proper name does not identify the agent only, hence the proper name as title. Something is identified beyond the individual in Eliot's signing of the proper name. *Silas Marner* and *Adam Bede* gather to them the cultural existences of specific communities, *in the names of* their privileged agents. The figure of the artisan provides a specific cultural activity and a form of work intrinsic to the community, whilst also being a signature of the historical moment, the 1830s. In the first third of the nineteenth century, and during Eliot's childhood years, the figure of the artisan was taken up by radical political theorists as the ideal figure for English Identity and as a resistance to industrial capitalism.[12]

Eliot takes up the artisan, making that figure ethically responsible for the health of the community within which the artisan lives. Eliot employs the proper name as an ethical signature guaranteeing a type of work that is beneficial to the community in which the work is carried out. The work is not exploitative as is large-scale capitalist enterprise. Instead, the artisan expresses a material concern through his mode of production for the accumulation of community and, therefore, shared property. The artisan produces from the community's resources community capital, whilst also existing in and taking from the society.

The artisanal project is, then, mapped by a constant reciprocity. It is concerned with identifying what is acknowledged communally as skilled work through the practical application of received competencies in the service of the community to which the artisan belongs. George Eliot's texts mime this project because Eliot, in artisanal fashion, takes from her imagined community only to re-form it, make it healthier, and give it the possibility of survival. The author grounds the beliefs and enunciation of the artisan in local, material experience, thereby displacing a more abstract and metaphysical concept of human subjectivity. The idea of the individual is re-written, traced through the cultural specificity of the artisan. The figure of the artisan is the signature of Eliot's socially grounded design, which we can read as a bourgeois materialism (having possible roots in Thomas Paine, via Wordsworth). Eliot projects the growth of the middle-classes "[c]onfigured as a mix of rural and urban occupations not yet mediated by 'suburbia,'"[13] through the exempla of artisans, whose prowess takes on a larger significance than that of their particular crafts.

Furthermore, the artisan undergoes a moment of sublation. Eliot sacrifices the specific artisan, causing a tragic event to be inflicted on him, as a means of preserving or spiritualizing the idea of the artisan for the good of the community. This is not to say that the artisan dies or is removed. This happens only to the local gentry, whom Eliot leaves without the hope for regeneration. Silas and Adam are changed somehow from what they were, made into different men through tragedy, in order that the community (and in this I include the community of readers always implied by Eliot) may benefit from the agon of their transcendent moments.

Yet at the same moment in which Eliot situates the artisan as experiencing epiphany and losing something of himself, she also undertakes to hold on to the larger significance of the artisan's Being-as-work. The "transcendent artisan" takes on national importance in the attempted conservation of a particularly English way of life. Through this, parochial community life is apparently enriched and made safe momentarily from the dehumanizing and reifying conditions of mass production and the Tory-capitalist enterprise at work in those towns that always impinge on Eliot's rural worlds.

The figure of the artisan is, then, a figure of national importance, being important both within the Victorian mythology of national identity and to George Eliot's conceptions of art and society. The artisan can be thought of thus: as a character to whom disparate energies and materials come in an "untold" or chaotic fashion. From that figure such materials emerge, transformed and shaped, given aesthetic meaning and a broader, cultural importance. For Eliot, the artisan creates a narrative thread from nothing, weaving that thread into the fabric of identity. Eliot's artisan is not the heroic actor in conventional terms because his role is more crucial, more radically social than that of the hero who is merely an agent, albeit a privileged one who moves and is moved amongst others.

Eliot's inscription of the stillness of the artisan who works away quietly at his loom or lathe amidst social upheaval, either in the village or in the country at large during the period of these novels, is a countermove to the loss of spirit attendant on industrial, urban alienation. The inscription of repose-in-work is a counter-move, a resistance on Eliot's part, because, like the inseparability of a text-ile weave (which must also be the dominant metaphor for Eliot's fictions), Eliot's re-marking of artisanal stillness is also the enunciation of the dynamic between work and life, a dynamic that, for Eliot is indivisible. Eliot reads—and writes— the continual mobility between "the system and the subject of the system."[14] This mobility, which is also an indivisibility, extends from the artisan to the community, and back again. There is no separation, properly speaking.

To write "artisan" is to remark a double moment: of stillness, and of continual, repeated action. The repose allows for productive action, such as sitting at a desk to write. Eliot is an artisanal novelist, a singular, skilled and skillful producer of text-ile fabrications, manufactured from the discursive weaves available to her.

Psycho-biographically speaking, we may even be tempted to read the presence and influence of Marian Evans's father in a such a mode of production. For Eliot, motion out of stasis, creative, repetitious movement unfolding out from the still centre (one of many such centres in the community), produces the tracing of continuity, perpetuation and preservation. Eliot maps out what she perceives as the organicity or connectedness of social elements that, in the ideology of the author, are indivisible from spiritual ideals. Her purpose is to conserve the spirit of communal identity, whilst reforming that same community after her own displacement of feudal hierarchies through her narratives. In doing so, Eliot strives to construct a vision of the survival of (the ideal of) community, given voice in the figure of the artisan, a figure of re-figuring.

George Eliot's figures of re-figuring are written through those who are employed in manual crafts and who are not yet divested of or estranged from the means of production. In turn, the tracing of such characters remarks in the use of pen and paper the writer as artisan. The writer as artisan belongs implicitly to a community whose duty is to labour for the conservation of a disappearing social order, and its national-cultural moment of materiality; hence Eliot's constant fictional return to the rural 1830s from the "reality" of the urbanized, mass-produced '60s as a profoundly ideological double gesture, of affirmation and resistance.

Eliot's investments in the figure of the artisan and her own artisanal labouring affirm the singular, creative life as involvement in the community, and as emergent from that community. This affirmation is also a resistance to industrialism and the dry academic efforts of "high culture" as commented on through Casaubon in *Middlemarch*. In the social displacement of manorial control, which both *Silas Marner* and *Adam Bede* register, the nurturing, caring artisan appears as the bourgeois ideal of the (disappearing) English world, and of the world of the word.

III

I want now to look at a few of the ways in which the figure and the writing of Daniel Deronda/*Daniel Deronda* shakes apart in order to reveal ideological-narrative concerns with the illusion of bourgeois English identity, described by Homi Bhabha as "a form of social and textual affiliation."[15] Such concerns were frequently in discursive circulation among liberal intellectuals such as George Eliot throughout the middle years of the nineteenth century. The apparent unfolding of issues at stake that the novel partakes of is, however, closed ultimately; a conservative recuperation *pace* Eliot's desires is effected through the final displacement of any continued internal critique.[16]

In *Daniel Deronda* Eliot writes a fictionalisation of the ideological-narrative concerns of Englishness through the ploy of making a merely reflexive trace of that which may be read as most archetypally English. Eliot makes the life of the English into art, a hackneyed art eaten through with anachronistic, self-referential and self-enclosing clichés. Yet a model of Englishness related to the clichéd archetype that Eliot seeks to reject is finally valorized. Indeed, it is never wholly dismissed as such by Deronda; for he does say, as part of an apologia to Sir Hugo, that:

> I want to be an Englishman, but I want to understand other points of view. And I want to be rid of a merely English attitude in studies.[17]

"A merely English attitude": Daniel's critical response articulates both the desire to maintain a cultural connection, and a simultaneous questioning and distancing from the identity which that same culture has provided. This dis/continuity of Deronda's opens for the reader the way into a revision of Englishness. Of course, one can also read this revision as positing a reformation of the culture, rather than being the expression of any genuine longing for an alternative culture; still, such a gesture does have great political import. Daniel proposes a cosmopolitan variation of English identity, an other Englishness.

But this is still only yet another version of the Authorised Englishman, when taken in the context of the novel as a whole. Not all Englishness is necessarily politically reprehensible. In the context of the Mallinger family and the cultural/political matrix of which the family, its friends and associates are representatives, this particular version of Englishness is so heavily overdetermined and overdetermining that, like Deronda, one cannot help but feel that this is the only Englishness open to us. Unlike Deronda, however, we need not feel the necessity to maintain an allegiance with the Tory-liberal culture which we witness Eliot performing. And, however critical a performance Eliot's is, it is still one ultimately which valorizes the dominant culture in the face of a lack of—for Eliot—any alternative vision of English identity.

If the figure of Daniel does provide a means of access to an analytical critique of the moribund postures of the English, then because of that selfsame culture, and (in)formed as it is by that culture's ideologies, Deronda's projected philosophical and real journey beyond the English culture and the close of the novel becomes problematised. Daniel Deronda's desire is transcribed through and through by the spectre of the English imperial imperative. Furthermore, this situation is problematic because, at the same time that we might read Deronda's gesture as a desire for an imaginary space of nationhood, of nationality and of national identity greater than the individual's desire, we also have to comprehend this as a somewhat violent dismissal of Deronda. We are not reading a simple and unequivocal inscription of a positive search for alterity. Deronda is revealed through the textual structures as the figure of the Other-within, the always foreign, who is referred to by Gwendolen as the "stranger,"[18] and of whom she asks, "is he an Englishman"?[19] Dismissal for Deronda is inevitable because, thus understood, as the Other-within, is disturbing not only for Gwendolen, but also for the conservative reader.

Daniel's presence is always disturbing. The text appears constructed so as to evade culpability in the act of making Daniel foreign and therefore threatening, by writing the question of national identity as one largely of self-interrogation, self-translation. Daniel's enquiry into (his) Being is performed by Eliot as marked by the inevitability of an essentialist drive, something specific and supposedly individual emanating from Daniel's psyche.

It is no accident then that our first encounter with Daniel is with the contents of his enquiring mind. On the first page, he asks himself about the nature of Gwendolen.[20] Even in this instance, where Daniel's analysis frames Gwendolen as an object for enquiry, Daniel's fictive, analytical and essentialist status is unveiled. In the double context of her fictional *oeuvre* and the quest for a narrative of national being, Eliot thus defines Daniel as the single most self-determining agent of her novels, thereby marking a break from the performance of her other fictive subjects, such as Adam Bede or Silas Marner. Once Daniel's Jewishness is announced as a result of his pursuit of meaning, his attempts to read himself and a suitable cultural text to which he can belong, the novel would seem to be so constructed as to allow him to see that he cannot be admitted into the culture which has written his outward signs, as it were. And so Daniel or, more precisely, what he has come to be refigured as must be displaced. He is closed off from textual activity through the promise of an ideal space.

Despite the troubling closure of the text, Daniel's interventions with English culture make it plain that a particular hegemonic model of a national identity does not exist *as such*. Whatever power bourgeois English culture may have possessed can be read in *Daniel Deronda* as part of, and constituted by, a precarious, shifting textual world. The English identity of the Mallingers, of Gwendolen and her social set is not rooted; its "center" is composed of moving simulacra. This text-world situates the image of its own illusory cultural centrality through the figuring of often paradoxical, worn out figures, discursive effects and performances. As Simon Dentith puts it, "the England of this novel is one of mannered and cultivated sterility . . . the hero's aspirations . . . directed to Zionism and a flight from England . . . [are] the final consequence[s] of the crisis in Liberal thought."[21]

This crisis, historically registered by the Liberal economic compromise between the 1820s and 1870s,[22] is constituted through the figure

of Sir Hugo who, as a self-admitted *rentier*, is both product and producer of that conservative-liberalism so forcefully and eminently *the* discourse of the English middle class. This crisis, mapped as it is in both the
economic-historical and moral position of Hugo, is at least partly the
result of what Eliot identifies, with a pithy directness, as "aristocratic
seediness";[23] which aristocracy has, in Sir Hugo's words, "a little disinterested culture."[24] Daniel is used to read the seediness, the disinterest-
edness of his culture and its inhabitants. This is a gesture by which Eliot
effects a displacement of the crisis from the liberal intellectual (such as
herself) but to which, in Daniel's remark cited above, she must return
inevitably.

This attempted displacement is double-fold, caught up also in the
aesthetics of realist narrative. The novel, *Daniel Deronda*, reads the running to seed of The Novel as Victorian epistemological paradigm, its history and plots as dying or, at least, decaying forms. There is a question of
reflection here that needs to be engaged, because reflection—the condition of the form of the form—is what is precisely at stake in the representations and performances of the English to themselves. With this is
mind, does Daniel mime the practice of his text? Or does *Daniel Deronda*
perform a mimetic remarking of its central figure's analyses and actions?
Perhaps the answer to both is yes; but, whichever we may decide on,
both the figure and the novel can be read as responses to the failure of
a particular intellectual-ideological project in the Victorian England of
the Second Reform Bill.

In order to continue this reading, it is necessary to return to the
(make-believe) of a beginning:

> Men can do nothing without the make-believe of a beginning.
> Even Science, the strict measurer, is obliged to start with a make-
> believe unit, and must fix on a point in the stars' unceasing journey
> when his sidereal clock shall pretend that time is at Nought. His
> less accurate grandmother Poetry has always been understood to
> start in the middle; but on reflection it appears that her proceeding
> is not very different from his; since Science, too, reckons back-
> wards as well as forwards . . . and . . . really sets off *in medias res*. No
> retrospect will take us to the true beginning.[25]

Eliot's motto, that which is the pretext to the first chapter, concerns
both story-telling and history; narrative *as* history, and vice versa. Not
just any story-telling either. What is being commented on, in the margin
between title and text that we often overlook, is a particular identity of
narrative prose. The motto is a concise meditation on, and mediation of,

"the English novel," or *histories*. This meditation is also a deconstructive disavowal, however; a rejection of previously dominant "historical" modes of story telling, of the English representing themselves to themselves. Something, perhaps a certain model or performance of the illusion of national identity, is being banished. As the figure of Daniel Deronda seeks an other space, a place of "philosophical enunciation" which grows as a resistance to the deadening structures of Englishness, its society and narratives, so too does the novel.

The motto outlines, unequivocally, the desire for origin, for some logocentric moment, a recuperable presence or what Deronda calls a "national centre"[26] from which comes truth and to which all subsequent events can be made somehow proper through an imagined—that is to say narrated—familial relationship. Thus, there is a focusing of desire. And this desire, the motto informs us, is masculine. We are in the presence of the desire, not of that universal figure, Man, but of those subjects of history, *men*. We then witness the establishment of a provisional dialectic between the masculinity of Science, "the strict measurer," and the femininity of grandmother Poetry; which dialectic is, however, swiftly displaced in favour of what we might read (or misread) as a theory of supplementarity that admits to the fragmentary, partial and provisional status of all texts.

The pre-text as reflexive supplement is crucial to the function of Daniel Deronda, both the character and the novel. If we comprehend the motto as a rethinking of "The Novel" (a particular instance of the aesthetic performance of the ideology of Englishness), it can also be read as mapping out, in advance, the aleatory randomness of *Deronda*'s stories, and Daniel's wanderings. There is a self-reflexive gambit at work here, a structural de-structuring, that we would do well to keep in mind because here is inscribed both opening and closure, both the dismissal and the recuperative translation of the fictional-historical form. And it is this double bind that plays the novel throughout.

III

Reflection works in *Daniel Deronda* to displace the self, to insist that the self is a condition of cultural instance or a range of cultural and social discourses and practices read as national identity. Yet reflection goes further. Reflexivity, (which is also self-reflexivity) a deliberate foregrounding of its own strategies, challenges the cultural boundaries of identity by displaying the fictitious, often paradoxical nature of those boundaries; in short, as *merely* modes of representation. Gwendolen is a condition of Daniel's internal reflection in the opening of the novel.

And, to take the example of Gwendolen, it is the condition of her "selfhood" that she is written as having no authentic self, but is instead subject to, constructed by, a range of English fictions, attitudes and beliefs.[27] As Klesmer observes to Gwendolen, her notions have "no more resemblance to reality than a pantomime."[28] The level of Gwendolen's reflection is such that she is engulfed by her own performance in a "labyrinth of life"[29] and a "labyrinth of reflection."[30]

When talking with Grandcourt, Gwendolen has recourse to remember "experiences . . . in novels."[31] Her performances throughout the novel bespeak the fictive attitudinizing of English identity. As can be seen in the presentation of Gwendolen, Eliot's narrative hermeneutic of national Being refigures the English upper middle class, displacing this class from their self-appointed role as the *Herrenvolk* of nineteenth-century western civilization to being merely walk-on players in a stale *pièce bien fait.*

At one moment, Gwendolen projects herself into such a theatrical performance, delivering a monologue on the imagined melodrama of courtship. Hers is a speculative narrative-performance riddled with the most clichéd terms:

> He will declare himself my slave—I shall send him round the world to bring me back the wedding ring of a happy woman—in the meantime all the men who are between him and the title will die of different diseases—he will come back Lord Grandcourt—but without the ring—and fall at my feet. I shall laugh at him—he will rise in resentment—I shall laugh more—he will call for his steed and ride to Quetcham, where he will find Miss Arrowpoint just married to a needy musician, Mrs Arrowpoint tearing her cap off, and Mr Arrowpoint standing by. Exit Lord Grandcourt, who returns to Diplow, and like M. Jabot, *change de linge.*[32]

In what sounds like the scenario of a play by T. W. Robertson or one of his contemporaries, Gwendolen announces the existence of Grandcourt and herself as solely textual devices. Her speech, written as a series of disconnected phrases strung together by dashes, mimes the written form of the stage direction. The various characters referred to, the imposed mission for Grandcourt and the sub-plot of the needy musician marrying into a wealthy family, are all suggestive of popular Victorian drama. The use of the word "exit" is also supportive of this reading.[33]

Thus Eliot manipulates the direct discourse of the character in order to suggest the idea that Gwendolen writes herself into an essentially fictive mode. The metalanguage of the text is also employed to re-enforce the notion of self-inscription:

Gwendolen's uncontrolled reading, though consisting chiefly in what are called pictures of life, had somehow not prepared her for this encounter with reality. Is that surprising? It is to be believed that attendance at the *opéra bouffe* in the present day would not leave men's minds entirely without shock, if the manners observed there with some applause were suddenly to start up in their own families.[34]

In a passage that intimates the arguments of Eliot's essay, "Silly Novels by Lady Novelists,"[35] Gwendolen's "nature" is revealed as formed in part by her reading. Eliot remarks in a somewhat Arnoldian tone a conservative shock at the Philistinism engendered by "uncontrolled" (unpoliced?) reading habits. The implication is that the middle classes, if left to themselves, will invariably attain to the lowest common denominator in aesthetic pleasures (the argument is not only redolent with Arnoldian echoes but also infers the possibility of Leavisian arrogance). Left to their own willful individualistic tastes, the bourgeoisie will establish the premises for their own demise; Gwendolen reads "bad" literature, without discretion or advice, and so deserves her fate. Here is the trajectory of the entire novel, at least with regard to Gwendolen's narrative. Yet it is Eliot, nonetheless, who employs the hackneyed phrases of clichéd literature in order to construct for us the world of the upper middle classes played out in a vicious teleological structure of reflection and retribution (Eliot attempts to evade responsibility for her countrymen and women with something akin to a karma credit plan).

Gwendolen, therefore, embodies the paradox of the Englishness that is foregrounded in the novel, only to be disrupted. She is wholly fictional, subject to the texts of "mannered and cultivated sterility." Yet in showing herself as such, she can be read as dismantling any claim to veracity in the image of English cultural identity in the latter half of the Victorian epoch. Described as without passion,[36] Gwendolen, a specular being, is often remarked by a negation of qualities, while being referred to and referring to herself through a range of arch-metaphors pertaining to theatricality, drama, artifice, fiction and performance; writing herself, as it were, into one of Meyrick's paintings, even before he has come to describe her repeatedly as the Van Dyke Duchess.

Yet Gwendolen is not the sole subject of English identity's reflexive enclosure. Meyrick, something of an archly referential parody of the "Will Ladislaw-Bohemian figure in Victorian Literature," is, like Gwendolen, recuperated into the systems of Englishness—an Englishness of an earlier age—through his use of culturally reflexive figures of speech, and in his becoming an "English" portrait painter in the

Gainsborough tradition.[37] He is a painter of the English, of markedly English representations of the English to and for themselves. The level of reflection is remarked in the text by the use of quotation marks ("in the Gainsborough style") that sign a certain forcefully symbolic English signature that, at the moment of the novel, is a point in the fictive-historical past. The quotation marks rewrite the phrase as an English motto, the possible citation of some source. Eliot's text not only closes off Englishness within its own texts—from the "high" to the "low," from Gainsborough to Gwendolen's "uncontrolled reading"—but also traces the labyrinthine weave of such textuality, played out socially and in its endless reference to itself.[38]

So it is that the metaphors and other figures referential to the discourse of bourgeois Victorian art become re-written by Eliot as synecdoches for her characters' Being-English. These figures govern and thereby translate the social/narrative activity of the English society of *Deronda*. So frequent are Gwendolen's self-reflexive statements, and so similar are they to those of the metalanguage,[39] that we are witness to the foregrounding strategy of which I have already spoken. It is precisely this strategy that dissolves the divisions between narrative voice and character reflection in the overall performance of the self as text, as performance or illusion.[40]

This is a figure in a mobile structure, (the *in medias res* of the motto) revealing to us that cultural or national identity has no truth to it *other than its truth as untruth*. The mobility of this structure is labyrinthine in its lack of discernible origins. This is registered in the novel through both its framed, extended flashback sequences and through the already noted similarity between narrative voice and character's discourse. In Gwendolen, we see the most (stereo)typically English of fictional characters. So typical, so fictional is she, that she comes close in characterization to those heroines of the mind and millinery species, defined by Eliot in the "Silly Novels" essay. Eliot's performance of the stereotype[41] counters realist ideology, distancing readerly engagement with Gwendolen, and thereby forestalling the tragic dimension, read by Barbara Hardy.[42] Furthermore, in Gwendolen's case her foregrounded reflexivity serves to read some of the major images of English identity as *solely fictional* and outmoded.

And the function of Gwendolen is a polemically exploited one, for she is representative of her class and its culture, the same culture that Deronda analyses and apparently rejects. Her life throughout Book I is comprised of a series of rituals and clichéd fictional plots belonging to an anachronistic world. And this is also true of the other characters who inhabit this world. Rex, for example, gives a stereotypical perfor-

mance—a piece of pure melodrama—as the jilted lover who initially looks
to the colonies for an honourable escape. This inclusion of the colonies
is not a single instance. It has already been remarked that Gwendolen's
family had made its money through her Grandfather's involvement with
the colonies at the end of the previous century.[43] And it is at the end of
the previous century and the beginning of the nineteenth century that
Gwendolen, Sir Hugo, Grandcourt, and all the other figures of the
English plot are caught. Historically, they are anachronistic. And fic-
tionally they also belong to other, earlier novels. Their plots are worthy
only of already familiar narrative structures. Eliot's liberal critique of aristocratic seediness would seem to have a somewhat radical thrust. But its
rejection of Tory-liberal redundancy is tightly caught up in its own
unspoken agendas, which have to be thought through in terms of mastery.

IV

　　Which issue brings us back then, to the quotation with which the
chapter began. Daniel, who has previously said of himself, "I am Daniel
Deronda. I am unknown"—a comment that both fixes identity through
the value of the proper name, then immediately erasing that identity
through the naming of Being as "unknown"—states that he is possessed
by an idea.
　　"I am," he says twice, using a verb form that articulates all that is
problematic in this novel. This form—I am—is possessed with an idea, *the
idea*, of presence, of presence presenting itself, to itself, through the
narration of Being in the self-identical statement—I am—that seeks to
erase difference. Daniel's reiteration of Being cancels the former
remark. Here we have the paradox of the English culture, its political
identity being caught up in the impossibility of its definition, except
through the identification of the foreign and the strange. Daniel figures both the domestic and the strange in a single figure, and seeks to
think through the paradox written here, a paradox that is bound up in
the questioning of (the questing after) Being. But as Heidegger has
asked, how can "'Being' ever present itself as 'Thought'"? To Be, in the
sense of English national identity, is not to question national identity as
such. Yet to assert one's Being as other than the dominant national
identity is to call the conditions for that identity into question. To question Englishness in such a radical fashion is to call Englishness to
account, to question its unquestioned legitimacy, on which it depends as
a founding principle. Here is both Daniel and the novel's dilemma, the
dilemma of the liberal intellectual, whose very thought is enmeshed in

the paradox, the running contrary to belief, of the political unthought of accepted identity and its reified cultural manifestations (that comprise the national unawareness foregrounded by Wilkie Collins, and discussed in the previous chapter). As Daniel's expression of his vision to Gwendolen shows, albeit inadvertently, obliquely, the *doxa* of the political unconscious is inescapable.

Throughout the novel, Daniel has been possessed by ideas; from the first chapter in fact, when his mind is possessed with the idea of the female (as) enigma, and given the form of Gwendolen.[44] Daniel is a creature of imagination, of thought, of mind and interpretation. These words—imagination, thought, mind—are in constant circulation around Deronda throughout the novel as definitions and translations of his figure and character. As a figure of thought (one who thinks the world, and who seeks actively to constitute himself, his Being through thought), he is always subject to his own analytical self-enquiry.

This self-reflection has its price however, in terms of an inability to engage in social action as a medium for change. As Neil Hertz has pointed out in quoting *Deronda*, Daniel is a "sympathetic but impotent observer."[45] And it is perhaps because of his impotence to do anything but observe, that Daniel turns to the idea(l) of nation, of national identity; to the pure idea of an imaginary nation with the possibility of being narrated, and thus mastered, by himself, Daniel Deronda. Yet in this desire for mastery—which speaks of the English colonial desire, thus marking Daniel as ineluctably English—which is also a desire for origin, for the narration of origin as the potentiality of an ideal future (from the make-believe of origin to ideal closure, Daniel's mind is understood to read a teleological project), Daniel must have recourse to an exemplary, lived narrative form. Thus as analogy, analogy as the ideological excuse for mastery, Daniel's mind grasps paradoxically the discourse and *episteme* of the national centre that he has rejected, that of England.

Daniel is therefore used, ultimately, not to aid the idea of Jewishness, nor to propose an alternative to the dead, closed book of English high culture; he has, instead, a certain purpose. The figure and the novel of Deronda/*Deronda* are used to familiarize and domesticate the Other, to deny alterity by framing the foreign in English terms in a gesture amounting to a colonial imperative, writing foreignness otherwise so as to displace any fear that exists at the illusory heart of English culture in crisis. Daniel's remark with which I began, is a form of discursive colonialism; it is the expression of the thinking of the colonisation of Being. Daniel's statement does not only capture but also engulfs; not a country but a nation, the idea of a nation, the *other* nation, nation of otherness, the other nation of narration, of a textual tradition that is supposedly vital through being constantly other; through being, in short, a narrative of dissemi*nation*. This gesture on Daniel's part leads us to speculate that Eliot regards English narrative—a narrative of expressly narrative concerns deemed to be English—as a hackneyed form, capable only of a ritualistic repetition of self-reflexive tropes that deny any survival. Daniel's commentary on his political purpose constitutes a double act of colonialism and the desire for empire. Daniel's remark is spoken with a revitalized passion that continues in other words another version of the story of the English traditions of Empire and commerce, which had been remarked upon in passing earlier by Gwendolen and Catherine Arrowpoint in their comments on their respective grandfathers,[46] and also by Rex Gascoigne, as I have suggested. The function of Daniel comes to seem not so at odds with that of other characters. Despite the "strangeness" of his name, despite his self-appointed "foreignness," Daniel's manner of interpretation is as recognizably English as is the condition of the other English characters.

In order to show this, a brief digression at this point; but *to the point* concerning identity and reflection. The digression is one concerning the proper name, its functions and interpretations:

Daniel's function of performing cultural analyses for the reflexive purpose of creating a valid alternative identity involves him in a naming process, a process of translation as naming. Naming as identity through cultural reference is yet one more textual device. This is most obviously the case though, not in a particular analysis of Deronda's, but in the example of Gwendolen's interpretation of Daniel. When she hears his name, she remarks on its strangeness (in terms presumably of her idea of nationality's relationship to signature), asking whether Deronda is English, as I stated earlier.

Names throughout the text have important national-ideological-philosophical resonances beyond their immediate uses and contexts concerning questions of broader identity and Being. Klesmer's surname refers us to a traditional Jewish music, the ethnological or, more properly, ethnographic identity and genealogy of which is understood to be at odds with the "High German" musical/national tradition that the musician ostensibly represents and interprets. Whether or not Eliot's readers would have known what klesmer music was is unknowable; but it is almost certain that Marian Evans, given her research, would have been familiar with the term, hence its use in the novel as a proper name for what we can read as a somewhat subversive purpose.

Rex Gascoigne's name, with its monarchical Latin and geographical-familial medieval French, remarks a displaced desire for some origin, even though that origin may well have been foreign (the name effectively gives the lie to the national myth that all worthwhile origins are English origins; the name displaces the English nation as a founding principle, re-writing them as merely the accidental supplement to French medieval territorialism). And we can read in this name, with its appropriation of the foreign, the historical project of the English, a project which from the time of French invasion had been concerned with the domestication of the foreign, both at home and abroad.

Grandcourt's name suggests a manorial inheritance and palatial (or even Palladian) splendour that has long gone, while the origins of Sir Hugo's family name—Mallinger, Mallingre—is of importance. From its French origins (like Rex's last name, Sir Hugo's name tells the story that the English aristocracy are only the remnants of feudal, baronial Gallic power staked out at the marginal beginnings of the early modern period), the name has come down to a mere homophonic pun, indicative of decadence. Indeed, this is not idle speculation, as the French translates as "sickly." The idea that the family malinger is re-enforced by the inability of Sir Hugo and his wife to produce sons, while the first syllable of the name reiterates the French for "bad," which, it is suggested, has been "in the family since its earliest history." The play that is available in the names seems to write the characters of the figures they name. The characters are inscribed indelibly, embedded by their names as merely the figures of a particular fictional economy that is on the verge of being exhausted, erased through being re-written constantly.

Thus English identity is made available as an effect of translation, and a bad translation at that, one relying for its effect on cliché and stereotype. This is even the case somewhat with Daniel's name, which carries in it the signature of the Judge of the Old Testament, the Judge of his own people. Daniel Deronda is to judge his people, by which I mean the English and not the Jewish people; for Daniel is inescapably English, despite or, perhaps, because of his desire, a desire larger than his own, overdetermined by the traces of national identity. In particular, Daniel judges Gwendolen. In fact, she asks him to judge her, so convinced is she that he has the right to do so. Yet Daniel does not judge according to any Hebraic insight. This Daniel is an English judge, whose name has therefore been domesticated, its orientalism transformed into comfortable, safe English: the Queen's English.

V

Homi Bhabha has suggested that, "Nations, like narratives, lose their origins in the myths of time and only fully realize their horizons in *the mind's eye.*"

Such an image of the nation—or narration—might seem impossibly romantic and excessively metaphorical, but it is from those traditions of political thought and literary language that the nation emerges as a powerful political historical idea in the west. An idea whose cultural compulsion lies in the impossible unity of the nation as *symbolic force*.[47] (my emphasis)

Daniel's cultural compulsion is the impossible idea of national unity, and he attempts to realise his own horizon in his mind's eye with a degree of symbolic force. The unconscious of this text, an unconscious with clearly national concerns of its own, cannot countenance this project, a project which had been the inevitable outcome of the novel's own conscious project, a critique and subsequent dismissal of redundant English culture.

So the text plays a double displacement, a displacement that is also a recuperation *in its own terms*. Daniel's foreignness is not wholly domesticated and so poses a threat to English identity, and all the more so because that identity is partly his own. He is then deferred, expelled from England onto an imaginary site, a site which is also the unending narrative of the quest for a homeland. Yet at the same moment, this quest is brought home because it is to be a quest in terms that the English can understand: Daniel's project is one of colonialism, as has already been mentioned.

If Daniel is displaced because of his foreignness, that which is English in him, that which writes him as English is valorized by the text, as Daniel, at the make-believe of the end of the novel, begins a recovery of nationhood from the English centre; a sort of inverse diaspora which promises the closure of identity (to itself), that closure signed by authority *such as the English have*, to quote Eliot once more. In these words, Daniel makes clear the paradox of English liberal thought, unable to give up the desire for mastery. If the problem, politically, is one of colonialism, then philosophically it is one of humanism too.

In writing of Eliot's agenda in *Daniel Deronda*, Christine Crosby states that Eliot misreads the "texts and traditions" of Jewish culture, seeing in them only a "single, serious truth, the truth of humanism":

> *Daniel Deronda* is thus symptomatic, displaying the workings of a humanism which will do whatever is necessary to consolidate one standard, one reality, the humanity of western, white bourgeois man.[48]

I would agree with Crosby's assessment of the novel, even though I would not claim so certainly that the concerns at stake are necessarily identifiable and, therefore, available for definition as Eliot's *per se*. The concerns, from which Eliot may well have sought to dissociate herself, are those of English identity. I would therefore want to read the agenda in question as part of a broader intellectual current in which Eliot is at work. The current is involved not only with the assertion of history as truth, as Crosby correctly affirms. It is also deeply involved with what it perceived to be at stake in the production of national identity. If the novel narrates the history of humanist man as Crosby states, then politically, specifically, the narration has a national identity; the narration is that of the Englishman who asserts Englishness everywhere by hiding its particularities in the universal folds of humanism. For Eliot, humanism is inescapably a condition of enlightened English identity; and a reflexive identity at that, confronting its own selfhood with the self-as-absolute-knowledge, which effectively closes off identity from internal self-critique.

Whatever objections may be raised to Daniel not really "looking like an Englishman" (the twin model of "native looks" are Rex and Grandcourt; for the Victorian reader, Deronda is too dark) are not valid. He may well be dark-skinned and somewhat oriental (in Said's sense) according to Eliot's descriptions of him; but these descriptions have more to say about the English discourse and its preconceptions on non-English otherness, than they do about Deronda. They partake of a degree of racial stereotyping in which Eliot is herself involved, in having recourse to such external details. However, importantly, what is at stake throughout this novel is Daniel's cultural Being, the ways in which he is inscribed by the culture within which he is raised; the question is one of Being attempting to think itself, articulate itself to itself as thought, as a presence equivalent of and reflecting Being. Daniel is the sum of his intellectual processes, his thoughts and imagination which trace this text so forcefully, and which are themselves not originary, generative discourses but the products of discourse themselves. After all Daniel does have an education *such as the English have*; this is the cultural context that overdetermines his identity.

While Daniel can say to Sir Hugo, "I want to be an Englishman," with a certainty that is unmistakable despite any qualifications he may put forward, his first remark about his Jewish identity in response to his mother is articulated as a question, rather than a statement: "Then I *am* a Jew?"[49] The questioning mode articulates another voice, one that echoes even at this instance with incredulity. The first statement of identity, manifesting desire (the desire to be English) is connected with that other expression of closure, "I am," the previous certainty of which is now undercut by the challenge that the form question presents. "I am" is now an interrogative remark opening an aporia in identity that cannot be filled by any amount of evidence, precisely because identity in the guise of intellect questions the very possibility of its own enunciation. And it is Jewish rather than English identity which is held up to uncertainty, unknowability, being displaced in and through the grammatical structure, foreignness being marginalised once again, because this question cannot stand against the certainty of earlier statements of Englishness. Thus the potential radicality of the openness of the question is undermined because its fragility cannot be turned into a questioning to be turned back against Englishness. In the form of the question is written the anticipation of Daniel's final removal to that imaginary space of nationhood as alterity and symbolic force that the Englishness of the text cannot accommodate.

So the paradox is still there. So bound up is the philosophical-national agenda of this book in the liberal-conservative culture of England that it seeks to criticize, that its only language is that of the self-same culture, a culture the idea of which is predicated on hegemonic simulation. The premise of an opening allowing for the critical analytic is so troublesome to contemplate that self-analysis (that which Daniel's presence initially promises) is deflected onto an idealized utopian space, safe from political engagement. However, even though Eliot cannot position the political engagement, it can be read that she comprehends both its necessity and possibility. As Sally Shuttleworth argues, in *Deronda* Eliot's struggle is in part to find a "language and narrative methodology that could express her radical social vision."[50] We can read a struggle for both struggle and comprehension in the following words from *Daniel Deronda*; words which seem to recognise, against themselves and obliquely, that very paradox that Eliot struggles to resolve, but which she only succeeds in re-establishing by making it more apparent:

> . . . human experience is usually paradoxical, if that means incongruous with the phrases of current talk or even current philosophy.[51]

7

READING TROLLOPE:
WHOSE ENGLISHNESS IS IT ANYWAY?

It should not be possible to read nineteenth-century literature without remembering that . . . [it] was a crucial part of the cultural representation of England to the English. The role of literature in the production of cultural representation should not be ignored.

—Gayatri Chakravorty Spivak

Clearly a regard for "tradition," which is, above all, a cultural construction, where what is "right" and "makes sense" is preserved in historical memory and identified with the fate of the community, with a social group or class, and ultimately with the nation, has much to do with the formation of a native "common sense" and a historical cultural bloc.

—Iain Chambers

Ideological domination—the everyday acceptance of the world and its existing relations of power and social relations—is not imposed from "above," but established across the shifting fields of relations that constitute a shared "consensus." This consensus has to be continually constructed and produced inside the different fields of public representation and social life; it involves not merely political but also "intellectual and moral leadership." In other words, the exercise of power becomes a decentred and profoundly cultural affair.

—Iain Chambers

I

This chapter is concerned with the question of Englishness and its problematised mapping in the Palliser novels of Anthony Trollope. The novels in question are heavily traced by crises of identity, rooted specifically in the local, the political and the discourses of cultural *realpolitik* that inform the hegemonic situation of the English bourgeoisie in the

1870s. Crisis and situation are inseparable; and both have a particular resonance for readers today, after the 1980s and the discourse of Thatcherism, especially with the Thatcherite call for a return to Victorian values.

This imperative on the part of Margaret Thatcher and her Tory-liberal disciples, which has led to the deep economic confusion of John Major's government resulting in subsequent systematic sacrifice and callous betrayal of the working class,[1] is an imperative founded on acts of highly selective, ideological memorialisation. Involved in remembering the past is a capitalisation on favoured fictions, a narrative re-telling of events and a narrative retailing of those events through the currency of Tory-liberal discourse. Such retail has been effected in order that the past may be made to conform somehow to an idea of what the past is, in accordance with a particular dominant ideology in the present. This project is something that we all participate in, either willingly or unwillingly, at one time or another. Narrative reformation is crucial to any project of national identity, but especially so for the New Right, in their dream of a post-empire England; which dream consists in an homogenisation of past situation and present crisis. Trollope, on the other hand, can be read as comprehending such projects and questioning the ideal of unity as political strategy. Trollope's questioning is presented at times with a ferocious irony, as he dismisses supposedly eternal values and the narratives that support them.

The figure of Anthony Trollope imagined behind this essay is one who resists narrative and other forms of co-optation. This Trollope is "comprehensible, hence complex and fragmentary and not the solid referent of a traditional art discourse, a Hollywood film or a neat historical tale."[2] Such a Trollope might seem an estranged figure, especially given his own often repeated political beliefs in Tory-liberalism (a discourse which, in another study, could be seen as differing greatly from the 1980s variety). But I insist on this estranged characterisation because, if we are to move towards a consistently dissident series of readings that manoeuvre counter to the "[i]deological domination" of which Iain Chambers writes above, then it is important that our reading should make strange that which is supposedly familiar; that which, in Chambers's words again, has been said to "make sense" and thereby deployed in the construction of a "shared 'consensus.'"[3]

In 1991, Prime Minister John Major "made sense" of Trollope, appropriating him as the preferred author of Downing Street, and suggesting to the Archbishop of Canterbury that Trollope be given recognition in Poets's Corner at Westminster Abbey (which happened, finally, in March, 1993). The only thing missing from this anecdote is the Master of an Oxford college, and we have a scene worthy of Trollope himself. But this is just one instance of attempted ideological re-writing of the past, leading to various forms of cultural domination. Chambers's talk of ideological domination, and the formation through culture and nationality of a historical cultural bloc, rewrites in broader terms what Spivak alerts us to above with regard to the "role of literature in the production of cultural representation."[4] John Major's comments constitute a single example of the way in which a familiar and domesticated Trollope is constructed. This domesticated Trollope is a particular figure belonging to a particular set of texts and discourses which constitute a "history," an ideological fiction, to which bourgeois-right literary culture has had the "proper access code."[5]

This Trollope is conventionally represented as an author of gently humorous, safe depictions of the everyday. This Trollope is accorded a position in the second division of Victorian authors; not as imaginative as Dickens, nor as philosophical as Eliot; safe ultimately, because he seems to be a mere documentary narrator, more easily—i.e., less troublingly—comprehensible in terms of conservative values.

There are other readings, other Trollopes however, that are, and must be, retrievable. Trollope's texts are our texts, displaced across a field of cultural, political and semantic play. They are crucial to any analysis of the modern palimpsest of national identity, not because they are objects for study that reveal an other('s) epoch but because their "ubiquitous signs" drawn from English culture and identity perform the "illusion and the aesthetization of the world that . . . *is also us.*"[6] (my emphasis)These texts can be read also as one instance of a working out, an uncovering, of the construction—and the constructedness—of a supposedly dominant identity, whilst simultaneously being available as both critique and revelation of the fallacious and illusory nature of the construct.

For even as we read these texts as playing the tropes of a specific identity—for example, that of the English Gentleman, or the English Parliamentary system as the suggested collective identity figured in the lives and relationships of certain sets of characters—we can also remark the mockery of that same identity. This is because identity is understood not as the true statement of national identity, but merely as one more position within Trollope's mapping of a political and cultural centre which, in Trollope's novels, is already decentred. The decentred centre is the pretext of Trollope's writing.

If we acknowledge this, we can produce a Trollope for whom politics is both "the exercise of power" and a "profoundly cultural affair."[7] Trollope reveals that there is no heart at the heart of the British Empire, and Englishness has nothing solid, its identity being a simulacrum. National identity in the Palliser novels is constructed and given repeated performances based on an imagined threat to the self-perceived centre of the upper middle class, a threat which is understood dimly by the members of this class as having something to do with social, political difference; and with this threat, and with the idea of difference itself, Trollope works to produce his decentring fictions. In order to understand this fully, and in order to intervene with Trollope's questioning of Englishness, it is important that we first consider the use of the proper name.

II

Something is always at stake, ideologically, in the proper name and its uses, in the proper name's propriety, and in the property that the name gathers to it. The name fixes a textual body, and the apparent unity of such a body; such has been the case with the domestication of "Anthony Trollope." The name is thus part of an economic question. This is true of course of the cultural assimilation of any novelist's name and works. But Trollope can be read as having anticipated this in the writing of *Phineas Finn*.

So I want to question a particular proper name as a way of undoing the very unity which the name supposedly assigns; I want to play the name as a type of gambit, in order to comprehend how Trollope uses the proper name in order to open up the textuality of English identity.

Phineas Finn/*Phineas Finn*. This signature is both character and title. However, in this case, it is also an agency of refusal (I shall return to this). The use of the name as title is a ploy on the part of novel writing to locate its subject, to insinuate a centre, to compose a textual body that is proper and properly defined within the limits of narrative and ideological convention that is particular to (the subject of) English writing. But Phineas is not an English subject. What then, can be read in this signature? The proper name would seem to make matters simple, announcing the limits, the propriety of that which is to be discussed. This is conventionally the case; but can we read the signature for what it hides? We can perhaps read it for the excesses and the transgressions that the propriety of the signature attempts to silence. We can also read an insertion made by this proper name, made in the name of some other for which this name stands. In such a reading, the proper name becomes somewhat improper. This name, "Phineas Finn," complicates instead of simplifying, its insertion being a breach by Trollope of the "natural order" of English identity; the name effects an incision that refuses closure.

The name of Finn is located centrally, whilst also being a marker of the edge. As a title indicative of a fictional unity—the supposed unity of a fiction and the fictionality of the idea of unity—it is remarked as a preface to its subject (the narrative of the novel) on the border of the text that bears its name. This text, the text that is *Phineas Finn*/Phineas Finn, is always already doubled: the name names the subject, the one to whom the proper name is assigned, and the broader textuality of a cultural artefact and narrative, within which the agent of discourse, subject(ed) to his own signature, is situated. Subject, artefact and narrative: this, more than mere doubling and redolent of the economy of the fictional unity and narrative motif of the dialectic, performs a manoeuvre that cannot be resolved. But listen also to what else is signed in the fantasy of this name.

With its classical propriety and Gaelic impropriety that speaks of the tensions between national identities, the name refuses to be settled into one place. This is true of the figure to whom the name belongs. He refuses to vote according to the directive of the Cabinet over the issue of Irish reform and so resigns, re-signing himself as being not subject to the authoritarian discourses and agendas of the English Government. His resignation is an affirmative refusal of English identity. It is also the mark of a signature belonging to a non-place, both politically and nationally. Ireland is a non-site in the fantasy of the English Empire; In Tory-liberal discourse, it does not exist outside of the empire. Its autonomy can never be other, because, sitting at the border of national identity, it always speaks of otherness to English identity, an otherness on which such identity is violently founded and, without which such identity cannot maintain its existence.

The name, "Phineas Finn," like Ireland from which Finn comes, and like the character whose name this is, exists on borderlines, socially, culturally, politically. The name also survives as a sign of movement between cultures, between dominance and subjugation, between authority and subversion. There is no accident in the choice of the last name, the name that writes over again the first syllable of the classical first name, offering to begin that name again, but from an Irish perspective. With this second beginning however, the supplement with its Gaelic remarking revokes the authority and propriety that the Greek spelling confers and seeks to keep in place. Finn is a good Irish name, suggesting the Irish patriot Finn McCool, from whom the Fenians took their collective name and identity. Phineas Finn is therefore bothersome; like his name and its contexts, he refuses either to go away or be placed, sliding between meanings, between Englishness and Irishness. And Finn's provisional locations and the slippage written in his name are denials of the simplistic, reductive dialectic that English ideology constructs in terms of itself and its neighbour.

The slippage within the structure of the name, the elision that dismantles the laws of that structure, is curiously appropriate to the subject of politics; which is also to say appropriate to the one who is subject to the political and, in this case, the subject—Finn—who is a politician. Finn is political, an Irish Catholic whose name suggests an other national history and identity of resistance and refusal; one also of subversion, of *sub versions* (of dominant narratives, told otherwise). Within Finn's lifetime, Catholic emancipation has been legislated by a Protestant parliament. His voice is thus authorised by the dominant discourse, the language and law of his colonial masters; and is it not ironic that Finn, an Irishman, works at the Colonial office?

However, Phineas traces a fin-like trajectory, between English and Irish, Catholic and Protestant, inside and outside, the colonist and the colonised, self and Other. The figure of Finn charts the sometimes surfacing, sometimes submerged textualities of the mid-nineteenth-century *realpolitik* of the performance of identity, in being part of the mechanisms, structures and institutions of the political aspects of Englishness, whilst also standing at a somewhat oblique angle to that identity; which angle throws identity into relief. Finn's signature is that which for us negotiates a range of positions that are never solely his own, but always readings of a "centre," an example of which is his move from the Irish to the English borough, from Loughshane to Loughton. And the connections, not specifically his own but available within the English Government's reading of Ireland and its own positions during the 1860s, are played from the possible echoes in his name, from the Fenian to the fainéant.

Here are named the possible extremes or borders of political life that we can read from the text. The Fenian and fainéant are not of course the finite limits of ideological situation, anymore than is the name of Finn. But we can read in them, as in the Irish politician's (im)proper name, the epoch of the "violent" outside, made violent by the English reading of the Fenian's "eccentricity" (yet one more position of marginality constructed from the hub of the Empire). At the other extreme, we read the "absolute" inability for any oppositional action on the part of an individual such as Finn because of his being made fainéant politically, having been taken in as a member of a Whig Cabinet. Finn is obviously dangerous enough in the minds of his masters to warrant his promotion to the "heart" of government.

Yet these are brief readings of only the "external" structures of the narrative, a translation of the surfaces of *Phineas Finn*. We need to attend to the "internal" also. The purpose of Finn is, as I have stated, to provide an insertion which is also an opening out. Finn's presence displays the "natural" as ideological, this being uncovered as he moves between the structures of exclusion which operate the fragmented formation of English identity. His presence reads an absolute lack of unity and consensus amongst the upper middle class. Trollope also uses Finn to reveal the political games that are engaged in as part of English politics and Victorian society. And this is achieved in a self-reflexive manner:

> Indeed, when he came to think of it, there appeared to him no valid reason why he should not sit for Loughton. The favour was of the kind that had prevailed *from time out of mind in England*, between the most respectable of the great land magnates, and young rising liberal politicians. Burke, Fox and Canning had all been placed in Parliament by similar influence. Of course he, Phineas Finn, desired earnestly,—longed in his very heart of hearts,—to extinguish all such Parliamentary influence, to root out for ever the last vestige of close borough nominations; but while the thing remained it was better that the thing should contribute to the liberal than to the conservative strength of the House,—and if to the liberal, how was this to be achieved but by the acceptance of such influence by some liberal candidate? And if it were right that it should be accepted by any liberal candidate,—then, why not by him? The logic of this argument seemed to him to be perfect. He felt something like a sting of reproach as he told himself that *in truth this great offer was made to him, not on account of the excellence of his politics* . . .[8]

This passage, Phineas's "internal" reflections on the nature of English political preference, careers across much of what is crucial ideologically to the relationships and social performances engaged in throughout the Palliser novels. I will therefore take the time to unfold this somewhat slowly.

Thought, in the first sentence, has a realist or mimetic quality to it, in that there is suggested the possibility of "appearance," as though ideas were apparitions. Phineas's mind would seem to function as a magic lantern. The grammatical structure tricks us, however. The comic gesture is finely tuned to possible, ambiguous semantic tension. We can read in the sliding between internal and external positions of thought and feeling, this being a locus that is historically determined. The statement, "there appeared to him," is suggestive of an external or metaphysical representation or vision. Not only this, but the "externality" of appearance contradicts the internal location, framed by the process of thinking in the phrase "when he came to think of it." "It," which is very important throughout this passage, posits an empirical object available for enquiry, contradicting and confounding the site of thought as being solely within the subject (Trollope's prose breaks down the limits of both inside and outside). Further, to suggest that someone can "come to it" implies a spatial orientation that, once again, posits the externality of the object of thought.

What is "external" to Phineas is not "his" thought but the textual condition of his being which, as the grammar, syntax and vocabulary make clear, is culturally, historically grounded. Thus it is that the discourse is seen to perform the subject, rather than it being the other way around. We are able to read a denial of an essentialist or humanist concept of identity: "Phineas" is not the lantern so popular in the England of the novel; he is the blank screen on which the discourses of the period are projected. He is a condition of a conceptualisation which is not peculiar to him, but is comprehensible as the often contradictory shifts of Victorian bourgeois perception. It is important to insist on this specificity if we are to register the depth to which the critical insertion of Phineas cuts in the ideology of Victorian identity.

The hyperbole that is wrapped into the first clauses is let down immediately in the negation, "no valid reason," which is in fact what appears. The appearance to Phineas is that of a negation, of validity and reason, the latter intimating both excuse and logic. There is not merely an absence as a simple binary opposite to the subject's self-presence, but the implicitly visual external presentation of the image of negativity.

And as if to counter this positive erasure, what follows immediately is recourse to the texts of both myth and history, both of which are governed by the dominant discourse of Englishness. As if to compensate for the lack of a pure theoretical or abstract logical model—one that we can assume is, in this case at least, unavailable because of its contamination by the local specificity of English liberal politics—textuality attempts to recover a historically valorised moment of subjective unity through the idea of English political narrative as precedent. The phrase, "from time out of mind," implies a continuous history of conferred privilege in the donation of parliamentary seats which has its obscured origins *before* history in a mythical and, therefore, indefinable space.

This being so, such a practice pre-dates any parliamentary or democratic system. It is instead a native tradition, part of the culture and identity of England and the English; and, and part of English consciousness also, as the use of the word "mind" implies. The parties involved in such political transactions are revealed as great magnates and rising liberal politicians. What is interesting is that, throughout the passage, "liberal" is spelt with a lower case "l," thus presenting the term as being related in the English tradition to an ideology rather than, more narrowly, a party. It is not the new money of industry and commercial enterprise that backs the young politicians. Instead, funding and other forms of backing come from those land owners who in conventional wisdom are figured in historical and fictive discourses as Tories.

Here we can read a deal being made between political situations in order to maintain a particular social order that accommodates differing ideologies in favour of a continuing social structure; and that deal is agreed on *in the name of England.* This is clearly an England of a certain group, and not all classes. There is an attempted justification of such a practice (presumably in Phineas's thoughts) by the citation of political figures such as Burke, Fox and Canning. This meeting of the fictive and the real offers us a textual opening up to the reader of English cultural practices supposedly external to the limits of the novel. The figure of Phineas, the figure of his contaminated logic which seeks an unethical justification through a remembrance of English political history, effects an insertion into the social formation that admits of a critical questioning as to the "nature" of the control of power in England. The control of power and the maintenance of Tory-liberal hegemony comes down to something as elusive and as hard to define as "influence" which, as we are witness to here, has little or nothing to do with either a particular part or personality.

Of course in opening up this perspective and in bringing into question the problematic of political manipulation and mediation as discourses of compromise and co-optation, Phineas himself immediately begins to close up the same structure; such is the coercive condition of a right-liberal hegemony. As we can see from this passage, the hegemonic model is effective because it is capable of convincing the majority of the reasonable and pragmatic nature of its appeals and formulations. Even those such as Phineas who initially see the corrupting nature of the system become entrapped. And we can read the effectiveness of such silent coercion in the final line of the passage quoted, where Finn hardly feels the sting at all, but only something like it. Finn's own position within the social/political world and the textual economy of the period does partially cloud his own critical insights into the nature of political compromise, even while his cultural marginality allows him to raise questions that, otherwise, would not be articulated. This drift between clouded vision and critical questioning is a vital part of the formation of identity.

Phineas is able at least to begin the enunciation of the mystified structures of political power. Should this beginning not be available to us, then the novel might well be recuperated into the positions against which this reading seeks to position it, with Phineas being merely one more romantic hero—such as Daniel Deronda, for example—unable to act in any engaged manner, his fate being sealed by some seemingly essential fault. Trollope side-steps such an essentialist teleology to a degree, however, through the performance of a range of voices from various social groups, all of which raise complicating articulations of their own ideological contexts. It is in such pronouncements that we can read the subtle control of, and resistance to, liberal hegemony; it is the function of Phineas Finn that, in being inserted into the discourses of liberal Englishness, he is used by Trollope to reveal the ideological situation of such discourses through his placement and critical understanding of events. Other characters also unfold the mysteries of the political.

III

In Chapter 32, "Lady Laura Kennedy's Headache," it is remarked that, "everyone of those Loughton tradesmen was proud of his own personal subjection to the Earl."[9] The language reveals a feudal mentality that helps maintain a cultural *status quo*. It is the same mentality that ensures Lord Silverbridge's election in *The Duke's Children*,[10] because the tenants understand their subjection to the manorial family, rather than to a political party or ideology. The language of the sentence also reveals a specific section of the middle class—the petty-bourgeoisie in the form of "tradesmen"—whose insertion into the performance of individuality ("his own personal subjection") as "self made men" is particularly strong. This position is further enunciated by Mrs. Low, whose name and husband's status are suggestive of her location within the class system.

Commenting on a letter of Mr. Monk's read to her and her husband by Phineas (in an act of democratic feeling, Phineas takes political discourse to the "people," only to find that the "people" in the shape of the Lows reject the radical agenda), Mrs Low says:

It's [the letter's contents] what I call downright Radical nonsense . . . Why should we want to have a portrait of ignorance and ugliness. What we all want is to have things quiet and orderly.[11]

Radical nonsense. Ignorance and ugliness. Quiet and orderly. The pairing of terms is telling. The first of these three pairs is an almost tautological structure, in the context of Mrs Low's conservatism. The phrase is one of those conjunctive dismissals so beloved by the bourgeois Right, where the development runs as follows: If it's Radical then it must be nonsense; and if it's nonsense then it must be radical.

However, behind this it is clear that the nonsense is not entirely nonsensical but constitutes some type of threat. This is made evident by Mrs. Low who feels the need to continue after her put-down by further rhetorical amplification which questions a mimetic image of unpalatable reality—"why should we want to have a portrait of ignorance and ugliness—in favour of a "reality" which is not real but an ideological construct, one which is quiet and orderly, polite and policed: in short, bourgeois. And what is under threat is the version of national identity to which Mrs. Low subscribes.

It is also of interest to note the mapping of the subject position in this extract. Initially, Mrs. Low qualifies her put-down as her own. "What I call" suggests a naming process, one that is understood by the speaking subject as peculiar to herself. to her articulations. By the end of the statement, the first-person position has been superseded by the plural, liberal community of consensus, "what we all want." The use of "what" as a predicate common to both subject positions aids the easy transference from the individual to the communal. Nominalisation—the indirect desiring function expressed in naming something so as to fix it as a possible possession of the speaker—is replaced by the enunciation of direct desire ("want").

The use of "all" has various effects. It re-enforces the implied community; it suggests a totality and unity to that community from which "radical nonsense" is excluded; and, in the context of the phrasing, pinpoints grammatically Mrs. Low as one of the socially mobile petty-bourgeoisie who has recently moved "up" in the class pecking order, while not having left behind the speech patterns of a lower class group, a group represented in the novel by the Bunces. And the Bunces are represented to us through Phineas's presence as their lodger.

IV

Phineas has a certain social duality. On the one hand, he is an M.P., initially outside the Cabinet, who dines with the aristocracy and other influential political and financial figures; on the other, he is an Irishman in London, a Catholic in a world of Protestant power, not having an income compatible with his social activities. He must take lodgings with people who go unrecognised and unremarked for the most part by his professional colleagues. Thus, he moves along various boundaries, making incursions into mutually exclusive worlds.

One such world is that of the Bunces who, if not poor, exist at the outer limits of petty-bourgeois society. Whilst Mr. Bunce does have a trade, not owning property he cannot vote. Thus Phineas is in a position to allow the reader an understanding of an other England. The representation of the Bunces and their position through Phineas is somewhat problematic however. It partakes of a traditional figure of the "masses." In the middle class imagination, the masses—to borrow Baudrillard's description—"drift somewhere between passivity and wild spontaneity, but always [as] a potential energy."[12] Passivity and wild spontaneity: Jane and Jacob Bunce. Trollope's text is historically recuperated through its representation of the working class couple by the Imaginary of liberal identity and its definitions of its other. In the writing of the Bunces we can read a (sometimes comic) artifice, a crude performance (the working classes are usually comic in middle class representations of them; comedy diffuses both political threat and the nakedness of alterity), the energy of which runs the risk of dehumanising the characters, thereby manipulating our readings.

We thus become read as bourgeois readers, in our efforts to escape the politics of dehumanisation The ideological production of our own reading practices is unveiled in the moment that we comprehend the delegitimising agenda of making a caricature and thus seek for an alternative, more humane reading. The double bind is that, as we try to make Mrs Bunce "more human" for example, we can do so only by reading from the text her motherly and tender-hearted qualities. In doing this we stereotype working class women in a reductive manner by reading only their maternal, feminine energies. Trollope gives only a partial view through Phineas, a middle-class figure whose presence guides our readings of the Bunces, as we, like Finn, like Trollope, are constrained by the provisional limits of the discourses that are at work. We thus need to negotiate the various positions—of the text, of Finn, of the Bunces, and of our readings—with care. With these concerns in mind, one passage proves illuminating:

> "For myself I don't think half so much of Parliament folk as some do. They're for promising everything before they's elected; but not one in twenty of 'em is as good as his word when he gets there."
>
> Mr. Bunce was a copying journeyman, who spent ten hours a day in Carey Street with a pen between his fingers; and after that he would often spend two or three hours of the night with a pen between his fingers in Marlborough Street. He was a thoroughly

hard-working man, doing pretty well in the world, for he had a good house over his head, and could always find raiment and bread for his wife and eight children; but, nevertheless, he was an unhappy man because he suffered from political grievances, or, I should more correctly say, that his grievances were semi-political and semi-social. He had no vote, not being himself the tenant of the house in Great Marlborough Street. The tenant was a tailor who occupied the shop, whereas Bunce occupied the whole of the remainder of the premises. He was a lodger and lodgers were not as yet trusted with the franchise. And he had ideas, which he himself admitted to be very raw, as to the injustice of the manner in which he was paid for his work. So much a folio, without reference to the way in which his work was done, without regard to the success of his work, with no questions asked of himself, was, he thought, no proper way of remunerating a man for his labours. He had long since joined a Trade Union, and for two years past had paid a subscription of a shilling a week towards its funds. He longed to be doing some battle against his superiors, and to be putting himself in opposition to his employers;—not that he objected personally to Messrs. Foolscap, Margin and Vellum, who always made much of him as a useful man;—but because some such antagonism would be manly, and the fighting of some battle would be the right thing to do . . .

Mrs. Bunce was a comfortable motherly woman who loved her husband but hated politics. As he had an aversion to his superiors in the world because they were superiors, so she had a liking for them for the same reason. She despised people poorer than herself . . . the world had once or twice been almost too much for her . . . but she had kept a fine brave heart during those troubles, and could honestly swear that the children always had a bit of meat, though she herself had been occasionally without it for days together.[13]

The image we read of the Bunces is one that, on the surface of things, is very sympathetic, understanding, moderate. Mrs. Low would not object (except, possibly, for the "bit of meat"). But the passage is also very English; it is marked by a middle-class liberal identity because of those self-same, "typically English" qualities: sympathy, moderation, understanding. Trollope's gentle prose invites us to invest these feelings in this uncomplaining, hard-working family and, in doing so, renders critical thinking on the social inequity on which the dominant model of Englishness is founded difficult by engaging our emotions.

Unlike other passages on the lower classes, such as Bunce's arrest outside the Houses of Parliament, this description largely avoids comic effect. The arrest of Mr. Bunce is described somewhat farcically, and this does tend to delegitimise workers' rights. We can speculate that the scene is farcical because of the supposed "threat" of an organised proletariat is too great a challenge psychically to the middle class. Also, Trollope focuses on the individual, whose character we are already familiar with. Such a focus tends towards depoliticising the scene which also again denies the potential power of the workers. Unlike the farcicality of the arrest, there is a touch of humour in Jane Bunce's references to "a bit of meat" for the children, but the humour is warm, designed to elicit from us a sympathy toward the mother for her valour, self-denial, "natural instincts" and "Dunkirk spirit" manifested against the world in general, and her husband's politics in particular. Like Mrs Low, Jane Bunce respects order and social hierarchy, hating politics.

Thus the question of national identity is bound up in the narrative mediation of that identity with a question of gender, and I shall return to this issue in a moment. Notice how Bunce's fight for his rights is a "manly thing" to do. Trollope divides the Bunces through the gendered political attitudes, leaning towards Mrs. Bunce's fuzzy conservatism, rather than her husband's macho radicalism (notice, though, how the sympathetic narrative direction is not present in scenes concerning Mrs. Low; Trollope's is not a blanket conservatism). However, the Bunces are united in the reading of them as a typical English couple of their class and historical period. The passage can be read as promoting that vision through the very identification of their gendered qualities, of tenaciousness, self-consciously fuzzy thinking, tender-heartedness and fortitude (remove Trollope's satirical edge and his sharp political observation, and you end up with Noel Coward). And the problem with this vision is that it is the middle-class image of the working people that has survived with minor adjustments for over 150 years. Inadvertently or not, Trollope has recourse to re-present the heavily loaded image, beloved of the New Right in the 1980s and '90s, of the family-as-national-identity, an image perpetuated in the self-interest of the right-liberal ruling order.

This passage is disturbing because, though I read it as wanting to be honest and sympathetic, honest because sympathetic, it finally gives way to the dishonesty of emotional proximity and familiarity. The cultural construction of the identity of the "family" relies on the relationship between female feeling and social *status quo*. The woman's supposed illogicality—and, by inference, lower class women as a definable group—becomes the fictitious site of the family's stability (registered through food and respect), despite the husband's politics. Bunce's activities become somehow unpleasant because it is implied that his wife suffers as a result of them. Because the woman feels, we are susceptible to ignoring her emotional responses as a text written onto her engendered figure, a text hostile to oppositional and dissident political activity; so, the traditional reading of woman is deployed by conservative discourse, in order to displace and mystify its own political activities which are involved in keeping the husband a docile, subservient worker.

We would be wrong though, to blame Trollope for the ideological "fault" that we perceive. What happens in this passage is a result of cultural contingency, of historical and cultural situation; the passage is written, in short, by the discourses of Englishness that Trollope is seeking to interpret and question through the figure of Phineas Finn. Importantly, the passage does at least offer a limited intervention into areas of social life that are grey and to which the middle class Victorian reader might well be ignorant or hostile. While Bunce's response to "Parliament folk" is a stock enunciation of "the common man," his "raw" thinking of the conditions under which his work is produced is more finely tuned, albeit momentarily. This becomes overwritten by the metaphor of battle that would seem to make the issue less serious for its being somewhat clichéd. We read the passage as tracing with some difficulty an issue of considerable complexity that the dominant discourses of the period gather up ultimately. What we can read, and that very clearly, is a typical instance of the bourgeois formation of national identity, and its efforts to domesticate and make safe its Other. This formation is one still being strategically deployed in the last decade. And it is such a formation against which Phineas is written as struggling.

However, before turning to Phineas, we need to look at the question of gender as Trollope uses it in relation to national identity and in the complication of ideological positions across class.

The problem of the "female position on politics" is further complicated by Glencora Palliser. While Mrs. Low and Mrs. Bunce express conservative views about society and class position, Glencora is given one of the more "progressive" or "radical" speeches in *Phineas Finn* (and we are witness to this because of Phineas's presence at Loughlinter). In Chapter 14, Glencora follows through the logical thread of certain liberal thinking, challenging the "liberalism" of Mr. Monk and Mrs. Bonteen.[14]

Glencora states her reading of "our political theory," which is to make "men and women all equal." This shocks Monk, the proponent of "radical nonsense," who "cries off" from the discussion. Glencora responds, "If I were in the Cabinet myself I should not admit so much . . . there is an official discretion." Glencora's remarks illuminate the silencing that is effected by being at what is supposedly the centre of political power. From her constantly shifting position on the fringes of that centre, Glencora, like Phineas, is empowered in her relative marginality to read the unarticulated premises of English bourgeois hegemony. She goes on to spell out these premises to Mrs Bonteen in didactic fashion. Taking Mrs Bonteen's comments as criticism of "me and my politics"—a phrase important for its connection of the personal and/as political in any definition of identity—Glencora states that liberalism is concerned with :

> making the lower orders comfortable . . . and educated, and happy, and good . . . make them as comfortable and good as yourself . . . I am not saying that people are equal; but that the tendency of all law-making and of all governing should be to reduce the inequalities.

Glencora's speech reveals the furthest limits of a particular reformist ideology, and also its own blindness to its own order and the power it attempts to wield. The economic necessity of liberalism is to create subjects, to subject the "lower orders" to a state of control and policing through jurisdiction and governmental legislation (Glencora's belief is in a trickle-down theory of government).

Education, happiness, comfort and moral well-being are the cornerstones to the effectiveness of the hegemonic maintenance of a docile proletariat. Notice that nowhere does Glencora suggest an actual change of class position for the others of England; nor are her "radical" proposals founded on any suggestion of concrete social change. Instead she invokes a certain indirect political discourse that encompasses the working class through a range of easily changeable theoretical positions. And it is a sign of the conservatism of the liberals listening to Glencora that they think Glencora's politics "too fast and furious."

Given statements such as Glencora's, which we should always read against the grain, and the positions of women such as Mrs. Low or Jane Bunce, it is difficult, if not impossible to suggest a final position of authority at which Trollope comes to rest on the subject of women's political attitudes. Certainly Trollope complicates the issue by ranging issues across both gender and class in such a fashion that we can fix no final political position to his understanding of national identity and the political mediations of Englishness.

There is, I believe, a degree of political irony, a playful but "responsible" anarchy with which Trollope infects his text; this ironic resonance suggests the impossibility of absolute authority and the redundancy of any effort to assume such a position of mastery. This could of course be merely another ploy of liberal humanism, which states that this is the way things are, and that there are no right or wrong positions, only beliefs and collective systems of beliefs which come to be refigured in the form of identity. However, this double bind of undecideability seems to undercut itself in offering such didactically stated moments of antagonism. Trollope constructs the textual antinomies in such a way that we are forced as readers to come to a political decision based on the contradictory choices offered us by Trollope, for which we are ultimately responsible. Reading any of Trollope's fictions, we come to comprehend the necessity for continued interventions into the culture of our identity.

V

It is the problematic condition of Phineas Finn's interventions into the cultures of England which keep the text alive for us. For, although Finn's presence ultimately offers a liberal reading (which is not necessarily ours) of historical currents, against this reading's implied recuperation of social difference and antagonism (which antagonism Trollope does not resolve other than in terms of Phineas's narrative), there is always to be remembered Phineas's own otherness. If Finn coalesces, it is because he has no other choice; he is unable to interpret his contexts in any other way.

At the beginning of Chapter 25,[15] Phineas's return to London precedes the narration of the political troubles, involving troops, the 40-50,000 strong "mob," and the possible dissolution of the government over the issue of the Ballot. We may perhaps see Phineas's presence as the generator of events; not in the sense that he actively contributes to or causes unrest, but that, in terms of the narrative, he is placed so as to be an involved witness, moving between the "inside" and "outside" of events. His identity is constituted as a narrative performance that does not admit of fixture, but is deliberately floated so as to "read" the various events. This allows us to comprehend both the inside of the House and Mildmay's position, and the situation of the "man in the street" as performed by Bunce. Finn's articulation in the narrative, and his deployment throughout the text, is a sustained reading and writing of the tensions within English culture, subject position and the exigencies of national identity. Without Finn the foreigner, it would not be possible to encounter Bunce's activism, or his reasons for agitation.

At the request of Mrs. Bunce, Phineas tries to intervene with Bunce, in order to prevent him being involved in the political disruption. It is typical of Finn's political blindness that he identifies the working class as "all the roughs of London."[16] However, Bunce, whose interest is in getting the vote—to him a crucial factor in the constitution of his Englishness, and the recognition by the upper classes of his stake in national identity—and who is described as a "respectable member of society" prior to Phineas's remark, is able to articulate his political thoughts so as to dismiss Phineas's summing up of the proletariat as "roughs":

> If everybody with a wife and family was to say so, there'd be none there but roughs, and then where should we be? What would the Government people say to us then? If every man with a wife was to show hisself in the streets to-night, we should have the ballot before Parliament breaks up, and if none of 'em don't do it, we shall never have the ballot. Ain't that so? . . . If that's so . . . a man's duty is clear enough. He ought to go, though he'd two wives and families.[17]

Turning Finn's own language against him (as Wilkie Collins points out in his preface to *Man and Wife*, the term "rough" belongs to middle class discourse for keeping the working class in their place; at least in the bourgeois imagination[18]), Bunce makes a clear and direct appeal for political activism, and for not shying away from the political responsibility that every person has as a member of civil society.

Civil society for Bunce has, as its basis, the nuclear family. He seeks a political voice in the name of that family and every family, and regards his responsibility as common to every "man." For Bunce, the question of political responsibility is a gendered, heterosexually normative one. We may mistakenly criticise Bunce for the ideological import of his position. But we must remember that we are reading the statement of a poorly educated, working class male of the 1870s, who holds a belief in fair democratic change, founded on the rights of workers and the systematic, legislated protection of those rights. Despite the humorous portrayals of Bunce elsewhere, commentaries such as the one above cut through the humour to make a valid and politically urgent point which, instead of being criticised, can be adapted to include the rights of all oppressed groups.

As a Tory-liberal, Trollope may well have been antipathetic to the idea of unions and reform of suffrage, but what his intentions were do not compromise the picture. As Antonio Gramsci has put it:

[a]lthough the author's specific aims must be considered when judging his work, this does not mean therefore that some other real contribution of the author should be omitted or disregarded or depreciated, even if it is in opposition to the ostensible aim.[19]

If we do not recognise this and, in recognising it, historicise the scene of writing, then we read carelessly, not seeing the valency of articulations by those who are otherwise culturally elided. Bunce's statement posits the potential for the construction of a national identity—through political action—that is positive. It is positive because it imagines the enunciation of an identity which hitherto had no voice. It is a measure of the strength of Bunce's speech that Phineas has no argument against it; indeed, he cannot even speak. Bunce carries the point, and the conversation closes with the silence of the representative of politics in the face of the powerless man.

VI

Having presented cultural structures which are prolematised by the positioning of Phineas, I want to imagine a certain crisis foregrounded by *The Prime Minister*.[20] The crisis is not "in" the narrative in any simple way. It exists as an instance of the cultural unconscious that we can attempt to map, from this novel and across other texts. The crisis is located across issues of definition and the impossibility of translation. It is also registered between two entirely interchangeable and moveable poles, the personal and political. The personal and political are bound up with each other, each dependent on the other. Both can be questioned in the context of Trollope's writing through a questioning of Trollope's uses of the categories "Gentleman" and "Coalition."

In *The Prime Minister*, the question of Ferdinand Lopez's origins is overdetermined by the insistent dalliance around his ambiguous status as a "gentleman." If he can be read as being a gentleman then, in Abel Wharton's eyes at least, Ferdinand can also be read as being an Englishman. And herein lies the danger for Wharton's sense and conceptualisation of national identity; if the foreign is admitted as being on an equal footing with Englishness, then the cultural value of English identity is debased. This is because, as Terry Eagleton has suggested, "to acknowledge someone as a subject is at once to grant them the status as oneself and to recognise their otherness and autonomy."[21] For Wharton, a "gentleman" and an "Englishman" are one and the same, the questions of breeding, heredity and national identity being linked inextricably.

Wharton's fears, therefore, are not peculiar to him, but figure the very question of the sovereignty of the subject. But opposed to Wharton, to open a gap in the text that allows our thinking on the subject, is the remark that:

> It was admitted on all sides that Ferdinand Lopez was a "gentleman." Johnson says that any other derivation of this difficult word than that which causes it to signify "a man of ancestry" is whimsical. There are many, who in defining the term for their own use, still adhere to Johnson's dictum;— but they adhere to it with certain unexpressed allowances for possible exceptions.[22]

In this passage, Dr. Johnson and his dictionary are invoked by Trollope in a game of cultural semantics that refuses to fix the issue. Despite the fact that Lopez's social status and performative identity are "admitted on all sides" (the passive voice of the first sentence obscures the origin of the remark, slipping it into the doxical coinage of cultural discourse), nothing could be further from definition.

Throughout the passage, indeterminacy opens up the reliability of definition to vague contradictions and gaps. As we know from reading the "all sides" of Trollope's texts, such sources are notoriously unreliable and, in some cases, redundant, because the "collectively expressed ideas of the bourgeoisie"[23] are seen to be paradoxical; this is the case with Wharton's objections to Lopez's cultural mapping and the general ambiguity surrounding Lopez's social position. This is a textual world caught up in the failure to comprehend textuality; a world where members belonging to the same club as Lopez only "pretend to read"[24] and "people don't read Pope now, or if they do they don't take the trouble to understand him."[25] And if such is the standard of comprehension amongst those who inhabit the world, then what is admitted on all sides need not be taken seriously, because the definition of a gentleman would seem to rely on the protocols of reading and interpretation.

As we see here, the skills of reading and interpretation are spectacularly absent. The only person who once read is Abel Wharton, who can no longer complete a reading, but can only "try" the novels (as he does his cases), unsuccessfully.[26] When thinking of Lopez, Wharton 'feels' that he must refrain from "talk in ambiguous language of what a 'gentleman' would or would not do,"[27] and tells Lopez that he wants "no definitions."[28] Abel is un-Abel, unable to read and scared of the consequences of interpretation. Note that, in the passage in question, Wharton's thought is not fixed dogmatically as are his remarks. "Internally," the discourses with which he presents and constructs his identity in his social context are altogether equivocal. He 'feels' rather than states, recognising his own inability to translate and define in the ambiguity of his statements on the subject of the "gentleman." The quotation marks employed by Trollope write silently the re-marking of the "gentleman" as a dubious and provisional category, which Wharton fails to assert so unsure is he in the context of his reading. He makes plain that he wants no definitions, thereby testifying to his own internal acknowledgement that his own identity is in a process of deconstruction.

Wharton's cultural identity is at stake. He is not even able to assert his own Being-as-gentleman, so called into doubt is the cultural text. Reading and, therefore, translation are faced with the threat of the foreign and new, and are passing away. The resolution of the question of "gentleman-ness" is deferred infinitely, displaced and consumed even as it is foregrounded and made excessive, something larger than and beyond translation (into English), just like the "Englishness" that Wharton insists on as the corollary definition of the "gentleman."

In the context of politics then, which is the context of the Palliser novels, that context by which Trollope unfolds for us the question of (the crisis of) national identity, what should the Government of England be composed of, if not "gentlemen"?

VII

If the category of "gentleman" is always already placed by Trollope in the abyss of the not-read, how are "gentlemen" to read themselves in terms of their public duty to their country, given that they too are unable to read? Perhaps the possibility of a partial interpretation, an interpretation involving compromise, lies in the category of the "coalition."

We understand Trollope revealing that no one authoritative definition of the state is possible, so dispersed are the party readings—dispersed within party structures and from one party to another—of the national text. The parties in question must therefore form a "coalition" from both Tory and Whig camps, in order to re-read national identity, such is the crisis of textuality. And our readings of the crisis in Trollope as a moment of fracture is due in part to what Terry Lovell defines as "comic implausibility" and "authorial intervention"[29] which are perceivable as undermining the authoritarian figure of the Gentleman, as reader and writer of Englishness. Yet Tory liberal identity on which the Gentleman depends for self definition is only possible through a coalition of ideologies; this is given political form, and thereby made visible, by Trollope, through the Coalition of *The Prime Minister*. At the head of this political compromise is Plantagenet Palliser.

Palliser's name is as significant as Phineas Finn's. Palliser's first name recalls a patronymic which carries in it a founding moment for the English aristocracy. The name also suggests a narrative of that aristocracy as a particular trace in the historical formation of an exclusive and hierarchical Englishness. So, perhaps Palliser can be called "a gentleman." Trollope wrote of his character that, "I think that Plantagenet Palliser, the Duke of Omnium, is a perfect gentleman. If he be not, then I am unable to describe a gentleman."[30] Trollope's statement carries an implied uncertainty that the author's cultural context—that out of which Trollope brings the whole category of "gentleman" into question in his novels—will undo his effort to describe a "gentleman." This ambiguity can be read in Palliser's names and the title of Prime Minister.

Palliser is not only himself. His identity is spread across a range of public and national signatures that are always in the service of a larger identity. Not only does his first name speak a narrative of English history, but his title also denies him a private, unified subjectivity. As Prime Minister, Palliser is re-written as the subject of Englishness, the representative of that identity and the ideologies of his party, and, as an elected figure, the property of "the people." In this issue of public names, we can begin to comprehend how "bourgeois theories of universal liberty and individualism are ideological,"

for they conceal the property-based interests of civil society. Despite its "appearance of guaranteeing individual freedom," civil society actually guarantees merely the freedom of private property's interests to carry on a running battle to extract surplus value.[31]

This "running battle" is carried out in the public and private names of Plantagenet Palliser. His names are the signs of bourgeois ideology's investment; they guarantee the continued extraction of surplus-value which, in the case of nineteenth-century literature and across the site of the "gentleman," is the continued production of (the meaning of) the ideology of Tory-liberal Englishness. The plurality of names and the confidence they are meant to inspire are a confidence trick in the service of hegemony. Trollope shows that the figure of the aristocratic gentleman as leader of and servant to his country is a political performance. Through its implicit appeals to inheritance, heredity, continuity and the maintenance of social divisions, the performance suggests a "natural" or "given" order. This in turn hides the exploitation of the concept of the individual.

Plantagenet is mobilized by Trollope in order to promote, albeit ironically, the Englishness of the English middle classes to themselves.

Yet Trollope's writing refuses the invisible suturing that would suggest the natural order (and, therefore, mark Trollope's texts with an unthinking conservatism and coalescence with the dominant ideology) through devices such as those identified above by Terry Lovell. And we can read the gaps opened by the stitches in the suture. As "The Prime Minister" (the definite article erases the personal in favour of the performative personality), Palliser is a doubled body, doubly read as leader both of the two parties in the form of the Coalition, and of the English people. His other, hereditary title, the Duke of Omnium, is translatable as a pun suggesting that he has command over all. This we know to be untrue. In his private life, Palliser has no command over Glencora or his children, other than that which they allow him. Certainly, he has no control over the government he supposedly leads. His titles, rather than being the signatures of centred power, are the authorisation of powerlessness. He is the subject of a writing that shows his own helplessness and marginality as a fainéant politician. Yet, because he is a "gentleman," his image is supposedly invested with power; here is the internal contradiction that Trollope plays out, and which we can read as the constant paradox of bourgeois ideology, from which come the crises of right-liberalism. And the figure of the "coalition" is merely the grouping of the powerful-helpless, of the political(ly) powerless; of gentlemen unable to read the crisis of their own identity.

The crisis is one of historical transition and epistemological discontinuity. Which is precisely why so many are unable to read; and why the Liberal club—named, ironically, the "Progress," given the political impotence Trollope reveals—to which Wharton's son and Lopez belong is unable to muster a unified front or identity for support of the party. The concept of the club, which had done "little or nothing"[32] as a unifying organisation, offers a social remapping of the political failure of gentlemen in misreading the epochal transition within which they are caught, and by which, paradoxically, they are produced. These same men, who belong to the Progress Club, are also those who support the Coalition.

"Coalition" is yet one more name for a club, and speaks of the similarities and homogeneity of traditional political discourse, whatever its party stripes or ostensible differences. We can read the failure of the gentlemen of the Coalition to read their own situation. Even though they perceive something of the crisis, they are unable to perceive the crisis as of their own making; instead of turning to self-analysis, they look outwards to a metaphysics of illusory unity. Thus, they form a cabinet that takes the moderates of both parties, whilst attempting to avoid Church reformists, Home Rulers and "philosophical Radicals."[33] Yet again, Palliser is typical of the failure to perceive the problem of liberal identity. Plantagenet's particular blindness to his own situation as a crisis of cultural and social making is registered in a remark to Glencora: "Cora, there are different natures which have each their own excellencies and their own defects."[34] So immersed is Plantagenet in the discourses that read and write him, that he can only find fault within himself with his running of the Government, perceiving the trouble as that of human nature. Palliser proposes a theoretical model of human existence, reliant on an atomistic and essentialist view of humanity. His view reveals to us the moment of self-unawareness in liberal humanist ideology. Thus his identity is enmeshed by liberal humanist belief, which blinkers him to comprehending the material conditions that inform the turmoil and insularity of English society in the 1870s,[35] a turmoil produced by the economic policies of successive Tory and Whig governments, and by gentlemen such as Palliser. This turmoil led to a round of ever deepening recessions, widespread unemployment and "chronic anxiety" in public opinion.[36]

So, we come to read that the "heads of the parties were at a standstill."[37] Palliser feels unequal to the task of writing the list of Cabinet members, so ambivalently does he regard the power that is not his. We can comprehend from our reading of Trollope an apparent stasis and impotence. This lack of movement is Trollope's registration of an epistemic break, focused for late Victorian culture by Trollope in the problematic status of the category of "gentleman." As Trollope makes us aware, both the problem and the cultural reliance on the concept of the "gentleman" inform the ideologies of both parties in their attempts to represent the "true" politics of national identity. And it is this incestuous, familial resemblance between ostensibly different party-political positions that constitutes the momentary ends of a particular form of paternal authoritarianism that, during the 1870s and 1880s, found itself unable to stand before or against the strategies of the slowly emergent petty-bourgeois hegemony which it had helped to produce. Trollope's governments shuffle from one muddle to another, as did the governments of Trollope's England, and as is the current administration of John Major, unable to effect change in the face of social problems comparable to those in the 1880s.

VIII

If Trollope does not offer us a clear political position in opposition to the dominant Tory-liberal model of his time, this does not mean a retreat from politics on Trollope's part. Rather, we should read his resistance to position as an engaged play, the inconclusiveness of which is, to quote James R. Kincaid, "characteristic of the ironic form."[38] Such open-endedness determines the possibility of hope for a new and fairer politics of Englishness, a politics of the margin and other Englishnesses.

Reading Trollope is a small enough beginning in the attempted determination of rethinking national identity. But from reading Trollope's complications of Victorian culture, we may be able to comprehend our own performed and performative functions, and so start to interfere with the political processes that mediate our identities. These suppositions are not necessarily hopelessly utopian or naively idealist. It is, after all, out of a desire for articulation through the figure of an alternative political community looking after the interests of the marginal that Jacob Bunce joins a trade union, the idea of which was in the 1860s and '70s not that much more fanciful that Septimus Harding's imaginary 'cello.

We need to imagine an articulation as a reaction to the discursive re-runs of the "Victorian" epoch that the authoritarian ideology of the New Right has financed and invested in, in the name of national identity. This "normative Victoriana" is a phantasm of our own culture, rather than being some truth of a bygone age. That which is presented to us is really the work of a political economy desirous of maintaining its power through the tyranny of a fictive unity.

This tyranny, manifested as the evocation of the previous century's identity, belongs to an effort on the part of the New Right to deal with the paradoxes of its own corporate-liberal beliefs. In Alan Sinfield's words:

> Margaret Thatcher's calls for a return to "Victorian" values are intended to deal with this difficulty by evoking a time when aggressive competition co-existed with tradition, family, religion, responsibility and deference . . . New-right economic policy encourages selfish social attitudes, but community feeling cannot be invoked or acknowledged because it is likely to sound like socialism . . . Thatcher's difficulty in specifying the right kind of individualism makes it all the more necessary to harp on about Englishness, respectability, family and nation.[39]

Finn cannot build a "family" of his own in England, his nation and religion held at arm's length as just one more barely tolerated property of the English. His first, Irish wife dies in childbirth and he cannot marry into the society around which he hovers, at times despairingly. At the centre of that society is Plantagenet Palliser, who is just as caught as

Finn. Both men foreground the problems of liberal ideology, rather
than celebrating it. Economic competitiveness, selfishness and aggressive
individualism are the direct consequences of Palliser's political philosophy, and it is these same negative aspects—of Tory-liberalism—that undo
Palliser, and not "human nature" as he seems to think.

But more importantly, what Trollope can be read as unravelling
are the subtly written protocols that hide their ideological chicanery
underneath the speculative concepts such as "family," "nation" and "gentleman" which are still the stock in trade of the New Right's polemic.
Trollope can make us laugh at the deadpan earnestness of the Right, as
he writes its figures larger than life. Nationalist liberalism is made farcical; and the political value of farce in our reading is that an alternative
"reality" is not offered. Trollope leaves things up in the air as the structures and institutions are revealed as shaken. The margins are opened to
us. Those who inhabit the margins seek to articulate their identities
beyond the Tory-liberal ethos. Whether or not they realise their desire is
not important, for to understand this would be to read one more closure; and closure is still closure, the conservative recuperation of the
other effected, the old order re-established. Trollope "lets go" of control.
In doing so, he intimates to us that there is always another story, others'
stories, to be told.

(In) Conclusion:
Towards a New Victorianism?

We cannot yet trust what I've been calling "national identity."

—Jacques Derrida

. . . a "past" that has never been present, and which will never be.

—Jacques Derrida

The close attention to which Englishness has been submitted in this study may seem, at times, overly concerned with apparently inconsequential details. Similarly, the narrow focus on Englishness alone, as opposed, say, to Britishness, may be conceived or misread as somewhat parochial. But if we cannot yet trust national identity—and by "trust" I mean place uncritical faith in any simply defined version of national identity—or if the term "national identity" is to be opened to any kind of ongoing critique, then it is crucial that closely, slowly, we begin to come to grips with the minutiae of a specific "national identity," if only to comprehend that what is being questioned is not "national identity" but, rather, national identit*ies*. And what better place to start than with that "identity" which is arguably the most resistant to questioning? What nation, more than the English, relies on its well constructed performance of reasonableness, ordinariness, everydayness, naturalness? Such qualities are aggressively impervious to questioning, "rooted" as they are in seemingly organic traditions.

What I have sought is to effect ways through such polished performances of the ordinary, to look at Englishness at a particular moment by getting behind the façades; amplifying, caricaturing, magnifying and, in some cases, distorting, precisely so that the ordinary should seem that much more a performance capable of being thought and articulated differently, and much less natural, immutable, fixed and resistant to change. This in itself is not a new technique. Indeed, I perceive it to be a very "Victorian" mode of analysis. Think of any Dickensian "distortion" of "human nature" and you will see what I mean. Think also, for a moment, of a text such as Elizabeth Barrett Browning's *Aurora Leigh*.

The poem's reception in England was, in many instances, hostile, and for this reason: precisely because Barrett Browning was calling into question national, class-based assumptions about the "nature" of women in relation to Englishness. The "woman question" was fiercely debated in the mid-Victorian period, as is well known. But Barrett Browning's treatment of the question within an always specifically spelled-out context of national identity heightens the polemic and forces us to address the issue of Englishness as the material and spiritual condition which formulates the "woman question" in the first place. As Cora Kaplan points out in her introduction to the poem, several "reviewers object[ed] to *Aurora Leigh* as being 'not a genuine woman.'"[1] Barrett Browning's technique is successful because she raises the issue of gender directly, that is to say "unnaturally," by doubling Aurora's identity making her both Italian and English, Catholic and Church of England. And it is significant that the Italian mother is sacrificed—she dies when Aurora is four—in order that the very English father, an "austere Englishman" who muses on "English questions" such as the raising of taxes,[2] can be seen to have the greater influence on Aurora, thereby introducing the tensions of national identity that torment the poem throughout.

The example of *Aurora Leigh* raises the question of other national identities and of the contest between Englishness and the "foreign." This study may well have implications for other national identities and their study, but it is neither my place, nor my intention to seek to tell others how to pursue those analyses; the questions to be asked must of necessity be different for every identity. Thus, where I have had recourse to talk of the foreign, as in the chapters on Wilkie Collins, George Eliot and, to a lesser extent, Elizabeth Gaskell, the foreign has not been my focus *per se*. Foregrounding the foreign would mean running the risk of reducing all other identities to a single "foreign identity," unless this study were dedicated to reading the signs of specific national identities. Rather, where the "foreign" has been read it has already been filtered through the lens of the writer, text and culture that I am reading. The "foreign" has already been deployed, by Eliot and Collins for example, in order to focus on Englishness from another position, in order to avoid a degree of parochialism. In terms of this study, parochialism in a postmodern age may well be a provisionally suitable self-conscious posture against nascent or immanent colonialist tendencies that the English have always deployed so effectively in the past.

Taking Marx's famous dictum, that in order to understand his methods it was necessary for his readers to follow him from the particular to the general, as a guideline, I have begun, again and again throughout these readings with particulars in order to perform a fragmented sense of identity that repeatedly, and in different contexts, estranges English organic wholeness. And this particularity has involved the choice of "nineteenth-century literature" as one possible starting point.

Performances of "national identity" in the nineteenth century constitute a contesting field of discursive and social activities, as the preceding chapters show. The situations of identity enunciated by the literature of the last century are broadly dispersed. Following these readings, we can suggest with a degree of certainty that "Victorian values," understood as the philosophies, knowledge and abstracts of lived practices, are not reconstructable in any seamless, logical fashion. There is not a restricted economy that can be given the name of Victorian ideology or Victorian identity. Rather, there is a general economy of national identity that is self-contradicting, knowingly self-assertive, constantly questioning and simultaneously blithely unaware of its own conditions of being. This identity—these identities—is/are "modern," "romantic," "classical" and "postmodern," among the various names which can be alternated and/or conjoined (Polonius had a point perhaps). Englishness is perceivable only as a structure inhabited by, and constructed out of, difference. Fear and desire mark domestic identity as much as ironic laughter in the face of attempted conservative consolidations of the key markers of that (those) identity (identities).

The literature of the nineteenth century does speak to us of national identity, however, and positively, of difference-in-identity, of the possibility of Being-Other within the gaps in (any narrow definition of) Englishness. This study has moved from fear of the other, through critiques of domestic identity to laughter in the face of domestic fear and incomprehension, as a means by which to set out towards other English identities from a domestic perspective. This is a journey into, rather than away from, the structures of identity; this conclusion is really not a conclusion, but a departure point, unlike the disguised detours and returns of Coleridge and Wordsworth with which I "began," and to which, it can be argued, we have been returned by the discourses of the New Right.

The literature by which this study opened the question of identity provides an opening itself; through these readings onto a common space for the complication of the articulation of Englishness. This common space, understood as being always open (to risk a Derridean pun, how can Being be anything other than always open, open to the other, to otherness itself, as part of an ethical understanding of alterity?), always unfixed, suggests, to borrow a term of Derrida's, other headings[3] for identity, founded on an understanding of national identity as being marked indelibly by heterogeneity and difference.

The figure of the other heading is multiple. It posits alternatives, and alterity also, as a political necessity for the reformation or deconstruction of identity. The question of the other heading, which this study has sought to indicate throughout, positions new starts, new directions from conventional sites, fields and spaces already established (such as "national identity," "Victorian values," "Literature," "close readings"). In fact, each chapter, whilst working as part of the general "other heading" that the study moves towards, constitutes an other heading in itself. This is so inasmuch as each chapter is itself an example; an example not of an analysis of this "thing" called "national identity," but an example of an analysis of "the discourses that assume a certain relationship to the particular" subject, and "of the forms and means by which opinion becomes visible and effective."[4] Each chapter constitutes not a landing point, such as Dover Beach, but a jetty[5] which points both out and in, traversing and destabilising the boundaries of national identity. Each chapter renders a different identity, another Englishness, an *other* Englishness. Each calls to mind headings, directions, all of which are part of the heading "national identity." Yet all demand that even identity is simultaneously part of and other than this heading, this title which gathers together these readings.

Derrida puts it this way:

> The expression "The Other Heading" can . . . suggest that another direction is in the offing . . . that it is necessary to change destinations. To change destination can mean to change goals, to decide on another heading . . . Indeed, it can mean to recall that there is another heading, the heading being not only ours . . . but the other . . . not only that which we identify, calculate, and decide upon, but the *heading of the other*, before which we must respond, and which we must *remember, of which* we must *remind ourselves*, the heading of the other being perhaps the first condition of an identity or identification that is not an egocentrism destructive of oneself and the other.
>
> But beyond *our heading*, it is necessary to recall ourselves not only to the *other heading*, and especially to the *heading of the other*, but also perhaps to the *other of the heading*, that is to say to a relation of identity with the other that no longer obeys the form, the sign, or the logic of the heading . . .[6]

In seeking to analyse the "Victorian" responses to Englishness, to national identity, this study has tried to respond to the otherness that is

"Victorian," an other identity/identities, the otherness of which we must remind ourselves, as Derrida puts it. For the point here is that, if we are to understand ourselves, we must recall to ourselves our other, our "Victorian other" if you will, recalling it without appropriation or the dream of mastery. We must recall it as an *other* Englishness, speaking of itself as an identity constituted not by the closure of selective representation, but alive, living on, contesting, playing between its discourses and performances of what has been a convenient, provisional "heading" for this study, "Englishness."

In discerning such "Victorian" alterity in the very heart of nineteenth-century English culture, in its mainstream representations of itself to itself, I have sought to demonstrate how the headings—Englishness, national identity—cannot be referred to with absolute equanimity, authority or reverence, as though there were some final Truth to identity. In returning to Victorian identities, we find ourselves at the point where we must recall the otherness of the Victorian heading, so as not to seek control over this differentiated, deferred (non-)identity. Victorian identity cannot, does not, *will not* be made to perform either a teleology or eschatology for those in search of both euphoric consolation and nostalgic consolation. The Victorian discourses that bear a certain relationship to the question of identity are too questioning and too questing amongst themselves, within *their selves*, to be thus shackled. Victorian identity (an identity which, to borrow from Luce Irigaray, is not one;[7] it is not "Victorian" as such, reconstituted unproblematically as "Victorian" by any totalising mythopoesis in the late twentieth century, nor is it a single identity) is, and *must be read* as the *other of the heading* "national identity," and our relation to "the Victorian" must be one that no longer either seeks to colonise or obey restrictive and restricting logics and economies.

What we can read from Victorian literature therefore, and which readings counter implicitly and explicitly the closure of "literature" in the service of national heritage and tradition *as* national identity, is the necessity of displacement, through polyvocal narratives, of difference-in-identity that "offers us new resources of analysis."[8] The New Right versions of "Literature" and "Victorian values" are constructed in the form and image of gifts, being handed down to those worthy of receiving it. But the logic of the "gift"[9] belies its status as gift, in that it has always already entered into an exchange mechanism, a market culture in which cultural identity is the property of the highest bidder. The idea of the gift is always compromised by the implicit demand on the part of those who give that something be given back in return for this authorised version of national identity; and what is demanded back is conformity to a particular narrative of Englishness. This selective narrative of the recent past, a past which, strictly speaking, never existed, has been "popularised and commodified" as part of "a new vision of Britain . . . rooted in the memory of the great industrial entrepreneurs of the nineteenth century . . . [and] a celebration of the values of the Victorian age."[10]

But, as has been argued, this is not the only story available. The various, sometimes contradictory discourses on national identity that are available to us are notable for their ability to speak to one another and across each other, at least partially. Our own recent past has emptied out the energies of cultural identity to form a nostalgic sepulchre, and we, unlike the "Victorians," can no longer communicate. If the "Victorians" felt the threat—or promise—of the death of God, it was an event to be discussed on many different levels. The failure of communication in the late twentieth century has come about for many reasons, not least the imposition of monolithic narratives of identity, the dismantling of community through a politics explicitly against the idea of community (for the idea of community denied at an implicit level a central focus, a heart of power from which the official word on cultural identity could be disseminated), and the loss of a radical vision of "fusing art and social life."[11] We have become the Victorians that 1960s' permissive and democratic discourse set up in opposition to its own apparent openness. And we have become these other Victorians because of a fear of the other-within. Alterity, and a respect for the alterity of alterity is absolutely necessary however to the vitality of identity. This is best illustrated through one final example. One of many on-going battles between the Conservative government and certain sectors of the nation throughout 1992 and 1993 has been over the issue of a standard curriculum in schools throughout Great Britain (and not just England). At the heart of this curriculum was to have been the "proper" teaching of standard English and, of course, Shakespeare from the age of eleven onwards. Clearly the issue at stake has been one of the consolidation of national identity through the legislated enforcement of a hegemonically dominant variant of the English langauge, with the canonical figure of "English literature" *par excellence* as the bulwark and mainstay of this policy. Yet it is—or should be—obvious that such a policy is aimed at the suppression of both dialects—"improper" Englishes—and the cultures enunciated through such other English speech. To smother anything which does not conform to some knee-jerk and hide-bound notion of what a language should be is to deny that very thing on which so much of identity is predicated: the heterogeneity of discourse in all its cultural manifestations, relations and interactions. As Sleary says so insistently to Thomas Gradgrind, in his delightfully non-standard English, and as if to remind Gradgrind (and us) of the importance of otherness to identity:

You *muth* have uth . . .[12]

NOTES

Introduction: The "Seemingly Indecipherable Metaphysics of Being" English or, Where to Begin?

1. This first sentence is suggested, as is the last part of the subtitle of this introduction, by the essay of the same name by Roland Barthes, "Where to Begin?," *New Critical Essays*, trans. Richard Howard (Berkeley: University of California Press, 1990), 79-91. Although the concerns of the essay are directed towards a strictly structuralist analysis of any literary text, they do bear pertinently on the question of a point or points of entry faced when writing what is called an introduction or preface.

2. Benedict Anderson, *Imagined Communities*, (19) cit. Homi K. Bhabha, "Introduction: Narrating the Nation," *Nation and Narration*, ed. Homi. K. Bhabha (London: Routledge, 1990), 1. This collection referred to hereafter as *NN*.

3. Bhabha, "Introduction," 1.

4. Anna Marie Smith, "A Symptomatology of an Authoritarian Discourse: The Parliamentary Debates on the Prohibition of the Promotion of Homosexuality," *New Formations*, 10 (Spring 1990: 41-66), 62.

5. Etienne Balibar and Immanuel Wallerstein, *Race, Nation, Class: Ambiguous Identities*, Etienne Balibar trans. Chris Turner (London: Verso, 1991), 87. Referred to hereafter as *RNC*.

6. Robert Young, *White Mythologies: Writing History and the West* (London: Routledge, 1990), 37. Referred to hereafter as *WM*.

7. Ibid.

8. See, for example, Jacques Derrida, *The Other Heading: Reflection on Today's Europe*, trans. Pascale-Anne Brault and Michael B. Naas, int. Michael B. Naas (Bloomington: Indiana University Press, 1992), referred to hereafter as *OH*; Robert Young, *WM*; Homi K. Bhabha, ed. *NN*; Gayatri Chakravorty Spivak, *In Other Worlds: Essays in Cultural Politics* (London: Methuen, 1987); Balibar and Wallerstein, *RNC*; Vron Ware, *Beyond the Pale: White Women, Racism and History* (London: 1992). With reference to Derrida on identity and otherness in the context of Western thought see note 13, below.

9. Peter Mason, *Deconstructing America: Representations of the Other* (London: Routledge, 1990), 4.

10. Ibid.

11. Terry Eagleton, "A Culture in Crisis," *The Guardian*, Friday November 27, 1992. Referred to hereafter as "CC."

12. Mason op. cit., 4-5.

13. In certain ways, as Derrida might say, his work has always concerned itself, and always been involved with questions of identity and its philosophical articulations. Those texts by Derrida which have been of most immediate importance to this study are *Margins of Philosophy*, trans. Alan Bass (Chicago: University of Chicago Press, 1982), referred to hereafter as *MP*; *Of Spirit: Heidegger and the Question*, trans. Geoffrey Bennington and Rachel Bowlby (Chicago: University of Chicago Press, 1989), referred to hereafter as *OS*; "'Eating Well,' or the Calculation of the Subject: An Interview with Jacques Derrida," trans. Peter Connor and Avital Ronnell, *Who Comes After the Subject*, ed. Eduardo Cadava, Peter Connor and Jean-Luc Nancy (London: Routledge, 1991), 96-120, referred to hereafter as *EW*; Derrida, *OH*; *Given Time: I. Counterfeit Money*, trans. Peggy Kamuf (Chicago: University of Chicago Press, 1992), Referred to hereafter as *GT*; "Onto-Theology of National Humanism (Prolegomena to a Hypothesis)," *The Oxford Literary Review: Frontiers*, ed. Geoffrey Bennington and Barry Stocker, (14: 1-2, 1992), referred to hereafter as "OT."

14. Iain Chambers, *Border Dialogues: Journeys in Postmodernity* (London: Routledge, 1990), 14. Referred to hereafter as *BD*.

15. Rosalind Brunt, "The Politics of Identity," *New Times: The Changing Face of Politics in the 1990s*, ed. Stuart Hall and Martin Jacques (London: Verso, 1990), 156.

16. Ibid.

17. Ibid., 158.

Chapter 1. Of Detours, Returns, Addictions and Women: Coleridge, Wordsworth and National Identity

1. The layout of this essay is suggested by particular works of Jacques Derrida, notably *Glas*, trans. John P. Leavey, Jr., and Richard Rand (Lincoln: University of Nebraska Press, 1986), *Cinders*, trans. Ned Lukacher (Lincoln: University of Nebraska Press, 1991), and "Living On • Border Lines," *Deconstruction and Criticism*, Harold Bloom *et al* (New York: Continuum, 1987: 75-177). See "Introduction" above for an explanation of the purpose.

2. All references to the poem are taken from *Coleridge: Poetical Works*, ed. Ernest Hartley Coleridge (Oxford: Oxford UP, 1969), pp. 295-99. All further page references are given in the notes as *C:PW*. Line references will be cited parenthetically in the text.

For an alternative reading of subjectivity and the female image in *Kubla Khan*, see Jane Moore, "Plagiarism with a Difference: Subjectivity in 'Kubla Khan' and *Letters written during a short residence in Sweden, Norway and Denmark*," *Beyond Romanticism: New Approaches to Texts and Contexts 1780-1832*, ed. Stephen Copley and John Whale (London: Routledge, 1992), 140-160.

Moore's essay offers a convincing argument that Coleridge silently interpolated extracts from Mary Wollstonecraft's *Letters*. Less persuasive, however, is her reading of Coleridge's attempted—and failed—mastery of the female other. It is not that Coleridge does not attempt to master the female (although I would argue that he returns to the female as a more familiar subject for mastery because he fails to master the Oriental other); rather, Moore fails to take into account the dream structure, the narrative of addiction and the imperial context, all of which are crucial in understanding the presence of the female simulacra. Thus her argument, for being so focused, falls short of her Lacanian trajectory in ignoring those elements which would be so vital in any fully rigorous Lacanian reading of the poem.

3. I am indebted, throughout this essay, to the recent work on addiction and its metaphors by Avital Ronell in her *Crack Wars: Literature Addiction Mania* (Lincoln: University of Nebraska Press, 1992). Referred to hereafter as *CW*.

4. John Barrell, *The Infection of Thomas De Quincey: A Psychopathology of Imperialism* (New Haven: Yale UP, 1991), 17. All further references to this book are given as Barrell.

5. Geoffrey Hartman, *The Unremarkable Wordsworth* (London: Methuen, 1987), 93.

6. The doubling of the figure of the cottage as both title and poetic object/subject, has a resonance for both the "Tintern Abbey" poem and *Kubla Khan*. Both Wordsworth and Coleridge work with a form of "resonance imaging" about architectural structures and spaces as "poetic" structures and spaces; and vice versa, whereby the poem becomes written as an architectonic form allowing for meaningful—and even excessive—reverberation.

By "poetic" I mean that which is "in" language that is almost irreducibly idiomatic; that which carries meaning, and the possibility of translation, but which keeps meaning to itself, The "poetic" cannot be translated fully, always holding back something, in excess of interpretation as the poetic trace itself. Architecture is a form of writing, of dimensional inscription, which bears something within it despite the poet's use of the architectural image and figure, as though it were the silent memorial of other writings that resonantly ghost the poet's structure. The question of architecture's writing, a writing resistant to mastery and, therefore, the object of desire, is closely analogous with the female trace.

7. The question of "errors" in dating occurs in both Coleridge and Wordsworth's writing at this time. As Theresa Kelley points out in her analysis of "Lines composed a few miles above Tintern Abbey," documentary evidence would suggest that either Wordsworth was incorrect in his dating of the poem (July 13) by two days, or he was in another place altogether, being approximately 80 miles upstream at Llyswen farm (Theresa M. Kelley, *Wordsworth's Revisionary Aesthetics* [Cambridge: Cambridge UP, 1988], 59).

Kelley remarks that the date given by Wordsworth is actually the fifth anniversary of Marat's assassination, and that Wordsworth often resorted to "quasi-fictional topography." (59) Coleridge, like Wordsworth, is not necessarily interested in historical, geographical or temporal verisimilitude. Poetry for both men is not ever merely a record or just a document. H. W. Piper's argument for the composition of *Kubla Khan* in 1797 is reasonable to a point (Piper, *The Singing of Mount Abora: Coleridge's Use of Biblical Imagery and Natural Symbolism in Poetry and Philosophy* [London: Associated University Presses, 1987], 60). The point is, however, only external and historical. It does not—it cannot—account for the "psychological" error on Coleridge's part, which is of a piece with both the poem and its preface.

E. S. Shaffer also raises the issue of the date, referring to other debates that opt for various months within 1797 (Shaffer *"Kubla Khan" and The Fall of Jerusalem: The Mythological School of Biblical Criticism and Secular Literature* [Cambridge: Cambridge UP, 1975], 327, n.24). Whether Coleridge composed this poem in the summer of 1797, as late as May of the following year, or at some point in between is not important in this essay. What is of interest is that there is error, involving slippage, displacement, or an amnesiac erasure as the supplement to opium, and that this error is a signature of the fallibility of the historical as documentary truth. Coleridge's elaborate concatenation of possible dates—and that it is elaborate is attested to by the number of essays that have considered the "true" date of the poem—suggests Coleridge's resistance to historical fixing and to his own being pinned down as his own subject, as subject either to history or his own desires.

8. *Poetical Works*, ed. Thomas Hutchinson, revised by Ernest de Selincourt (Oxford: Oxford University Press, 1988), 589.

9. Thomas De Quincey, *Confessions of an English Opium-Eater and other writings*, ed. Grevel Lindop (Oxford: Oxford University Press, 1992), 70-71. All further references to *Confessions*.

10. *Confessions*, 70

11. Jacques Derrida, *GT*, 7.

12. *C:PW*, 296.

13. Alan G. Hill, ed., *Letters of William Wordsworth: A New Selection* (Oxford: Oxford University Press, 1988), 94-96. All quotations are taken from this letter.

14. *C:PW*, 296.

15. Poppies, from which opium is produced, are essentially a farm crop. The poppy farmer is not that different from the farmers, land-workers and artisans who suffer in and drift through Wordsworth's domestic landscapes. The poppies are often grown by subsistence farmers in areas of Asian countries (especially on the Indian sub-continent) where the soil is either too poor to support the growth of other food or cash crops on a profitable or intensive level, or where the crop grains and seeds are of too high a price for the farmers to afford. The demonization of the poppy, its grower and its by-products, is clearly part of the general discourse of Orientalism, which, for the English, develops out of colonisation, trade, and imposed economic conditions from the mid-eighteenth century onwards.

The poppy/opium "trade" was introduced into China by the English as part of a general distribution of products from India under English rule. The "Oriental addiction" was largely, if not solely, an effect of British imperialism. For a detailed study of the English imagination, the opium trade and its cultural consequences, see Barrell.

16. *C:PW*, 295.

17. The fluidity of Venice undoes the certainties of economic structure, dissolving the circuits of exchange and with that, erasing the boundaries and limits of assured identity. See the chapter on Wilkie Collins, below.

18. *C:PW*, 295.

19. Barrell, 17.

20. Alun R. Jones, "Introduction," *Wordsworth's Poems of 1807*, ed. Alun R. Jones (Atlantic Highlands: Humanities Press, 1987, vii-xxvii), vii. Any references to poems from this edition are given in the notes as *1807*, followed by the page number. Line reference to a particular poem is given parenthetically, immediately after quotation in the text.

21. *1807*, 56-69.

22. Wordsworth's ideological shifts are responsible, at least in part, for certain revisions of *The Prelude*. For discussions of Wordsworth's politics, see Mary Jacobus, *Romanticism Writing and Sexual Difference: Essays on The Prelude* (Oxford: Clarendon Press, 1989), Nicholas Roe, *Wordsworth and Coleridge: The Radical Years* (Oxford: Clarendon Press, 1990) and Geoffrey Hartman, *Wordsworth's Poetry 1787-1814* (Cambridge, Ma.: Harvard University Press, 1987).

23. *C:PW*, 296.

24. Barrell, 149.

25. *1807*, 66.

26. Ibid., 67.

27. Ibid., 64.

28. See Derrida, *GT* (ch. 2, 34-70, passim.), in which Derrida discusses what he calls "the madness of economic reason."

29. *GT*, 36-37.

30. *1807*, 64.
The terms "blood" and "earth" or "soil" are used by Heidegger as the grounding for German identity and to invoke the destiny of the German people in his notoriously problematic "Rectorship Address." On this subject, and on the theme of "blood and soil" in the self-realisation of national identity, see Jacques Derrida, *OS*. On related issues, and from related perspectives, see also Philippe Lacoue-Labarthe, *Heidegger, Art and Politics*, trans. Chris Turner (Oxford: Basil Blackwell, 1990), and Jean-François Lyotard, *Heidegger and "the jews,"* trans. Andreas Michel and Mark Roberts, int. David Carroll (Minneapolis: University of Minnesota Press, 1990).

31. *C:PW*, 296.

32. Ibid., 63.

33. Ibid., 56.

34. Ibid., 63.

35. *1807*, 63.

36. Ibid.

37. Ronell, *CW*, 13.

38. Ibid., 23.

39. Ibid., 13.

40. Ibid., 25.

41. *1807*, 60.

42. Ronell, *CW*, 31.

43. For a full discussion of the politics and discourses of racism from a feminist perspective see Vron Ware, *Beyond the Pale: White Women, Racism and History* (London: Verso, 1992). See Also Rachel Bowlby, "Breakfast in America— Uncle Tom's Cultural Histories," *Nation and Narration*, ed. Homi K. Bhabha (London: Routledge, 1990), 197-213.

44. Robin Jarvis, "Wordsworth and the Use of Charity," *Beyond Romanticism: New Approaches to Texts and Contexts 1780-1832,* ed. Stephen Copley and John Whale (London: Routledge, 1992), 214.

45. After Freud, after Lacan and after Derrida, all of whom have come to bear in some way on this essay, we can read the signature of the abyss in the naming of the *Abyss*inian maid, where fear of sexual and foreign otherness resound endlessly.

46. Jacques Derrida, "OT."

47. Ibid., 17.

48. See Derrida, *GT,* 7; where Derrida interprets the return home of the *Odyssey* as an essentially economic structure.

49. Frances Ferguson, "History, Deconstruction, and Wordsworth," *Diacritics*, 17: 4 (Winter, 1987), 34.

50. Jacques Derrida, *EW*, 99.

51. *EW*, 96.

52. Ibid.

Chapter 2. Matthew Arnold, Englishness and a Question of Spirit

1. All references to the poems of Matthew Arnold are taken from *Arnold: The Complete Poems*, (second ed.) ed. Kenneth Allott and Miriam Allott (London: Longman, 1979). All line references are cited parenthetically, following the relevant quotation.

2. Chris Baldick, *The Social Mission of English Criticism 1848-1932,* Oxford English Monographs (Oxford: Clarendon Press, 1987).

3. Ibid., 24.

4. Baldick is quoting from W. E. Hough's essay "Victorian Anti-Intellectualism," *Journal of the History of Ideas*, xiii (1952), 296. The notion that the Victorian age was one of crass materialism and "anti-intellectualism" is now commonplace. I am not challenging the idea as such. What I shall go on to suggest in the following chapter is that we need to think through the accuracy of the term as it applies to Arnold's thought on his countrymen.

5. Jacques Derrida, *OH*, 72-73.

6. William Wordsworth, "Poems dedicated to National Independence and Liberty Parts I & II," *Wordsworth: Poetical Works*, 1904, ed. Thomas Hutchinson, revised by Ernest de Selincourt (Oxford: Oxford University Press, 1988), 241-264.

7. *The Observer*, 8th October, 1992. The copy from the advertisement speaks somewhat confusingly of rekindling memories from unforgettable years from which come songs that will never be forgotten with words that stay forever in the memory. If memory is so permanent, indelible even, why the need to rekindle it?

8. The tone is first noticed by Kenneth Allott in his edition of Arnold's poems (22).

9. Without wishing to push the reading too far, I am tempted to speculate that the loss of light on France is a metaphorical loss of hope for Arnold after the continental political disappointments of 1848.

10. "Frightful is it, to be the mortal vessel of your truth." Schiller.

11. Ruth apRoberts, *Arnold and God* (Berkeley and Los Angeles: University of California Press, 1983), 105.

12. In this marking of the text, Arnold's metaphors bear a resemblance to Wordsworth's historical/cultural "hedgerows" from "Tintern Abbey," which imply the Enclosure Acts. Importantly, in the case of both men, the metaphors deny their respective poets' attempts to distance themselves from the political and social worlds in which they lived.

13. Such an argument, that others are more fitted intellectually to discuss major issues such as "human rights" or "nuclear war," has no real ground on which to stand as the pretext for retreat in the face of the political. As Derrida has argued in "No Apocalypse, Not Now," (*Diacritics*, Vol. 14, No. 2 [Summer 1984], 20-33), our lack of immediate technological or strategic information should not stand in the way of our ethical engagement with those issues which concern us most directly.

14. Allott (ed.) *Arnold*, 58.

15. There is another possible reading of this figure of the heart. In traditional poetic discourse, the heart always belongs to a lover. The figure of "heart-wasting" suggests a love that is unrequited. Arnold has effected a violent displacement, albeit unconsciously, of a traditional poetic figure, tearing it out of its familiar context to politicise poetic subjectivity in a wholly estranging fashion. On the surface, Arnold cannot escape either the mesh of poetic language and its referents or the ostensible liberal response. What Arnold's access to poetic discourse does allow him, however, is this deconstructive movement.

16. Allott (ed.) *Arnold*, 109.

17. William Shakespeare, *King Richard II*, The Arden Shakespeare, ed. Peter Ure (London: Routledge, 1989), 50-53.

> This royal throne of kings, this scepter'd isle,
> This earth of majesty, this seat of Mars,

This other Eden, demi-paradise,
This fortress built by Nature for herself
Against infection and the hand of war,
This happy breed of men, this little world,
This precious stone set in the silver sea,
Which serves it in the office of a wall,
Or as a moat defensive to a house,
Against the envy of less happier lands,
This blessed plot, this earth, this realm, this England,
This nurse, this teeming womb of royal kings,
Fear'd by their breed, and famous by their birth,
Renowned for their deeds as far from home,
For Christian service and true chivalry,
As is the sepulchre in stubborn Jewry
Of the world's ransom, blessed Mary's son;
This land of such dear souls, this dear dear land,
Dear for her reputation through the world,
Is now leas'd out—I die pronouncing it—
Like to a tenement or pelting farm.

(II. i. 40-60)

18. The single speech most vividly recalled by Arnold's second clause is Prospero's "Revels" speech, which causes Arnold's passing paraphrase to offer us a glimpse of Arnold as the creator and ambivalent master, like Prospero, of an illusory world.

19. Gareth Stedman Jones, *Outcast London: A Study in the Relationship between the Classes in Victorian Society* (London: Penguin, 1984). The term "Outcast London" is not Stedman Jones's originally; an earlier use of the term is in the work of nineteenth-century writer Andrew Mearns, *The Bitter Cry of Outcast London*, ed. Anthony S. Wohl (Leicester: Leicester University Press, 1970). This work is interesting, inasmuch as it shows both a keen observation of working-class conditions in Victorian London, while also expressing the fear of which Stedman Jones speaks.

Another important and disturbing, right-wing study of the urban poor from the nineteenth-century is Arnold White, *The Problems of a Great City* (London: Remington and Co., 1886), which attempts a debunking of socialism and suggests sterilisation of the "unfit" as a remedy to the conditions of the poor (27-64).

20. Ibid., 1.

21. Matthew Arnold, *Culture and Anarchy*, 1869, ed. John Dover Wilson (Cambridge: Cambridge University Press, 1932), 193.

22. Friedrich Engels, *The Condition of the Working Class in England*, 1845, ed. Victor Kiernan (London: Penguin, 1988), 277.

23. Jones, 241-242.

24. Allott, ed., *Arnold*, 525.

25. Arnold's choice of profession for his proletarian figure is odd. The term "weaver" is suggestive of artisanal and semi-rural labour of the 1820s and 1830s, rather than of an East End worker of the 1860s. Gareth Stedman Jones' comprehensive tables and charts appended to *Outcast London* give no indication of weaving as being a trade in the East End of London. (358-395) Arnold appears to be caught in a moment of idealisation, so unpalatable to him is the reality of London's poor.

26. William Wordsworth, "An Evening Walk," *Wordsworth: Poetical Works*, 462 -469, ll. 241-300.

Wordsworth's fierce displacement of the picturesque with the narrative of the dire social, domestic consequences of the English waging war in foreign countries effects a powerful political intervention into poetry, by foregrounding the question of the role of poetry in an age of poverty and misery. After the death of the female tramp and her children, one cannot return with any complacency to the pastoral scene, unless one mis-reads the scene as merely a return to the gothic on Wordsworth's part. This reading seems to me, however, to be an effort to evade personal culpability through a translation of Wordsworth's intervention into a mere replay of a particular strand in the aesthetic tradition.

27. David Riede, *Matthew Arnold and the Betrayal of Language*, Virginia Victorian Studies (Charlottesville: University Press of Virginia, 1988), 2.

28. Matthew Arnold, "Preface to the First Edition of Poems," *Selected Prose*, ed. P. J. Keating (London: Penguin, 1987), 41-55. Also printed in Kenneth Allott's edition of the complete poems (652-674). Any further references to this essay in this and the following chapter are taken from Keating's edition.

29. Riede, 1.

30. J. Hillis Miller, *The Disappearance of God: Five Nineteenth-Century Writers* (Cambridge, Ma: Harvard University Press, 1963), 265.

31. Arnold, "Preface," (1853): 54.

Chapter 3. Arnold, Englishness and Critical Avoidance: A Reading of "My Countrymen"

1. Matthew Arnold, "My Countrymen," *Selected Prose*, ed. P. J. Keating (London: Penguin, 1987), 175-202.

2. Baldick, op. cit., 26.

3. Baldick's wording is curious. A "systematic suppression" would seem to imply a theoretical or pre-planned programme on Arnold's part. Given the

variations, contradictions and paradoxes that arise in Arnold's texts, reading such an ordered response is too strong an accusation.

4. Martin Heidegger, *Being and Time*, 1927, trans. John Macquarrie and Edward Robinson (New York: Harper and Row, 1962), 37.

Heidegger is discussing the means by which to formulate the question of Being. The passage continues:

> We must rather choose such a way of access and such an interpretation that the entity *can show itself in itself and from itself.* And this means that it is to be shown as it is . . . in its average *everydayness.* In this everydayness there are certain structures which we shall exhibit—not just accidental structures but essential structures. (37-38; first emphasis mine)

This provisional definition by Heidegger of the approach to the question of Being has a sympathetic resonance with Arnold's methodological construction of his essay. Arnold allows the dominant variant of Englishness to show itself in its everydayness through his re-citation of newspaper reports that circulate around the question of middle-class education.

Arnold has selectively produced these articles so as to draw a double focus: on language and Englishness. Through this initial approach to the subject of Englishness in general, as a form of Being-in-the-world, a Being-there-for-others, (which is always implicit in Arnold's investigations into the question of identity) Arnold is able to make plain what Heidegger terms the "essential structures." Such a critical activity has a more profound potential for unfolding Englishness (to itself) than does a merely external critique, whilst it also bears with it and in it the implication of an ethics of analysis that respects otherness, rather than seeking to master its material.

5. apRoberts, op. cit., 8.

6. William E. Buckler, *On the Poetry of Matthew Arnold: Essays in Critical Reconstruction*, The Gotham Library (New York: New York University Press, 1982), 182.

In his final chapter, "Arnold and the crisis of Classicism," (180-202) Buckler's concluding remarks on Arnold's critical Preface of 1853, and his reading of an "oblique confession of poetic inadequacy" (200) allied to a sense of ethical culpability in poetry's inability to intervene with history, intersect to a degree with my own reading of the Arnoldian sense of crisis. Where our arguments differ is in their focus; while Buckler seems intent on offering an argument for crisis rooted in Arnold's psyche as the motivating factor, I am suggesting that Arnold cannot help but engage with the crisis because of his being a privileged agent of Victorian intellectual culture.

7. *Unpublished Letters of Matthew Arnold*, ed. Arnold Whitridge (New Haven: Yale University Press, 1923), 15-16.

8. Baldick, op. cit., 24.

9. Ibid., 32.

10. Raymond Williams, *Culture and Society: Coleridge to Orwell*, 1958, (London: The Hogarth Press, 1990) 110-130.

11. Ibid., 128.

12. George Eliot, "A Word for the Germans," *Selected Critical Writings*, ed. Rosemary Ashton (Oxford: Oxford University Press, 1992), 333.

13. Arnold, *Culture and Anarchy*, cit. Williams, 129.

14. Williams, op. cit. 116.

15. Arnold, *Selected Prose*, 301-340.

16. Derrida, *OS* 5.

17. For further information on the context of the essay, see Keating's notes to his edition of "My Countrymen," 456 ff.

18. "My Countrymen," 200.

19. Williams, op. cit., 121.

20. Ibid., 119, 122.

21. Ibid., 118.

22. Ibid., 119.

23. Ibid., 117.

24. "Friendship's Garland," 329; in which letter, Arminius acknowledges the importance of Hegel's *Phenomenology of Spirit* to the subject of *geist*.

25. "My Countrymen," 175.

26. Ibid.

27. Ibid.

28. Ibid.

29. Ibid.

30. Ibid., 176.

31. Ibid.

32. Ibid.

33. Ibid.

34. Ibid.

In the footnote appended by Arnold, he cannot resist the comment "how very fine and striking is this language!" Arnold's use of the exclamation point leaves us in no doubt as to his real opinion of the language. Arnold was obviously concerned that his middle-class readers would miss the irony of his remark, and so provided the silent stage direction in order to direct his audience against the grain of the words themselves.

35. Ibid., 176.

36. Ibid., 176-177.

37. Ibid., 177.

38. Ibid.

39. Ibid.

40. Ibid.

Arnold's description of theory sounds almost Derridean to us today; or, perhaps, somewhat similar to the impatient criticisms of Derrida delivered by liberal pragmatists, critics in a hurry, and those (certain New Historicists) for whom the Real has become a fetish.

41. Ibid.

42. Ibid.

43. Ibid.

44. Ibid., 178.

45. Ibid.

46. Ibid.

47. Derrida, *OS*, 2.

48. Arnold, 178.

49. Ibid.

50. Ibid.

51. Ibid.

52. Ibid., 180.

53. Ibid., 179-180.

54. Ibid., 180.

55. Ibid.

56. Ibid., 181.

57. Arnold is playing with a phrase from the *Times* he had quoted earlier in the essay. (180) The *Times* had called Palmerston "the best type of our age and country" and "emphatically the *English* minister" (my emphasis).

58. Ibid., 181.

59. Ibid.

60. Ibid.

61. Ibid., 182.

62. Ibid., 184.

63. Ibid., 185.

64. Ibid.

65. Ibid.
Arnold's recourse to the word "genial" inadvertently recalls the *Telegraph*'s description of Thomas Bazley's speech.

66. Ibid.

67. Ibid., 186.

68. Ibid., 189.

69. Ibid., 189-190.

70. Ibid., 190.

71. Ibid.

72. Ibid., 191.

73. Ibid., 193.

74. Ibid.

75. Ibid., 198.

76. Ibid., 199.

77. Derrida, *OH,* 76. Derrida continues his discussion of duty to the re-thinking of European identity in terms that are appropriate to my reading of Arnold's efforts to think through the double question of spirit and Englishness:

> The *same duty* dictates cultivating the virtue of . . . *critique, of the critical idea, the critical tradition,* but also submitting it, beyond critique and questioning, to a deconstructive genealogy that thinks and exceeds it without yet com-promising it (77).

78. Arnold, 200.

79. Ibid.

80. Ibid.
Arnold is supposedly talking of another, nameless friend; this is of course another Arnoldian apparition, through which Arnold projects his voice.

81. In this sentence I am again echoing Derrida in *The Other Heading* (76-79 passim.).

82. Arnold, 200.

83. Ibid.

84. Ibid.

85. Ibid., 201.

86. Ibid.

87. Ibid.

88. Baldick, op. cit. 20.

89. Williams, op. cit. 116.

Chapter 4. Critical Nationalism and the "Truth" of (Identity in) Elizabeth Gaskell

1. Jacques Derrida, "Désistance," *Psyché* (Paris: Galilée, 1988). Translated by Christopher Fynsk as "Introduction: Desistance" in Philippe Lacoue-Labarthe, *Typography: Mimesis, Philosophy, Politics* (Cambridge, Mass.: Harvard University Press, 1989), 1-43.

2. Elizabeth Gaskell, "The Last Generation in England," *Cranford* (Oxford: Oxford University Press, 1972), 161.

3. Ibid., op. cit.

4. Jean-Luc Nancy, *The Inoperative Community*, ed. Peter Connor, trans. Peter Connor *et al* (Minneapolis: University of Minnesota Press, 1991): 80.

5. On the distinction between narrative and narratorial voice, see Jacques Derrida's introduction to Lacoue-Labarthe, cited above. See also Lacoue-Labarthe's essay in the same volume, "The Echo of the Subject." (139-208). The difference, broadly speaking, is that the narrative voice is that which is produced and fixed by the reader who brings certain assumptions and agendas to reading, who reads after a particular voice; the narratorial voice is that which speaks in the text of the narrative but which has, as yet, not been fixed by a single reading.

6. Nancy, op. cit.; 80.

7. Ibid., 80.

8. Ibid.

9. Edgar Wright, ed., Elizabeth Gaskell, *My Lady Ludlow and Other Stories* (Oxford: Oxford University Press, 1989), 433. All further references to this collection are to particular stories, unless otherwise indicated.

10. Appendix, *Ludlow*, 433.

11. Ibid., 439.

12. Ibid.

13. Ibid.

14. Ibid.

15. "The Poor Clare," *Ludlow*, 270-333. From this perspective, "The Doom of the Griffiths" (229-270) is also worth mentioning, opposing Englishness with Welsh identity. When Gaskell writes of Shakespeare putting words in Owain Glendwr's mouth (notice that Gaskell does not keep the Anglicised spelling of the Welsh name), which "is much the same thing" (229) as saying it himself, one cannot help but feel that this is not unqualified praise for the Bard, but has more to do with the English attitude to the Welsh.

16. "An Accursed Race": *Ludlow*, 211-229.

17. Ibid., 215.

18. Ibid., 218.

19. Ibid.

20. Ibid., 219.

21. Ibid., 220.

22. Ibid., 219.

23. Ibid., 213.

24. Ibid., 211.

25. Ibid., 226

26. Nicos Poulantzas, *Fascism and Dictatorship*, trans. Judith White (London: Verso, 1979), 107.

27. Interestingly, many of these bodies have recourse to textuality in order to authorize their xenophobia, seeking to dispute the lost origins of the Cagots

through pseudo-linguistic and etymological enquiries, seeking also to prove, amongst other things, that the Cagots are Oriental (in Edward Said's use of the term), being either Syrian or Jewish.

28. Nancy, op. cit. 81.

29. This term is taken from, and given full explication in, Jacques Derrida, "Survivre," *Parages* (Paris: Galilée, 1986), 117-219.

30. "An Accursed Race," *Ludlow*, 211.

31. Ibid., 229. Whether or not this epitaph is "real," there is a slight political irony for me in the burial place of Mary Hand, given England's several hundred years' investment in Shakespeare as *the* representative of national and cultural identity.

32. Appendix, *Ludlow*, 441.

33. I am drawing the term "underlabour" as an appropriate description of Gaskell's critical activity from John Locke, *An Essay Concerning Human Understanding*, ed. A. C. Fraser (New York, 1959), Vol. I, 14. Gaskell underlabours from various ideological situations to clear the philosophical grounds of identity for the reader so as to prepare for a more thorough thinking through of the issues of Victorian Englishness.

34. Nancy, op. cit., 80.

35. This is a passing reference to an essay by Jacques Derrida, "Le dernier mot du racisme," "Racism's Last Word," trans. Peggy Kamuf, *Critical Inquiry*, vol. 12 (1985), 290-99

36. Nancy, op. cit., 81.

37. With this in mind, one can easily read the title of this story as a reference not to the Cagots but to the English.

38. Elizabeth Gaskell, "Cousin Phillis" *Cranford/Cousin Phillis*, ed. Peter Keating (Harmondsworth: Penguin, 1976), 219-319.

39. Ibid., op. cit., 35-219.

40. Ibid., 248.

41. Ibid., 290.

42. Ibid., 302.
The sense we receive of Holdsworth is not that he is positively harmful to culture (although he does introduce an ambivalence concerning, indirectly, the intrusion of the railway, reflected the "harm" he causes Phillis), but that he is in search of an appropriate, and appropriately vital culture to which he can belong.
If this is so, then Canada, in its sometime uneasy connection between the

English and the French—a cultural dialectic as old as 1066—becomes the proper name for a new culture written by the heterodox concatenation engendered by the old cultural identities. This new culture survives, lives beyond the old because of the investment in the spirit of identities rather than their dead shells. However, also in the proper name of Canada is the worrying spirit of yet another culture, that of the American natives, violently suppressed in the name of Canada, at the hands of both English and French.

43. *Cousin Phillis*, 270.

44. Ibid., 264.

45. Ibid., 265.

46. Ibid., 236.

47. Ibid., 233.

48. Ibid.

49. Ibid., 222.

50. Ibid., 248.

51. Ibid., 254.

52. Ibid.

53. Roy Bhaskar, *Reclaiming Reality: A Critical Introduction to Contemporary Philosophy*, (London: Verso, 1989): 8.

54. Samuel Smiles, *Self-Help, with Illustrations of Conduct and Perseverance*, 1859, abridged edition by George Bull, int. Sir Keith Joseph (Harmondsworth: Penguin, 1986). Further references to Smiles are taken from the abridged edition, although the original has been consulted, and referred to as "S-H."
    "National progress," writes Smiles, "is the sum of individual industry, energy and uprightness . . . everything depends upon how [a man] governs himself from within"; (20) "The spirit of self-help, as exhibited in the energetic action of individuals, has in all times been a marked feature in the English character, and furnishes the true measure of our power as a nation." (22) Notice how Smiles moves effortlessly between a metaphysical conception of national spirit and the figure of the atomistic individual who is that spirit's prime mover. Society and culture are succinctly elided, as are the currents and traces of history. Englishness is a timeless quality evinced by its most successful representatives (i.e., most successful in capitalist terms). In turn, it is because of the spirit of national identity that certain individuals are so successful.
    The connection between this and Holdsworth's comments on Mr Manning are transparently obvious; and it is only a step—and a much too easy one at that—from Smiles and Holdsworth (though not Gaskell) to Margaret Thatcher, her often flaunted "Victorian values" and her dictum that "there is no such thing as society."

55. *Cousin Phillis* was first published in serial form by the *Cornhill Magazine* between November 1863 and February 1864. 1859, the year of Smiles's book, was also the year of publication for Darwin's *On the Origin of Species* and Mill's *Essay on Liberty*. Millsian liberalism is as equally an influence in the delineation of Holdsworth as is Smiles. Holdsworth's remark to Paul about his father's "good blood" may reflect a certain Darwinian influence.

56. S-H, 30.

57. S-H, 40-41.

58. Derrida, *OS,* 16.

59. The argument about Paul that follows can be extended to incorporate all fictional characters, as a means of resisting the dominance of realist ideology. Also, in talking of historicity, by bringing it into play, I am seeking to resist and move beyond the implied dialectic structure of a phrase such as "blindness and insight." Such pairing serves merely to recuperate the examination within a particular framework that I am, in part, arguing against.

60. Holman's reliance on the word is much greater than Manning's. However, even Holman's position to the Word is not fixed absolutely in the text. Gaskell makes Holman's relationship to textual authority relative by introducing Brother Robinson. The inference is, of course, that there are no absolute positions.

61. *Cousin Phillis*, 234.

62. Ibid., 235-236.

63. Ibid., 243.

64. Ibid., 262.

65. Ibid., 280.

66. Ibid., 226.

67. Ibid., 316.

68. Ibid., 308.

69. Ibid., 246.

70. Ibid., 317.

71. George Eliot, *Middlemarch*, ed. W. J. Harvey (Harmondsworth: Penguin, 1983): 890.

Chapter 5. Wilkie Collins and the (Secret) Heart of English Culture

1. Jenny Bourne Taylor, *In the Secret Theatre of Home: Wilkie Collins, Sensation Narrative, and Nineteenth-Century Psychology* (London: Routledge, 1988), 2. Hereafter referred to in the notes as STH.

2. François Bédarida, *A Social History of England 1851-1990*, revised edition 1990, trans. A. S. Forster and Jeffrey Hodgkinson (London: Routledge, 1991), 48.

3. Ibid.

4. There is a question of the canon raised here, of its genealogy and the assumptions—the unconscious discourses—at work in the gradual cultural accretion of what are deemed canonical works through retroactive reading gestures. Collins is a hitherto more neglected, certainly more marginal figure in the pantheon of "English Literature" than, say, George Eliot or even Charles Dickens, precisely because it is harder to "translate" him into an idiom-free aesthetic.
  Collins is somewhat marginalised *because* he is so English, because his writing is so contaminated by the often contradictory traces of national identity. This is not to say that Eliot and Dickens are not; no writer's language can escape its cultural context. The critical process has, however, found it easier to render their narratives in a manner which frees them from cultural "impurities."

5. Wilkie Collins, *The Fallen Leaves* (London: Chatto and Windus, 1879), 72.

6. Ibid.

7. See Bédarida, 48-56.

8. Wilkie Collins, *The Law and the Lady*, ed. Jenny Bourne Taylor (Oxford: Oxford University Press, 1992), 116.
  The terms of verdict in English law are interesting inasmuch as, although one is innocent until proven guilty, after one has been sent to trial, one can only be either guilty or not guilty. The defendant, once a defendant can never be "innocent" again. Thus, "not guilty," the phrase which the jury are commanded to express if such are their findings, seems to be a judgement implying the potential for guilt.

9. On this point, see Daniel Bivona, "Postscript: disposing of the surplus: capitalism and empire," *Desire and Contradiction: Imperial Visions and Domestic Debates in Victorian Literature* (Manchester: Manchester University Press, 1990), 113-128.

10. Taylor, STH, x.

11. *The Law and the Lady*, 286.

12. Ibid., 288.

13. Ibid.

14. Ibid., 379-381.

15. Wilkie Collins, *No Name*, ed. Virginia Blain, (Oxford: Oxford University Press, 1986).

16. Wilkie Collins, *The Guilty River* (Stroud: Alan Sutton, 1991), 9-10.

17. Wilkie Collins, *Man and Wife* (Stroud: Alan Sutton, 1990).

18. Wilkie Collins, *The Moonstone*, ed. J. I. M. Stewart (Harmondsworth: Penguin, 1986), 409.

19. Ibid., 408.

20. Wilkie Collins, *The Haunted Hotel* (Stroud: Alan Sutton, 1990).

21. Bivona, op. cit., 117-123.

22. Ibid., 122.

23. Ibid., 120.

24. Schumpeter, cit. Bivona, 120.

25. Bivona, 120.

26. *Haunted Hotel*, 89.

27. Today, the same can be said of Sheratons, Hiltons and other international hotel chains, except of course that one is in an outpost of the USA. Wherever you are, there is home; the same wallpaper, the same piped muzak, the same uniforms. Like the Coleridge of chapter 1, we have never really left home at all.

28. *Haunted Hotel*, 12.

29. Ibid., 71.

30. Ibid., 21.

31. In the sense that the reader feels Collins to be indicting the family and the idea of the bourgeois family as culpable in the unfolding of social events, this narrative bears a passing resemblance to Priestley's *An Inspector Calls*.

32. *Haunted Hotel*, 46.

33. Ibid., 48.

34. Ibid., 56.

35. At one point, Collins has one of the maids serve a "*customary* cup of tea" (128; my emphasis).

36. *Haunted Hotel*, 98.

37. Ibid., 94.

38. Ibid., 20.

39. Ibid., 32.

40. Ibid., 1-11.

41. Ibid., 1.

42. Ibid., 9.

43. Ibid., 97.

44. Given the post-modern context, and the Venetian location, *parages* is a suitable word at this juncture, meaning both "waters" and "regions." One meaning undoes the other, forcing us to think through the logic of boundaries, borders and their dissolution (on this subject, see Derrida, *Parages* [Paris: Galilée, 1986]).

Such boundaries are not ever only literal, but are the boundaries of identity. In effect, what Collins dismantles here, through the narrative of the English abroad, is the stability of English identity, and the certainties, the arrogance on which any such teleological identity is supposedly founded.

45. *Haunted Hotel*, 106.

46. Ibid., 145.

47. Ibid., 146.

48. Ibid., 156.

49. The public name around which the troubles of the narrative have occurred—Lord Montbarry —is reiterated. This has a double, paradoxical effect. On the one hand, the reproduction of the proper name suggests the effort to erase, to cover up any ghostly resonance; on the other hand, this very performative simulation invokes the weight of the past and the shadow of the dead, promising the eternal return of a particular, troubled identity to haunt the English family in the future.

50. *Haunted Hotel*, 164.

51. Ibid., 165.

52. Ibid., 166.

53. It is worth commenting that, today, the title should be read for what it can say about the hierarchical and proprietorial relationship that exists between man and woman in marriage.

A man is always "man," regardless of his marital status, such is the law that determines naming. Indeed, his right to the title of Man (the universal signifier of humanity) offers to hide from view his precise status; Man is thus protected by authority from being considered as property.

"Wife," however, makes clear the woman's subordinate position in the relationship. As Derrida has shown repeatedly, with concern to the structural nature of binarisms, the terms are not equivalent but are culturally co-ordinated in terms of an uneven power balance in which the former term of the title "man and wife" is always assumed superior to the latter.

54. My reading of *Man and Wife* touches on points already made with great clarity by Jenny Bourne Taylor in her analysis of the novel (213-217). I am indebted both to her readings and her discussions with me of the work of Wilkie Collins.

55. Jacques Derrida, "Force of Law: The 'Mythical Foundation of Authority,'" *Deconstruction and the Possibility of Justice*, ed. Drucilla Cornell, Michael Rosenfeld and David Gray Carlson (London: Routledge, 1992), 14. Further references to this essay are as follows: Derrida *FL*.

56. *Man and Wife*, xiii, xiv.

57. Ibid., xiv.

58. Ibid.

59. From Thatcher to John Major, we have been told that we live in a classless society; and this at a time when civil liberties have been eroded, when social services have been illogically and ruthlessly cut as part of the on-going ideological skirmishes in the name of free market-liberalism, and when poverty has increased more rapidly than at any other time in the twentieth century. Yet because the rhetoric of the "classless society" has caught hold so effortlessly, it has become increasingly difficult to identify the strategic, political nature of systematic depredations which are presented to us as naturally inevitable and therefore irresistible.

60. *Man and Wife*, xiv.

61. Ibid., xv.

62. Collins uses a similar polemical device in *The Fallen Leaves*, where the protagonist of the discourse is Amelius Goldenheart, a member of a Christian Socialist community in the United States of America. Perhaps because Amelius is so crucial to the narrative of *The Fallen Leaves* he is not so crude an ideological device as the nameless stranger of *Man and Wife*. The crudity does have its own purpose and strengths, however. It maintains an analytical distance between observer and observed that becomes at least partially dissolved in *The Fallen Leaves* as Amelius is somewhat Anglicised, contaminated by Englishness (which is, in a sense, "in his blood," his having been born in England]; though never stating this overtly, the novel does seem to be propelled by a conservative desire for the ideological recuperation of Amelius.

63. *Man and Wife*, 464.

64. Ibid., 464.

65. Ibid.

66. Ibid., 464-465.

67. Ibid., 465

68. Ibid.

69. Ibid.

70. Ibid.

71. Ibid.

72. Ibid.

73. Ibid.

74. Ibid., 466.

75. Ibid.

76. Ibid.

77. Ibid.

78. Terry Eagleton, "Nationalism: Irony and Commitment," *Nationalism, Colonialism and Literature* (Minneapolis: University of Minnesota Press, 1990), 28.

79. *Man and Wife*, 467.

80. Derrida *FL*, 13.

Chapter 6. The Ideology of Englishness: The Paradoxes of Tory-Liberal Culture and National Identity in *Daniel Deronda*

1. A shorter version of this chapter was presented at the "George Eliot and Community" Conference, North East Missouri State University, Kirksville, Missouri, in April 1991. My thanks to Dennis Leavens for inviting me to present this.

2. "But how can 'Being' ever come to present itself as 'Thought'"? Martin Heidegger, *Identity and Difference*, trans. and int. Joan Stambaugh (New York: Harper and Row, 1969). 57.

3. This is taken from the epigraph of the essay, which is from George Eliot, "Impressions of Theophrastus Such," *Theophrastus Such, Jubal, and Other Poems, and The Spanish Gypsy* (Chicago, New York and San Francisco: Belford, Clarke and Co., 1888), 153.

4. George Eliot, *Daniel Deronda*, ed. Barbara Hardy (Harmondsworth: Penguin, 1967), 35.

5. *Deronda*, 875.

6. For a full explication of the ideologies of this term, see Barry Gordon, *Economic Doctrine and Tory Liberalism 1824-1830* (London: Macmillan, 1979). On the question of the liberal compromise, see also Richard Price, *Labour in British Society: An Interpretive History* (London: Routledge, 1990). Referred to hereafter as Price.

7. *Deronda*, 224.

8. Ibid., 220.

9. Ibid., 212.

10. I am borrowing here from the title and concerns of a recent work, *Nation and Narration*, ed. Homi K. Bhabha (London: Routledge, 1990).

11. Peter de Bolla, *The Discourse of the Sublime: Readings in History, Aesthetics and the Subject* (Oxford: Basil Blackwell, 1989), 12-13.

12. Price, 29-49.

13. Alan Liu, *Wordsworth: The Sense of History* (Stanford: Stanford University Press, 1989), 237.

14. Jacques Derrida, *The Ear of the Other: Otobiography, Transference, Translation*. ed. Christie McDonald, trans. Avital Ronell and Peggy Kamuf (Lincoln: University of Nebraska Press, 1988), 5.

15. Homi K. Bhabha, "DissemiNation: Time, Narrative, and the Margins of the Modern Nation," *Nation and Narration*, 292.

16. It could be argued that Eliot's "failure" to structure the close of the text in a more radical fashion in keeping with the ethical deconstruction by which the narrative is so constantly informed is only the mark of Eliot's—or the text's—historicity.

Against this, however, one could offer texts by Collins and Dickens (amongst several writers) whose texts evince an almost postmodern sensibility in subverting and questioning traditional narrative structures in an open-ended fashion.

17. *Deronda*, 224.

18. Ibid., 49. Mirah will later introduce herself in a similar fashion: "I am a stranger. I am a Jewess" (241). George Eliot reads Jewishness as strangeness itself, it would seem.

19. Ibid., 42.

20. Ibid., 35.

21. Simon Dentith, *George Eliot* (Brighton: Harvester, 1987), 80.
I wish to qualify Dentith's use of the word "zionism." Dentith uses this as
a general term for Jewish spiritual identity, and it is not necessarily my own
choice. As William Baker has pointed out to me (for which I am grateful), much
of the Jewish source material for *Daniel Deronda* is not Zionist specifically, if at all
(for a fuller discussion of this issue, see William Baker, "George Eliot's Readings
in Nineteenth-Century Jewish Historians: A Note on the Background of *Daniel
Deronda*," *Victorian Studies*: 15 [June 1972], 463-473. See also, Baker, *Some George
Eliot Notebooks: An Edition of the Carl H. Pforzheimer Library's George Eliot Holograph
Notebooks, Volume 1–Ms 707* [Salzburg: Institut für Englische Sprache und
Literatur, Universität Salzburg, 1976]).
 However, for the purposes of my argument, the point is not focused on a
particular Hebraic tradition but the fact that, ultimately, whatever the sources of
the Jewish culture being used, they come to be read by Deronda in terms of the
English liberal intellectual tradition. Jewish culture is depoliticized, made over
and re-written within the paradigm of English humanist thought.

22. For a detailed and cogently argued reading of the compromise, see
Price, 49-93.

23. *Deronda*, 103.

24. Ibid., 217.

25. Ibid., 35.

26. Ibid., 875.

27. The authentic self would seem to be conditioned by an active life of
the mind, as represented through Daniel's thoughts and his philosophical knowledge. Eliot constructs Deronda as an Arnoldian subject, a figure of English
intellectualism, while the "purely" English are marked by their lack of internality.
In the first chapter (40), Eliot refers to the gambling English as "dowdy
Philistines." As Barbara Hardy points out in a footnote to her edition of the
novel, the word "Philistine" has a distinctly Arnoldian ring to it, which is in
keeping with the suggestion of Deronda as an Arnoldian figure.

28. *Deronda*, 301.

29. Ibid., 317.

30. Ibid., 664.

31. Ibid., 148.

32. Ibid., 127.

33. In her reading of the novel, Nancy Paxton argues, following Barbara
Hardy, that Gwendolen achieves "tragic splendor" and "the tragic consciousness
of time and loss" which, apparently, all English must experience "if they are to

avert the 'national tragedy' that seems to be threatening English society" (Nancy L. Paxton, *George Eliot and Herbert Spencer: Feminism, Evolutionism, and the Reconstruction of Gender* [Princeton: Princeton University Press, 1991], 225). Given Gwendolen's terms and the other archly theatrical references within which middle-class life is framed in the novel, Eliot would seem to think of the "national tragedy" as being more of the order of Colley Cibber than William Shakespeare.

34. *Deronda*, 193.

35. George Eliot, "Silly Novels by Lady Novelists," *Selected Essays, Poems and other Writings*, ed. A. S. Byatt and Nicholas Warren (Harmondsworth: Penguin, 1990), 140-164. The essay is also included in *Essays of George Eliot*, ed. Thomas Pinney (London: Routledge and Kegan Paul, 1967), 300-325.

36. *Deronda*, 135.

37. Ibid., 869.

38. Ibid., 857. In the context of referentiality, it is interesting to note that Deronda, in dismissing Hans's ideas about Mirah, refers to them as "a good-natured fiction." This accurate reading of Deronda's remarks the level of narrative enclosure that is middle-class Englishness.

39. The use of arch-metaphors in the novel (124, 127, 134) effectively counters any realist or mimetic transparency, leading us back to the figure of the text as labyrinth. The effect of a reflexive strategy is to make it difficult to pin down a singular narrative voice with any certainty. There does however seem to be a consensus of narrative voices in play.

40. After Gwendolen has imagined her tyranny over Grandcourt in her imaginary courtship scene, discussed above, the narrative asks, "was ever any young witch like"? (127) The difference between this question and those raised about Gwendolen in "Daniel Deronda's mind" (35) is one of degree rather than kind. Can we assert with any confidence that such enunciations are separable into clearly definable voices?

41. Gwendolen is a figurative stereotype, not because she displays often used characteristics (although this is also true), but because, in a more literal sense, hers is a written "character" cast as it were from other pieces of printing.

42. Barbara Hardy, *The Novels of George Eliot: A Study of Form* (Oxford: Oxford University Press, 1959).

43. *Deronda*, 43.

44. Ibid., 35.

45. Neil Hertz, "Some Words in George Eliot: Nullify, Neutral, Numb, Number," *Languages of the Unsayable: The Play of Negativity in Literature and*

Literary Theory, ed. Sanford Budick and Wolfgang Iser (New York: Columbia University Press, 1989: 280-297), 290.

46. *Deronda*, 288-292. The issue of the colonies bothers the narrative repeatedly, and thus the question of national identity and its foundations in unresolved ways. See, for example, Bult's comments (p. 283) and the discourse on Jamaica and Caliban (p.376). Daniel's remarks about Caliban are typical of the good intention of the liberal intellectual and the idealism that underwrites humanist thinking.

As the comment about Caliban shows, in relation to Daniel everything becomes more or less an artistic performance, its merit judged (by Daniel and the narrative voice) on the level of mimetic representation that it reaches. But for Daniel, the only reality is one of philosophical reflection: a truly metaphysical space determined by the humanist credo "I am," which for Daniel is the enunciation of an identity supposedly free of the snares of performance.

47. Homi K. Bhabha, "Introduction: Narrating the Nation," *Nation and Narration*, ed. Homi. K. Bhabha (London: Routledge, 1990, 1-8), 1.

48. Christina Crosby, *The Ends of History: Victorians and "the Woman Question,"* (London: Routledge, 1991), 40, 41.

49. *Deronda*, 689.

50. Sally Shuttleworth, *George Eliot and Nineteenth-Century Science: The Make-Believe of a Beginning* (Cambridge: Cambridge University Press, 1984), 182.

51. *Deronda*, 868.

Chapter 7. Reading Trollope: Whose Englishness is it Anyway?

1. As I write, this has been expressed most strongly in the Government's nefarious dealings with miners and the National Union of Mineworkers, and the attempted illegal closure of over thirty pits in 1992. This is just one narrative of Tory self-interest and power-brokerage, going back to 1984.

2. Iain Chambers, *BD*, 1.

3. Ibid., 44.

4. Gayatri Chakravorty Spivak, "Three Feminist Texts and a Critique of Imperialism," *A Feminist Reader*, ed. Catherine Belsey and Jane Moore (Oxford: Basil Blackwell, 1989).

5. Avital Ronell, *The Telephone Book: Technology, Schizophrenia, Electric Speech* (Lincoln: University of Nebraska Press, 1989), 273.

6. Chambers, *BD*, 88.

7. Ibid., 44.

8. Anthony Trollope, *Phineas Finn, the Irish Member*, ed. John Sutherland (Harmondsworth: Penguin, 1986), 319. Hereafter referred to in notes as *PF*. Also refer to Trollope's *Phineas Redux*, ed. John C. Whale(Oxford: Oxford University Press, 1990).

9. Ibid., 324.

10. Anthony Trollope, *The Duke's Children*, ed. Hermione Lee (Oxford: Oxford University Press, 1989).

11. *PF*, 361.

12. Jean Baudrillard, *In the Shadow of the Silent Majorities or, the End of the Social and Other Essays*, trans. Paul Foss, John Johnston and Paul Patton (New York: Semiotexte, 1983), 7.

13. *PF*, 106-107.

14. *PF*, 163-164. All quotations in the text concerning Glencora's argument are taken from these pages.

15. Ibid., 258-268.

16. Ibid., 261.

17. Ibid., 261-262.

18. Wilkie Collins, *Man and Wife*, xiv-xv.

19. Antonio Gramsci, *Selections from Cultural Writings*, ed. David Forgacs and Geoffrey Nowell-Smith, trans. William Boelhower (Cambridge, Ma.: Harvard, 1985), 134.

20. Anthony Trollope, *The Prime Minister*, ed. Jennifer Uglow (Oxford: Oxford University Press, 1989). Referred to hereafter as *PM*.

21. Terry Eagleton, *The Ideology of the Aesthetic* (Oxford: Basil Blackwell, 1990), 415.

22. *PM*, 3.

23. John Keane, *Democracy and Civil Society: On the Predicaments of European Socialism, the Prospects for Democracy, and the Problem of Controlling Political Power* (London: Verso, 1988), 214.

24. *PM*, 11.

25. Ibid., 16. From Johnson to Pope; Trollope's indictment of Englishness is focused on the nineteenth-century middle-class abandonment of English literary culture.

26. Ibid., 32.

27. Ibid., 26.

28. Ibid., 25.

29. Terry Lovell, *Consuming Fiction* (London: Verso, 1987), 23-24.

30. Anthony Trollope, *An Autobiography*, ed. Michael Sadleir and Frederick Page (Oxford: Oxford University Press, 1987) 361.

31. Keane, *op. cit.*, 214-215.

32. *PM*, 10.

33. Ibid., 107.

34. Ibid., 102.

35. On the crisis in Victorian values see, for example, François Bédarida, *A Social History of England 1851-1990*, trans. A. S. Forster and Jeffrey Hodgkinson (London: Routledge, 1991), 99-109.

36. Bédarida, op. cit., 103.

37. *PM.*, 45.

38. James R. Kincaid, *The Novels of Anthony Trollope* (Oxford: Oxford University Press, 1977), 175.

39. Alan Sinfield, *Literature, Politics, and Culture in Postwar Britain* (Berkeley: University of California Press, 1989), 296-297.

(In) Conclusion: Towards a New Victorianism?

1. Cora Kaplan, "Introduction," *Aurora Leigh and Other Poems*, Elizabeth Barrett Browning, (London: The Women's Press, 1978), 13.

2. *Aurora Leigh*, Book I, ll. 65-76, p.40

3. Jacques Derrida, *OH*.

4. Michael B. Naas, "Introduction: For Example," Jacques Derrida, *OH*, x-xi.

5. On the politics of the jetty as a non-theoretical "theory," see Jacques Derrida, "Some Statements and Truisms about Neologisms, Newisms, Postisms, Parasitisms, and other Small Seismisms," trans. Ann Tomiche, *The States of "Theory": History, Art, and Critical Discourse*, ed. David Carroll (New York: Columbia University Press, 1990), 63-94.

6. *OH*, 14-15.

7. Luce Irigaray, *The Sex Which is Not One*, trans. Catherine Porter (Ithaca: Cornell University Press, 1985).

8. Derrida, *GT*, 15.

9. On the politics and logic of "the gift" in the cultural context of Western thought, see Derrida, *GT*, 1-71.

10. John Horner and Sylvia Harvey, "Introduction: Great Britain Limited," *Enterprise and Heritage: Crosscurrents of National Culture* (London: Routledge, 1991), 14.

11. Eagleton, "CC."

12. Charles Dickens, *Hard Times*, ed. David Craig (London: Penguin, 1988), 308. This final quotation is not a direct attack on Gradgrind so much as a recognition of the importance of that which is perceived as marginal to any conception of identity.

SELECT BIBLIOGRAPHY

The first two parts of this bibliography deal with primary materials. The first section (a), lists texts by those authors who are the subjects of the chapters of this work. The second (b), records works of other writers from the eighteenth and nineteenth centuries consulted in the research for this book. First parenthetical reference in the primary texts refers to original date of publication. First parenthetical reference in secondary texts accompanies translations and refers to original date of publication in original language. All works referred to directly in the preceding chapters are given full bibliographical reference in the notes for the relevant chapter.

Primary Texts (a)

Arnold, Matthew. (1869). *Culture and Anarchy*, ed. John Dover Wilson, Cambridge, 1932.

———. (1923). *Unpublished Letters of Matthew Arnold*, ed. Whitridge Arnold, New Haven.

———. (1965). *The Complete Poems*, ed. Kenneth Allott, second ed. Miriam Allott, London, 1979.

———. (1987). *Selected Prose*, ed. P. J. Keating, London.

Coleridge, Samuel Taylor. (1817). *Biographia Literaria or Biographical Sketches of My Literary Life and Opinions*, ed. James Engell and W. Jackson Bate, Princeton, 1984.

———. (1912). *Poetical Works*, ed. Ernest Hartley Coleridge, Oxford, 1989.

———. (1988). *Selected Letters*, ed. H. J. Jackson, Oxford.

———. (1991). *On Politics and Society*, ed. John Morrow, Princeton.

Collins, Wilkie. (1852). *Basil*, ed. Dorothy Goldman, Oxford, 1990.

———. (1860). *The Woman in White*, ed. Julian Symons, Harmondsworth, 1985.

———. (1862). *No Name*, ed. Virginia Blain, Oxford, 1986.

———. (1866). *Armadale*, ed. Catherine Peters, Oxford, 1989.

——. (1868). *The Moonstone*, ed. J. I. M. Stewart, Harmondsworth, 1986.

——. (1870). *Man and Wife*, Stroud, 1990.

——. (1875). *The Law and the Lady*, ed. Jenny Bourne Taylor, Oxford, 1992.

——. (1879). *The Fallen Leaves*, London.

——. (1879). *The Haunted Hotel*, Stroud, 1990.

——. (1879). *A Rogue's Life*, Stroud, 1991.

——. (1883). *Heart and Science*, Stroud, 1990.

——. (1886). *The Guilty River*, Stroud, 1991 .

Eliot, George. (1858). *Scenes of Clerical Life*, ed. David Lodge, Harmondsworth, 1985.

——. (1859). *Adam Bede*, ed. Stephen Gill, Harmondsworth, 1986.

——. (1860). *The Mill on the Floss*, ed. A. S. Byatt, Harmondsworth, 1981.

——. (1863). *Romola*, ed. Andrew Sanders, Harmondsworth, 1986.

——. (1866). *Felix Holt, the Radical*, ed. Peter Coveney, Harmondsworth, 1982.

——. (1871–72). *Middlemarch*, ed. W. J. Harvey, Harmondsworth, 1983.

——. (1876). *Daniel Deronda*, ed. Barbara Hardy, London, 1986.

——. (1888). *Theophrastus Such, Jubal, and other Poems and the Spanish Gypsy*, Chicago.

——. (1963). *Essays of George Eliot*, ed. Thomas Pinney, New York.

——. (1990). *Selected Essays, Poems and other Writings*, ed. A. S. Byatt and Nicholas Warren, London.

——. (1992). *Selected Critical Writings*, ed. Rosemary Ashton, Oxford.

Gaskell, Elizabeth. (1848). *Mary Barton*, ed. Stephen Gill, Harmondsworth, 1983.

——. (1853). *Ruth*, ed. Alan Shelston, Oxford, 1985.

——. (1855). *North and South*, ed. Martin Dodsworth and Dorothy Collin, Harmondsworth, 1985.

——. (1863). *Sylvia's Lovers*, ed. Andrew Sanders, Oxford, 1989.

——. (1866). *Wives and Daughters*, ed. Frank Gloversmith, int. Laurence Lerner, London, 1986.

——. (1988). *Cranford/Cousin Phillis*, ed. Peter Keating, London.

———. (1989). *My Lady Ludlow and other Stories*, ed. Edgar Wright, Oxford.

———. (1992). *A Dark Night's Work and other Stories*, ed. Suzanne Lewis, Oxford.

Trollope, Anthony. (1855). *The Warden*, ed. David Skilton, Oxford, 1989.

———. (1857). *Barchester Towers*, ed. Michael Sadleir and Frederick Page, int. James R. Kincaid, Oxford, 1989.

———. (1858). *Dr Thorne*, ed. David Skilton, Oxford, 1990.

———. (1859). *The Bertrams*, ed. Geoffrey Harvey, London, 1991.

———. (1861). *Framley Parsonage*, ed. David Skilton and Peter Miles, London, 1988.

———. (1861). *Framley Parsonage*, ed. D. P. Edwards, Oxford, 1989.

———. (1862). *North America*, ed. Robert Mason, int. John William Ward, London, 1992.

———. (1862). *The Struggles of Brown, Jones, and Robinson*, ed. N. John Hall, Oxford, 1992.

———. (1864). *Can You Forgive Her?* ed. Stephen Wall, Harmondsworth, 1986.

———. (1864). *The Small House at Allington*, ed. James R. Kincaid, Oxford, 1988.

———. (1865). *Miss Mackenzie*, ed. A. O. J. Cockshut, Oxford, 1990.

———. (1865). *Marion Fay*, ed. Geoffrey Harvey, Oxford, 1992.

———. (1866). *The Belton Estate*, ed. John Halperin, Oxford, 1991.

———. (1867). *The Claverings*, ed. David Skilton, Oxford, 1991.

———. (1867/1868). *Nina Balatka/Linda Tressel*, ed. Robert Tracy, Oxford, 1991.

———. (1869). *He Knew He was Right*, ed. John Sutherland, Oxford, 1986.

———. (1869). *The Last Chronicle of Barset*, ed. Stephen Gill, Oxford, 1989.

———. (1869). *Phineas Finn, the Irish Member*, ed. John Sutherland, Harmondsworth, 1986.

———. (1870). *The Vicar of Bullhampton*, ed. David Skilton, Oxford, 1990.

———. (1871). *Ralph the Heir*, ed. John Sutherland, Oxford, 1990.

———. (1871). *Sir Harry Hotspur of Humblethwaite*, ed. N. John Hall, Oxford, 1991.

———. (1873). *The Eustace Diamonds*, ed. Stephen Gill and John Sutherland, Harmondsworth, 1986.

———. (1874). *Lady Anna*, ed. Stephen Orgel, Oxford, 1990.

———. (1874). *Phineas Redux*, ed. John C. Whale, int. F. S. L. Lyons, Oxford, 1990.

———. (1875). *The Way We Live Now*, ed. John Sutherland, Oxford, 1991.

———. (1876). *The Prime Minister*, ed. Jennifer Uglow, Oxford, 1989.

———. (1879). *Cousin Henry*, ed. Julian Thompson, Oxford, 1987.

———. (1879). *An Eye for an Eye*, ed. John Sutherland, Oxford, 1992.

———. (1880). *The Duke's Children*, ed. Hermione Lee, Oxford, 1989.

———. (1881). *Dr Wortle's School*, ed. John Halperin, Oxford, 1990.

———. (1882). *The Fixed Period*, ed. R. H. Super, Ann Arbour, 1990.

———. (1882). *Kept in the Dark*, ed. G. W. Pigman III, Oxford, 1992.

———. (1883). *An Autobiography*, ed. Michael Sadleir and Frederick Page, int. P. D. Edwards, Oxford, 1987.

———. (1884). *An Old Man's Love*, ed. John Sutherland, Oxford, 1991.

Wordsworth, William. (1807). *Wordsworth's Poems of 1807*, ed. Alun R. Jones, Atlantic Highlands, 1987.

———. (1904). *Poetical Works*, ed. Thomas Hutchinson and Ernest de Selincourt, Oxford, 1988.

———. (1971). *The Prelude*, ed. J. C. Maxwell, Harmondsworth.

———. (1977). *The Poems*, (2 Vols.) ed. John O. Hayden, London.

———. (1988). *Selected Prose*, ed. John O. Hayden, London.

———. (1988). *The Letters of William Wordsworth*, ed. Alan G. Hill, Oxford.

Wordsworth, William and Samuel Taylor Coleridge. (1798). *Lyrical Ballads*, ed. W. J. B. Owen, Oxford, 1990.

———. (1991). *Lyrical Ballads*, ed. R. L. Brett and A. R. Jones, London.

Primary Texts (b)

Barrett Browning, Elizabeth. (1857). *Aurora Leigh and Other Poems*, int. Cora Kaplan, London, 1987.

Braddon, Mary E. (1862). *Lady Audley's Secret*, ed. Jennifer Uglow, London, 1985.

———. (1863). *Aurora Floyd*, ed. Jennifer Uglow, London, 1984.

Browning, Robert. (1981). *The Poems*, vols. one and two, ed. John Pettigrew, supplemented and completed by Thomas J. Collins, Harmondsworth.

Butler, Samuel. (1872). *Erewhon*, ed. Peter Mudford, Harmondsworth, 1984.

———. (1903). *The Way of All Flesh*, London, 1953.

Carlyle, Thomas. (1836). *Sartor Resartus*, ed. Kerry McSweeney and Peter Sabor, Oxford, 1991.

———. (1839). *Critical and Miscellaneous Essays*, 7 volumes, London, 1869.

———. (1841). *On Heroes, Hero-Worship and the Heroic in History*, London, 1891.

———. (1851). *The Life of John Sterling*, London.

———. (1986). *Selected Writings*, ed. Alan Shelston, London.

Carroll, Lewis. (1987). *The Annotated Alice: Alice's Adventures in Wonderland and Through the Looking Glass*, ed. Martin Gardner.

Clough, Arthur Hugh. (1991). *Selected Poems*, ed. Jim McCue, London.

Cobbett, William. (1830). *Rural Rides*, ed. George Woodcock, Harmondsworth, 1987.

Conan Doyle, Arthur. (1887). *A Study in Scarlet*, Harmondsworth, 1985.

———. (1890). *The Sign of Four*, London, 1987.

———. (1991). *Sherlock Holmes Selected Stories*, Oxford.

Darwin, Charles. (1859). *On the Origin of Species by Means of Natural Selection, or the Preservation of Favoured Races in the Struggle for Life*, int. Ernst Mayr, Cambridge, Mass., 1964.

De Quincey, Thomas. (1821). *Confessions of an English Opium Eater*, ed. Alethea Hayter, London, 1986.

———. *Confessions of an English Opium-Eater and Other Writings*, ed. Grevel Lindop, Oxford, 1992.

Dickens, Charles. (1836-37). *The Pickwick Papers*, ed. Robert L. Patten, Harmondsworth, 1976.

———. (1837-39). *Oliver Twist*, ed. Peter Fairclough, Harmondsworth, 1986.

———. (1839). *Nicholas Nickleby*, ed. Michael Slater, Harmondsworth, 1978.

———. (1841). *The Old Curiosity Shop*, ed. Angus Easson, London, 1985.

———. (1848). *Dombey and Son*, ed. Raymond Williams, Harmondsworth, 1986.

———. (1849–50). *David Copperfield*, ed. Trevor Blount, London, 1985.

———. (1853). *Bleak House*, ed. J. Hillis Miller, Harmondsworth, 1977.

———. (1854). *Hard Times*, ed. David Craig, Harmondsworth, 1988.

———. (1857). *Little Dorritt*, ed. John Holloway, London, 1988.

———. (1860–61). *Great Expectations*, ed. Angus Calder, Harmondsworth, 1987.

———. (1864–5). *Our Mutual Friend*, ed. Stephen Gill, Harmondsworth, 1986.

———. (1985). *Selected Short Fiction*, ed. Deborah A. Thomas, Harmondsworth.

Disraeli, Benjamin. (1844). *Coningsby*, ed. Thom Braun, London, 1989.

———. (1845). *Sybil or, the Two Nations*, Harmondsworth, 1954.

Engels, Friedrich. (1845). *The Condition of the Working Class*, ed. Victor Kiernan, London, 1986.

———. (1884). *The Origin of the Family, Private Property and the State*, int. Michèle Barrett, Harmondsworth, 1986.

Gissing, George. (1884). *The Unclassed*, ed. Jacob Korg, Brighton, 1983.

———. (1886). *Demos: A Story of English Socialism*, ed. Pierre Coustillas, Brighton, 1982.

———. (1887). *Thyrza*, ed. Jacob Korg, Brighton, 1984.

———. (1889). *The Nether World*, ed. Stephen Gill, Oxford, 1992.

———. (1891). *New Grub Street*, ed. Bernard Bergonzi, Harmondsworth, 1985.

———. (1892). *Born in Exile*, int. Gillian Tindall, London, 1985.

———. (1893). *The Odd Women*, int. Margaret Walters, London, 1987.

———. (1894). *In the Year of the Jubilee*, int. John Halperin, London, 1987.

———. (1897). *The Whirlpool*, int. Gillian Tindall, London, 1984.

———. (1898). *The Town Traveller*, ed. Pierre Coustillas, Brighton, 1981.

———. (1903). *The Private Papers of Henry Ryecroft*, ed. Mark Storey, Oxford, 1987.

———. (1905). *Will Warburton, a Romance of Real Life*, ed. Colin Partridge, Brighton, 1981.

Godwin, William. (1793). *Enquiry Concerning Political Justice and its Influence on Modern Morals and Happiness*, ed. Isaac Kramnick, Harmondsworth, 1985.

Hazlitt, William. (1987). *Selected Writings*, ed. Ronald Blythe, Harmondsworth.

——. (1991). *Selected Writings*, ed. Jon Cook, Oxford.

Hopkins, Gerard Manley. (1985). *Poems and Prose*, ed. W. H. Gardner, Harmondsworth.

——. (1990). *Gerard Manley Hopkins*, ed. Catherine Phillips, Oxford.

Hughes, Thomas. (1869). *Tom Brown's Schooldays*, ed. Andrew Sanders, Oxford, 1990.

Inchbald, Elizabeth. (1791). *A Simple Story*, ed. J. M. S. Tompkins, int. Jane Spencer, Oxford, 1988.

Keats, John. (1988). *The Complete Poems*, ed. John Barnard, London.

Kingsley, Charles. (1850). *Alton Locke*, ed. Elizabeth A. Cripps, Oxford, 1987.

——. (1872). *Poems*, London, 1889.

Le Fanu, Sheridan. (1864). *Uncle Silas*, ed. W. J. McCormick, Oxford, 1988.

——. (1872). *In a Glass Darkly*, Stroud, 1990.

Locke, John. (1690). *An Essay Concerning Human Understanding*, ed. A. C. Fraser, New York, 1959.

Macaulay, Thomas Babbington. (1848-61). *The History of England*, ed. Hugh Trevor Roper, London, 1986.

Marx, Karl. (1847). *The Poverty of Philosophy: Answer to the "Philosophy of Poverty" by M. Proudhon*, Moscow, 1955.

——. (1887). *Capital, a Critique of Political Economy, Volume I: The Process of Capitalist Production*, trans. Samuel Moore and Edward Aveling, ed. Frederick Engels, New York, 1984.

——. (1898). *Wages, Price and Profit*, Moscow, 1947.

——. (1939). *Grundrisse: Foundations of the Critique of Political Economy*, trans. and foreword Martin Nicolaus, New York, 1973.

——. (1984). *Selected Writings in Sociology and Social Philosophy*, ed. T. B. Bottomore and Maximilien Rubel, trans. T. B. Bottomore, Harmondsworth.

——. (1988). *Economic and Philosophical Manuscripts of 1844 and the Communist Manifesto*, trans. Martin Milligan, Buffalo.

——. (1992). *Early Writings*, trans. Rodney Livingstone and Gregor Benton, int. Lucio Colletti, London.

Marx, Karl and Friedrich Engels. (1846). *The German Ideology*, ed. C. J. Arthur, London, 1970.

Mayhew, Henry. (1861–62). *London Labour and the London Poor*, ed. Victor Neuberg, London, 1987.

Mearns, Andrew. (1883). *The Bitter Cry of Outcast London*, ed. Anthony S. Wohl, Leicester, 1970.

Mill, John Stuart. (1848). *Principles of Political Economy with some of their Applications to Social Philosophy*, ed. Donald Winch, Harmondsworth, 1985.

——. (1859). *On Liberty*, ed. Gertrude Himmelfarb, London, 1985.

——. (1873). *Autobiography*, ed. E. John Robson, London, 1989.

——. (1989). *On Liberty with the Subjection of Women and Chapters on Socialism*, ed. Stefan Collini, Cambridge.

Mill, John Stuart and Jeremy Bentham. (1987). *Utilitarianism and other Essays*, ed. Alan Ryan, London.

Moore, George. (1894). *Esther Waters*, ed. David Skilton, Oxford, 1983.

Morris, William. (1890). *News from Nowhere or, an Epoch of Rest*, ed. James Redmond, London, 1983.

——. (1920). *Prose and Poetry (1856–1870)*, Oxford.

——. (1986). *News from Nowhere and Selected Writings and Designs*, ed. Asa Briggs, London.

Morrison, Arthur. (1896). *A Child of the Jago*, Harmondsworth, 1946.

Newman, John Henry. (1848). *Loss and Gain: the Story of a Convert*, ed. Alan G. Hill, Oxford, 1986.

Oliphant, Margaret. (1986). *The Doctor's Family and other Stories*, ed. Merryn Williams, Oxford.

Owen, Robert. (1991). *A New View of Society and other Selected Writings*, ed. Gregory Claeys, London.

Pater, Walter. (1973). *Essays on Literature and Art*, ed. Jennifer Uglow, London.

——. (1885). *Marius the Epicurean*, ed. Michael Levey, Harmondsworth, 1985.

Ruskin, John. (1985). *Unto this Last and other Writings*, ed. Clive Wilmer, London.

——. (1991). *Selected Writings*, Kenneth Clark, London.

Rutherford, Mark. (1896). *Clara Hopgood*, London, 1985.

Shelley, Mary. (1818). *Frankenstein*, ed. M. K. Joseph, Oxford, 1991.

Shelley, Percy Bysshe. (1905). *Poetical Works*, ed. Thomas Hutchinson and G. M. Matthews, Oxford, 1991.

Smiles, Samuel. (1859). *Self-Help, with Illustrations of Conduct and Perseverance*, int. Keith Joseph, Harmondsworth, 1986.

Stevenson, Robert Louis. (1886). *Kidnapped*, Toronto, 1982.

———. (1979). *Dr Jekyll and Mr Hyde and other Stories*, ed. Jenni Calder, London.

———. (1987). *Dr Jekyll and Mr Hyde and Weir of Hermiston*, ed. Emma Letley, Oxford.

Stoker, Bram. (1897). *Dracula*, ed. A. N. Wilson, Oxford, 1991.

Tennyson, Alfred. (1989). *Tennyson: A Selected Edition*, ed. Christopher Ricks, Berkeley.

Thackeray, William Makepeace. (1848). *Vanity Fair*, ed. J. I. M. Stewart, Harmondsworth, 1985.

———. (1848–50). *The History of Pendennis*, ed. Donald Hawes, int. J. I. M. Stewart, London, 1987.

Ward, Mary Augusta. (1888). *Robert Elsmere*, ed. Rosemary Ashton, Oxford, 1987.

———. (1894). *Marcella*, int. Tamie Waters, London, 1984.

White, Arnold. (1886). *The Problems of a Great City*, London.

White, William Hale. (1881). *The Autobiography of Mark Rutherford*, ed. William S. Peterson, Oxford, (1990)..

Wilde, Oscar. (1990). *The Soul of Man and Prison Writings*, ed. Isobel Murray, Oxford.

Wollstonecraft, Mary. (1792). *Vindication of the Rights of Woman*, ed. Miriam Brody, London, 1985.

———. (1992). *Mary / Maria* with Mary Shelley, *Matilda*, ed. Janet Todd, London.

Wollstonecraft, Mary and William Godwin. (1987). *A Short Residence in Sweden, Norway and Denmark and Memoirs of the Author of 'The Rights of Woman,'* ed. Richard Holmes, Harmondsworth.

Wordsworth, Dorothy. (1991). *The Letters of Dorothy Wordsworth*, ed. Alan G. Hill, Oxford.

———. (1991). *The Journals of Dorothy Wordsworth*, ed. Mary Moorman, Oxford.

Secondary Texts: Criticism, Theory, Politics

Althusser, Louis. (1965). *For Marx*, trans. Ben Brewster, London, 1986.

———. (1971). *Lenin and Philosophy and other Essays*, trans. Ben Brewster, New York.

———. (1990). *Philosophy and the Spontaneous Philosophy of the Scientists, and other Essays*, trans. Ben Brewster, James H. Kavanagh, Thomas E. Lewis, Grahame Lock and Warren Montag, London.

Althusser, Louis and Etienne Balibar. (1968). *Reading Capital*, trans. Ben Brewster, London, 1990.

Appignanesi, Lisa, ed. (1989). *Ideas from France: The Legacy of French Theory, ICA Documents*, London.

Armstrong, Nancy. (1987). *Desire and Domestic Fiction: A Political History of the Novel*, Oxford.

Attridge, Derek. (1988). *Peculiar Language: Literature as Difference from the Renaissance to James Joyce*, Ithaca.

Attridge, Derek, Geoff Bennington and Robert Young, eds. (1987). *Post-structuralism and the Question of History*, Cambridge.

Baker, William. (1972). "George Eliot's Readings in Nineteenth-Century Jewish Historians: A Note on the Background of *Daniel Deronda*," *Victorian Studies*, 15 (June 1972): 463–473.

———. (1976). *Some George Eliot Notebooks: An Edition of the Carl H. Pforzheimer Library's George Eliot Holograph Notebooks, Volume 1 – Ms 707*, Salzburg.

Baldick, Chris. (1983). *The Social Mission of English Criticism 1848–1932*, Oxford.

———. (1987). *In Frankenstein's Shadow: Myth, Monstrosity and Nineteenth-Century Writing*, Oxford.

Balibar, Etienne and Immanuel Wallerstein. (1988). *Race, Nation, Class: Ambiguous Identities*, trans. of Etienne Balibar by Chris Turner, 1991.

Barker, Francis. (1984). *The Tremulous Private Body*, London.

Barker, Francis, Peter Hulme, Margaret Iverson and Diana Loxley, eds. (1986). *Literature, Politics and Theory: Papers from the Essex Conference 1976–1984*, London.

Barreca, Regina, ed. (1990). *Sex and Death in Victorian Literature*, Bloomington.

Barrell, John. (1991). *The Infection of Thomas de Quincey: A Psychopathology of Imperialism*, New Haven.

———. (1991). *Poetry, Language and Politics*, Manchester.

Barret-Ducrocq, Françoise. (1989). *Love in the Time of Victoria*, trans. John Howe, London, 1991.

Barrett, Dorothea. (1991). *Vocation and Desire: George Eliot's Heroines*, London.

Barrett, Michèle. (1980). *Women's Oppression Today: Problems in Marxist Feminist Analysis*, London.

———. (1991). *The Politics of Truth: From Marx to Foucault*, Stanford.

Barthes, Ronald. (1972). *New Critical Essays*, trans. Richard Howard, Berkeley, 1990.

———. (1973). *The Pleasure of the Text*, trans. Richard Miller, New York, 1975.

———. (1984). *Image Music Text*, trans. Stephen Heath, London.

———. (1984). *The Rustle of Language*, trans. Richard Howard, Berkeley, 1989.

Baudrillard, Jean. (1972). *For a Critique of the Political Economy of the Sign*, trans. Charles Levin, St. Louis, 1981.

———. (1978). *In the Shadow of the Silent Majorities or, the End of the Social and other Essays*, trans. Paul Foss, John Johnston and Paul Patton, New York, 1983.

———. (1979). *Seduction*, trans. Brian Singer, New York, 1990.

———. (1988). *Selected Writings*, ed. and int. Mark Poster, Stanford.

Bédarida, François. (1991). *A Social History of England 1851–1990*, trans. A. S. Forster and Jeffrey Hodgkinson, London.

Beer, Gillian. (1983). *Darwin's Plots: Evolutionary Narrative in Darwin, George Eliot and Nineteenth-Century Fiction*, London.

Benjamin, Andrew, ed. (1989). *The Lyotard Reader*, Oxford.

Benjamin, Walter. (1955). *Illuminations*, trans. Harry Zohn, int. Hannah Arendt, New York, 1983.

Bennett, Tony. (1990). *Outside Literature*, London.

Bhabha, Homi K., ed. (1990). *Nation and Narration*, London.

Bhaskar, Roy. (1989). *Reclaiming Reality: A Critical Introduction to Contemporary Philosophy*, London.

Bivona, Daniel. (1990). *Desire and Contradiction: Imperial Visions and Domestic Debates in Victorian Literature*, Manchester.

Bloom, Harold, Paul de Man, Jacques Derrida, Geoffrey Hartman and J. Hillis Miller. (1987). *Deconstruction and Criticism*, New York.

Bocock, Robert. (1986). *Hegemony*, Chichester.

de Bolla, Peter. (1989). *The Discourse of the Sublime: History, Aesthetics and the Subject*, Oxford.

Bourdieu, Pierre. (1979). *Distinction: A Social Critique of the Judgement of Taste*, trans. Richard Nice, Cambridge, 1984.

Buckler, William. (1982). *On the Poetry of Matthew Arnold: Essays in Critical Reconstruction*, New York.

Budick, Sanford and Wolfgang Iser, eds. (1989). *Languages of the Unsayable: The Play of Negativity in Literature and Literary Theory*, New York.

Cadava, Eduardo, Peter Connor and Jean-Luc Nancy, eds. (1991). *Who Comes After the Subject?*, London.

Carroll, David, ed. (1990). *The States of 'Theory': History, Art, and Critical Discourse*, New York.

Chambers, Iain. (1990). *Border Dialogues: Journeys in Postmodernity*, London.

Connors, Steven. (1985). *Charles Dickens*, Oxford.

Copley, Stephen and John Whale, eds. (1992). *Beyond Romanticism: New Approaches to Texts and Contexts 1780-1832*, London.

Corlett, William. (1989). *Community without Unity: A Politics of Derridean Extravagance*, Durham.

Corner, John, and Sylvia Harvey, eds. (1991). *Enterprise and Heritage: Crosscurrents of National Heritage*, London.

Cottom, Daniel. (1989). *Text and Culture: The Politics of Interpretation*, Minneapolis.

————. (1987). *Social Figures: George Eliot, Social History, and Literary Representation*, foreword Terry Eagleton, Minneapolis.

Crary, Jonathan. (1992). *Techniques of the Observer: On Vision and Modernity in the Nineteenth Century*, Cambridge, Ma.

Critchley, Simon. (1992). *The Ethics of Deconstruction: Derrida and Levinas*, Oxford.

Crosby, Christina. (1991). *The Ends of History: Victorians and "the Woman Question"*, London.

Dean, Mitchell. (1991). *The Constitution of Poverty: Toward a Genealogy of Liberal Governance*, London.

Dentith, Simon. (1987). *George Eliot*, Brighton.

Derrida, Jacques. (1967). *Of Grammatology*, trans. Gayatri Chakravorty Spivak, Baltimore, 1976.

———. (1967). *Speech and Phenomena and other Essays on Husserl's Theory of Signs*, trans. David B. Allison, Evanston, 1973.

———. (1967). *Writing and Difference*, trans. Alan Bass, London, 1987.

———. (1972). *Dissemination*, trans. Barbara Johnson, Chicago, 1981.

———. (1972). *Margins of Philosophy*, trans. Alan Bass, Chicago, 1982.

———. (1972). *Positions*, trans. Alan Bass, Chicago, 1981.

———. (1974). *Glas*, trans. John P. Leavey, Jr. and Richard Rand, Lincoln, 1986.

———. (1976). *The Archeology of the Frivolous: Reading Condillac*, trans. John P. Leavey, Jr., Lincoln, 1987.

———. (1977). *Limited Inc.*, trans. Samuel Weber and Jeffrey Mehlman, Evanston, 1988.

———. (1978). *Spurs: Nietzsche's Styles/ Éperons: Les Styles de Nietzsche*, trans. Barbara Harlow, Chicago, 1979.

———. (1978). *The Truth in Painting*, trans. Geoff Bennington and Ian McLeod, Chicago, 1987.

———. (1980). *The Post Card: From Socrates to Freud and Beyond*, trans. Alan Bass, Chicago, 1987.

———. (1982). *The Ear of the Other: Otobiography, Transference, Translation*, trans. Peggy Kamuf and Avital Ronell, Lincoln, 1988.

———. (1982). *Signéponge/Signsponge*, trans. Richard Rand, New York, 1984.

———. (1983). "My Chances/*Mes Chances*: A Rendezvous with some Epicurean Stereophonies," trans. Irene Harvey and Avital Ronell, *Taking Chances: Derrida, Psychoanalysis, and Literature*, ed. Joseph H. Smith and William Kerrigan, Baltimore, 1984.

———. (1983). "Of an Apocalyptic Tone Newly Adopted in Philosophy," trans. John P. Leavey, Jr., *Derrida and Negative Theology*, ed. Harold Coward and Toby Foshay, Albany, 1992.

——. (1984). "No Apocalypse, Not Now," *Diacritics*, 14: 2 (Summer 1984): 20–33.

——. (1985). "Racism's Last Word" trans. Peggy Kamuf, *Critical Inquiry*, 12 (1985): 290–299.

——. (1986). *Memoires for Paul de Man*, revised edition, trans. Cecile Lindsay, Jonathan Culler, Eduardo Cadava and Peggy Kamuf, New York, 1989.

——. (1986). *Parages*, Paris.

——. (1986). *Schibboleth pour Paul Celan*, Paris.

——. (1987). *Cinders*, trans. Ned Lukacher, Lincoln, 1991.

——. (1987). "How to Avoid Speaking: Denials," trans. Ken Frieden, *Derrida and Negative Theology*, ed. Harold Coward and Toby Foshay, Albany, 1992.

——. (1987). 'Letter to a Japanese Friend', trans. David Wood and Andrew Benjamin, *Derrida and Différance*, ed. David Wood and Robert Bernasconi, Evanston, 1988.

——. (1987). *Of Spirit: Heidegger and the Question*, trans. Geoffrey Bennington and Rachel Bowlby, Chicago, 1989.

——. (1987). *Ulysse gramophone: Deux mots pour Joyce*, Paris.

——. (1988). "The Politics of Friendship," trans. Gabriel Motzkin, *The Journal of Philosophy*, 85: 11 (November 1988): 632–644.

——. (1989). *Psyche*, Paris.

——. (1990). "Some Statements and Truisms about Neologisms, Newisms, Postisms, Parasitisms, and Other Small Seismisms," trans. Ann Tomiche, *The States of 'Theory,'* ed. David Carroll, New York.

——. (1991). *A Derrida Reader*, ed. Peggy Kamuf, New York.

——. (1991). *Given Time: I. Counterfeit Money*, trans. Peggy Kamuf, Chicago, 1992.

——. (1991). *The Other Heading: Reflections on Today's Europe*, trans. Pascale-Anne Brault and Michael B. Naas, int. Michael B. Naas, Bloomington, 1992.

——. (1992). *Acts of Literature*, ed. Derek Attridge, London

——. (1992). "Force of Law: The 'Mystical Foundation of Authority,'" trans. Mary Quaintance, *Deconstruction and the Possibility of Justice*, ed. Drucilla Cornell, Michael Rosenfeld, David Gray Carlson, London.

————. (1992). "Onto-Theology of National Humanism," *The Oxford Literary Review* 14: 1–2 (Winter 1992): 3–25.

————. (1992). "Passions: 'An Oblique Offering,'" trans. David Wood, *Derrida: A Critical Reader*, Oxford.

————. (1992). "Post-Scriptum: Aporias, Ways and Voices," trans. John P. Leavey, Jr., *Derrida and Negative Theology*, ed. Harold Coward and Toby Foshay, Albany.

Docherty, Thomas. (1986). *After Theory: Post Modernism/Post Marxism*, London.

Dollimore, Jonathan. (1991). *Sexual Dissidence: Augustine to Wilde, Freud to Foucault*, Oxford.

Eagleton, Terry. (1978). *Criticism and Ideology: A Study in Marxist Literary Theory*, London.

————. (1984). *The Function of Criticism: From the Spectator to Post Structuralism*, London.

————. (1990). *The Ideology of the Aesthetic*, Oxford.

————. (1990). *The Significance of Theory*, Oxford.

————. (1991). *Ideology: An Introduction*, London.

————. (1992). "A Culture in Crisis," *The Guardian*, November 27.

Eagleton, Terry, Fredric Jameson and Edward W. Said. (1990). *Nationalism, Colonialism and Literature*, Minneapolis.

Easthope, Anthony. (1983). *Poetry as Discourse*, London.

————. (1991). *British Post-Structuralism: Since 1968*, London.

————. (1989). *Poetry and Phantasy*, Cambridge.

Edgley, Roy and Richard Osborne, eds. (1985). *Radical Philosophy Reader*, London.

Feltes, N. N. (1986). *Modes of Production of Victorian Novels*, Chicago.

Ferguson, Frances. (1987). "History, Deconstruction, and Wordsworth," *Diacritics*, 17: 4 (Winter 1987): 32–43.

Forgacs, David, ed. (1988). *An Antonio Gramsci Reader: Selected Writings 1916–1935*, New York.

Forrester, John. (1990). *The Seductions of Psychoanalysis: Freud, Lacan and Derrida*, Cambridge.

Foster, Shirley. (1985). *Victorian Women's Fiction: Marriage, Freedom and the Individual*, Totowa.

Foucault, Michel. (1961). *Madness and Civilization: a History of Insanity in the Age of Reason*, trans. Richard Howard, New York, 1988.

——. (1969). *L'archéologie du savoir*, Paris.

——. (1975). *Discipline and Punish: The Birth of the Prison*, trans. Alan Sheridan, New York, 1979.

——. (1976). *Histoire de la sexualité I: La volonté de savoir*, Paris.

Freud, Sigmund. (1963). *Introductory Lectures on Psychoanalysis*, trans. James Strachey, ed. James Strachey and Angela Richards, Harmondsworth, 1973.

Frow, John. (1986). *Marxism and Literary History*, Cambridge, Mass.

Gallagher, Catherine, and Thomas Laqueur, eds. (1987). *The Making of the Modern Body: Sexuality and Society in the Nineteenth Century*, Berkeley.

Gidal, Peter. (1989). *Materialist Film*, London.

Gordon, Barry. (1979). *Economic Doctrine and Tory Liberalism 1824–1830*, London.

Goux, Jean-Joseph. (1973). *Symbolic Economies: After Marx and Freud*, trans. Jennifer Curtiss Gage, Ithaca, 1990.

Gramsci, Antonio. (1971). *Selections from the Prison Notebooks*, trans. and ed. Quentin Hoare and Geoffrey Nowell Smith, London.

——. (1978). *Selections from Political Writings 1921–1926*, trans. and ed. Quentin Hoare, London.

——. (1985). *Selections from Cultural Writings*, ed. David Forgacs and Geoffrey Nowell Smith, trans. William Boelhower, Cambridge, Mass.

Haight, Gordon. (1985). *George Eliot: A Biography*, Harmondsworth.

Hall, Stuart. (1988). *The Hard Road to Renewal: Thatcherism and the Crisis of the Left*, London.

——. (1990). 'The Emergence of Cultural Studies and the Crisis of the Humanities', *October*, 53 (Summer 1990): 11–25.

Hall, Stuart and Martin Jacques, ed. (1990). *New Times: The Changing Face of Politics in the 1990s*, London.

Hamilton, Paul. (1983). *Coleridge's Poetics*, Oxford.

Hardy, Barbara. (1959). *The Novels of George Eliot: A Study of Form*, Oxford.

Hartman, Geoffrey H. (1967). *Wordsworth's Poetry 1787–1814*, Cambridge, Mass.

Harvie, Christopher. (1991). *The Centre of Things: Political Fiction in Britain from Disraeli to the Present*, London.

———. (1987). *The Unremarkable Wordsworth*, London.

de la Haye, Yves, ed. (1979). *Marx and Engels on the Means of Communication (the Movement of Commodities, People, Information and Capital)*, New York.

Heidegger, Martin. (1927). *Being and Time*, trans. John Macquarrie and Edward Robinson, New York, 1962.

———. (1969). *Identity and Difference*, trans. and int. Joan Stambaugh, New York.

Herbert, Christopher. (1991). *Culture and Anomie: Ethnographic Imagination in the Nineteenth Century*, Chicago.

Hindess, Barry, ed. (1990). *Reactions to the Right*, London.

Hobsbawm, E. J. (1990). *Industry and Empire: From 1750 to the Present Day*, Harmondsworth.

Irigaray, Luce. (1974). *Speculum of the Other Woman*, trans. Gillian C. Gill, Ithaca, 1989.

———. (1977). *The Sex which is not One*, trans. Catherine Porter, with Carolyn Burke, Ithaca, 1985.

Jacobus, Mary. (1989). *Romanticism, Writing and Sexual Difference: Essays on the Prelude*, Oxford.

Jameson, Fredric. (1981). *The Political Unconscious: Narrative as Socially Symbolic Act*, Ithaca.

Keane, John. (1988). *Democracy and Civil Society: On the Predicaments of European Socialism, the Prospects for Democracy and the Problem of controlling Social and Political Power*, London.

Keane, John, ed. (1988). *Civil Society and the State: New European Perspectives*, London.

Kearney, Richard. (1984). *Dialogues with Contemporary Continental Thinkers: The Phenomenological Heritage*, Manchester.

Kelley, Theresa M. (1988). *Wordsworth's Revisionary Aesthetics*, Cambridge.

Kincaid, James R. (1977). *The Novels of Anthony Trollope*, Oxford.

———. (1992). *Child-Loving: The Erotic Child and Victorian Culture*, London.

Kofman, Sarah. (1980). *The Enigma of Woman: Woman in Freud's Writings*, trans. Catherine Porter, Ithaca, 1985.

Krell, David Farrell. (1990). *Of Memory, Reminiscence, and Writing: On the Verge*, Bloomington.

Kristeva, Julia. (1974). *Revolution in Poetic Language*, trans. Margaret Waller, int. Leon S. Roudiez, New York, 1984.

Lacan, Jacques. (1966). *Écrits: A Selection*, trans. Alan Sheridan, New York, 1977.

———. (1973). *The Four Fundamental Concepts of Psychoanalysis*, trans. Alan Sheridan, New York, 1981.

———. (1975). *The Seminar of Jacques Lacan, Book I: Freud's Papers on Technique 1953–1954*, ed. Jacques–Alain Miller, trans. John Forrester, New York, 1991.

———. (1978). *The Seminar of Jacques Lacan, Book II: The Ego in Freud's Theory and in the Technique of Psychoanalysis 1954–1955*, ed. Jacques–Alain Miller, trans. Sylvana Tomaselli, notes by John Forrester, New York, 1991.

———. (1984). *Speech and Language in Psychoanalysis*, trans. Anthony Wilden, Baltimore.

———. (1986). *The Ethics of Psychoanalysis 1959–1960: The Seminar of Jacques Lacan Book VII*, ed. Jacques–Alain Miller, trans. Dennis Porter, London, 1992.

Lacan, Jacques and the école freudienne. (1985). *Feminine Sexuality*, ed. Juliet Mitchell and Jacqueline Rose, trans. Jacqueline Rose, New York.

Laclau, Ernesto. (1977). *Politics and Ideology in Marxist Theory*, London.

———. (1990). *New Reflections on the Revolution of Our Time*, London.

Laclau, Ernesto and Chantal Mouffe. (1985). *Hegemony and Socialist Strategy: Towards a Radical Democratic Politics*, London.

Lacoue-Labarthe, Philippe. (1986). *La poésie comme expérience*, Paris.

———. (1989). *Typography: Mimesis, Philosophy, Politics*, ed. Christopher Fynsk, int. Jacques Derrida, Cambridge, Ma.

———. (1990). *Heidegger, Art and Politics: The Fiction of the Political*, Oxford.

Langan, Mary and Bill Schwartz, eds. (1985). *Crisis in the British State 1880–1930*, London.

Larsen, Neil. (1990). *Modernism and Hegemony: A Materialist Critique of Aesthetic Agencies*, Minneapolis.

Lentricchia, Frank. (1983). *Criticism and Social Change*, Chicago.

Light, Alison. (1991). *Forever England: Femininity, Literature and Conservatism between the Wars*, London.

Liu, Alan. (1989). *Wordsworth: The Sense of History*, Stanford.

Loesberg, Jonathan. (1991). *Aestheticism and Deconstruction: Pater, Derrida, and de Man*, Princeton.

Lovell, Terry. (1980). *Pictures of Reality: Aesthetics, Politics and Pleasure*, London.

———. (1987). *Consuming Fiction*, London.

Lyotard, Jean–François. (1979). *The Postmodern Condition: A Report on Knowledge*, trans. Geoff Bennington and Brian Massumi, foreword Fredric Jameson, Minneapolis, 1985.

———. (1983). *The Differend: Phrases in Dispute*, trans. George Van Den Abbeele, Manchester, 1988.

———. (1988). *Heidegger and "the jews,"* trans. Andreas Michel and Mark S. Roberts, int. David Carroll, Minneapolis, 1990.

———. (1988). *Peregrinations: Law, Form, Event*, New York.

Macfarlane, Alan. (1987). *The Culture of Capitalism*, Oxford.

Macherey, Pierre. (1966). *A Theory of Literary Production*, trans. Geoffrey Wall, London, 1985.

Mason, Peter. (1990). *Deconstructing America: Representations of the Other*, London.

McGann, Jerome, ed. (1989). *Victorian Connections*, Charlottesville.

McKeon, Michael. (1987). *The Origins of the English Novel 1600–1740*, Baltimore.

Miami Theory Collective, ed. (1991). *Community at Loose Ends*, Minneapolis.

Michie, Helena. (1987). *The Flesh Made Word: Female Figures and Women's Bodies*, Oxford.

Miliband, Ralph. (1977). *Marxism and Politics*, Oxford.

Miller, J. Hillis. (1963). *The Disappearance of God: Five Nineteenth–Century Writers*, Cambridge.

Mooers, Colin. (1991). *The Making of Bourgeois Europe*, London.

Mort, Frank. (1987). *Dangerous Sexualities: Medico–Moral Politics in England since 1830*, London.

Mouffe, Chantal, ed. (1992). *Dimensions of a Radical Democracy: Pluralism, Citizenship, Community*, London.

Musselwhite, David E. (1987). *Partings Welded Together: Politics and Desire in the Nineteenth-Century English Novel*, London.

Nancy, Jean-Luc. (1982). *Le Partage des voix*, Paris.

————. (1991). *The Inoperative Community*, trans. Peter Connor, Lisa Garbus, Michael Holland and Simona Sawhney, foreword Christopher Fynsk, ed. Peter Connor, Minneapolis.

Nelson, Cary and Lawrence Grossberg, eds. (1988). *Marxism and the Interpretation of Culture*, Urbana.

Niranjana, Tejaswini. (1992). *Siting Translation: History, Post-structuralism, and the Colonial Context*, Berkeley.

Osborne, Peter, ed. (1991). *Socialism and the Limits of Liberalism*, London.

Paxton, Nancy L. (1991). *George Eliot and Herbert Spencer: Feminism, Evolutionism, and the Reconstruction of Gender*, Princeton.

Perkins, David. (1990). "The Imaginative Vision of *Kubla Khan*: On Coleridge's Introductory Note," *Coleridge, Keats, and the Imagination: Romanticism and Adam's Dream: Essays in Honor of Walter Jackson Bate*, ed. J. Robert Barth and John L. Mahoney, Columbia.

Peters, Catherine. (1992). *The King of Inventors: A Life of Wilkie Collins*, London.

Piper, H. W. (1987). *The Singing of Mount Abora: Coleridge's Use of Biblical Imagery and Natural Symbolism in Poetry and Philosophy*, London.

Poulantzas, Nicos. (1968). *Political Power and Social Classes*, trans. Timothy O'Hagan, with David McLellan, Anna de Casparis and Brian Grogan, London, 1987.

————. (1970). *Fascism and Dictatorship*, trans. Judith White, London, 1979.

Price, Richard. (1990). *Labour in British Society: An Interpretive History*, London.

Reide, David. (1988). *Matthew Arnold and the Betrayal of Language*, Charlottesville.

Richards, Thomas. (1991). *The Commodity Culture of Victorian England: Advertising and Spectacle, 1851-1914*, London.

apRoberts, Ruth. (1983). *Arnold and God*, Berkeley.

Robbins, Bruce. (1986). *The Servant's Hand: English Fiction from Below*, New York.

Roe, Nicholas. (1988). *Wordsworth and Coleridge: The Radical Years*, Oxford.

Ronell, Avital. (1989). *The Telephone Book: Technology, Schizophrenia, Electric Speech*, Lincoln.

——. (1992). *Crack Wars: Literature, Addiction, Mania*, Lincoln.

Roper, Michael and John Tosh. (1991). *Manful Assertions: Masculinities in Britain since 1800*, London.

Rose, Jacqueline. (1986). *Sexuality in the Field of Vision*, London.

Ryan, Michael. (1982). *Marxism and Deconstruction: A Critical Articulation*, Baltimore.

——. (1989). *Politics and Culture: Working Hypotheses for a Post–Revolutionary Society*, Baltimore.

Said, Edward. (1985). *Orientalism*, Harmondsworth.

——. (1983). *The World, the Text, and the Critic*, Cambridge, Ma.

Sallis, John. (1989). "Flight of Spirit," *Diacritics*, 19:3–4 (Fall–Winter 1989): 25–38.

Sedgewick, Eve Kosofsky. (1990). *Epistemology of the Closet*, Berkeley.

Shaffer, E. S. (1975). *'Kubla Khan' and The Fall of Jerusalem: The Mythological School of Biblical Criticism and Secular Literature*, Cambridge.

Shaw, W. David. (1990). *Victorians and Mystery: Crises of Representation*, Ithaca.

Shires, Linda M., ed. (1992). *Rewriting the Victorians: Theory, History and the Politics of Gender*, London

Shuttleworth, Sally. (1984). *George Eliot and Nineteenth–Century Science: The Make Believe of a Beginning*, Cambridge.

Sinfield, Alan. (1989). *Literature, Politics and Culture in Postwar Britain*, Berkeley.

——. (1992). *Faultlines: Cultural Materialism and the Politics of Dissident Reading*, Oxford.

Smith, Anna Marie. (1990). "A Symptomatology of an Authoritarian Discourse: The Parliamentary Debates on the Prohibition of the Promotion of Homosexuality," *New Formations*, 10 (Spring 1990): 41–66.

Soper, Kate. (1990). *Troubled Pleasures: Writings on Politics, Gender and Hedonism*, London.

Spivak, Gayatri Chakravorty. (1987). *In Other Worlds: Essays in Cultural Politics*, London.

——. (1989). 'Three Feminist Texts and a Critique of Imperialism', *A Feminist Reader*, ed. Catherine Belsey and Jane Moore, Oxford.

Sprinker, Michael. (1987). *Imaginary Relations: Aesthetics and Ideology in the Theory of Historical Materialism*, London.

Stallybrass, Peter and Allon White. (1986). *The Politics and Poetics of Transgression*, Ithaca.

Stedman Jones, Gareth. (1983). *Studies in English Working Class History 1832–1932*, Cambridge.

———. (1984). *Outcast London: A Study in the Relationship between the Classes in Victorian Society*, London.

Sutherland, J. A. (1976). *Victorian Novelists and Publishers*, Chicago.

Swindells, Julia and Lisa Jardine. (1990). *What's Left?: Women in Culture and the Labour Movement*, London.

Taylor, Jenny Bourne. (1988). *In the Secret Theatre of Home: Wilkie Collins, Sensation Narrative, and Nineteenth-Century Psychology*, London.

Thompson, F. M. L. (1988). *The Rise of Respectable Society: A Social History of Victorian Britain 1830–1900*, Cambridge, Ma.

Tivey, Leonard and Anthony Wright, eds. (1989). *Party Ideology in Britain*, London.

Trotter, David. (1988). *Circulation: Defoe, Dickens and the Economies of the Novel*, London.

Tuchman, Barbara. (1989). *Edging Women Out: Victorian Novelists, Publishers, and Social Change*, London.

Vološinov, V. N. (1929). *Marxism and the Philosophy of Language*, trans. Ladislav Matejka and I. R. Titunik, Cambridge, Ma., 1986.

Ware, Vron. (1992). *Beyond the Pale: White Women, Racism and History*, London.

Waters, Chris. (1990). *British Socialists and the Politics of Popular Culture 1884–1914*, Stanford.

Watt, Ian. (1983). *The Rise of the Novel: Studies in Defoe, Richardson and Fielding*, Harmondsworth.

Weber, Samuel. (1987). *Institution and Interpretation*, Minneapolis.

Weedon, Chris. (1987). *Feminist Practice and Poststructuralist Theory*, Oxford.

Weeks, Jeffrey. (1991). *Against Nature: Essays on History, Sexuality and Identity*, London.

Williams, Raymond. (1980). *Problems in Materialism and Culture: Selected Essays*, London.

———. (1984). *Writing in Society*, London.

———. (1989). *Resources of Hope: Culture, Democracy, Socialism*, ed. Robin Gable, London.

———. (1990). *Culture and Society: Coleridge to Orwell*, London.

Wood, Ellen Meiksins. (1986). *The Retreat from Class: A New 'True' Socialism*, London.

Young, Robert. (1989). *White Mythologies: Writing History and the West*, London.

Žižek, Slavoj. (1989). *The Sublime Object of Ideology*, London.

———. (1991). *For They Know Not What They Do: Enjoyment as a Political Factor*, London.

INDEX